A LIKELY STORY

Also by Rosemary Mahoney

THE EARLY ARRIVAL OF DREAMS
WHOREDOM IN KIMMAGE

One Summer with Lillian Hellman

A LIKELY
STORY

ROSEMARY MAHONEY

DOUBLEDAY

New York   London   Toronto

Sydney   Auckland

PUBLISHED BY DOUBLEDAY
a division of Bantam Doubleday Dell
Publishing Group, Inc.
1540 Broadway, New York, New York 10036

DOUBLEDAY and the portrayal of an anchor
with a dolphin are trademarks
of Doubleday, a division of
Bantam Doubleday Dell Publishing Group, Inc.

Book design by Jennifer Ann Daddio

Library of Congress Cataloging-in-Publication Data

Mahoney, Rosemary.
A likely story: one summer with Lillian Hellman /
Rosemary Mahoney. — 1st ed.
p.   cm.
1. Hellman, Lillian, 1906–   —Friends and associates.
2. Women dramatists, American—20th century—
Biography.   3. Women domestics—United States—
Biography.   4. Mahoney, Rosemary.   I. Hellman,
Lillian, 1906–   . II. Title.
PS3515.E343Z77   1998
812'.52—dc21
[b]   98-22116
CIP

ISBN 0-385-47793-7
Printed in the United States of America
October 1998
First Edition
1   3   5   7   9   10   8   6   4   2

AUTHOR'S NOTE
*I have changed the names of several private individuals who
appear in this book.*

for Nathaniel Kahn

ONE

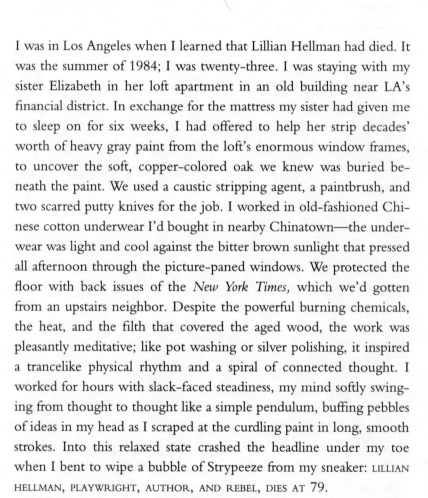

I was in Los Angeles when I learned that Lillian Hellman had died. It was the summer of 1984; I was twenty-three. I was staying with my sister Elizabeth in her loft apartment in an old building near LA's financial district. In exchange for the mattress my sister had given me to sleep on for six weeks, I had offered to help her strip decades' worth of heavy gray paint from the loft's enormous window frames, to uncover the soft, copper-colored oak we knew was buried beneath the paint. We used a caustic stripping agent, a paintbrush, and two scarred putty knives for the job. I worked in old-fashioned Chinese cotton underwear I'd bought in nearby Chinatown—the underwear was light and cool against the bitter brown sunlight that pressed all afternoon through the picture-paned windows. We protected the floor with back issues of the *New York Times,* which we'd gotten from an upstairs neighbor. Despite the powerful burning chemicals, the heat, and the filth that covered the aged wood, the work was pleasantly meditative; like pot washing or silver polishing, it inspired a trancelike physical rhythm and a spiral of connected thought. I worked for hours with slack-faced steadiness, my mind softly swinging from thought to thought like a simple pendulum, buffing pebbles of ideas in my head as I scraped at the curdling paint in long, smooth strokes. Into this relaxed state crashed the headline under my toe when I bent to wipe a bubble of Strypeeze from my sneaker: LILLIAN HELLMAN, PLAYWRIGHT, AUTHOR, AND REBEL, DIES AT 79.

Seeing these words was like discovering that the cool, slippery object you've crushed beneath your bare foot in the garden is a large pus-colored slug. I recoiled instinctively and my face tightened and my free hand flew up to cover my mouth. For several years I had supposed that Lillian Hellman was already dead, perhaps because for years I had been killing her off in my imagination. But the newspaper was only a few days old. I looked at the headline again to be certain I had read it correctly, then heard myself mutter, "Thank God." I called out to my sister that Hellman was dead. Lillian Hellman was good and dead. I clapped my dirty hands and made cracks about the pieties that were sure to be scattered about at her funeral.

After reading the obituary several times, kneeling over the newspaper with my elbows tucked into my lap, sneering and shaking my head, I stood up and returned to my work, humming and hoping to pick up my thoughts where I had dropped them off. I thought about what was immediately before me: this building, situated in the urban wasteland of Fourth Street and Main near the Indian mission, had once been the Canadian embassy and was now called the Bird House, because during the many years it stood empty, hundreds of pigeons had taken up residence in its vast, high-ceilinged rooms, mating and nesting and fouling the wooden floors, entering and exiting through broken windows in fluttering fat gray bundles. I scraped paint and thought about the pigeons' stringy pink feet the color of bubblegum, their tiny ball-bearing eyes and piebald eggs. I thought about the artists who had valiantly reclaimed the building, shoveling pigeon shit for months, hoping to render the space livable.

My sister, an artist, lived on the third floor of the building, and looking through her windows was like looking down from a lifeguard's chair onto the hazardous sea below. The oily streets shone slickly in the hazy heat, Indians fought and sang popular songs and smashed empty Thunderbird bottles in the narrow alley behind the building, hookers teetered about on comically high heels and used the alley as an office, jalopies oozing salsa music ran red lights. At night, police helicopters circled the neighborhood looking for criminals below: their searchlights swept over the buildings, up the side of one, down the side of another, flashed through our windows, and grazed my sister's pale face on the mattress near me. I thought about my sister's face; like mine, it was long-chinned and serious. I tried to conjure Johns Hopkins University, where I would be entering a graduate writing program at the end of the summer: I saw a sun-filled, linoleum-floored classroom, a brick dormitory with a domed clock tower, a wide shallow stairway of pale marble worn softly concave—like the rubber kneelers in the Capuchin chapel up the road from our house—by decades of leather soles. But I failed to regain the feeling of purposeless freedom I had enjoyed before coming upon that obituary; my thoughts were self-conscious and deliberate now, laboriously oversteered, as if by a battleship's great rudder. As the hot afternoon progressed, I began to experience a peculiar, nagging uneasiness. I was conscious of a hollow timbre in my rejoicing over Lillian Hellman's death, a sense that despite my outward joy I was disturbed by the news. I didn't like being reminded of her, didn't like thinking about the few months I spent in her house.

I scraped at the gray paint and hummed a stupid tune to distract myself, to keep my mind from slipping back into recollections of things that had happened six years before but were humiliating enough that they could still make me blush. It was easy to feel myself a teenager again in the little maid's room where I slept in Hellman's house in the company of the ironing board, the folding clothes rack, and the groaning of a chest freezer that was parked, most certainly, just outside my room but that in my memory lies persistently inside it, against the north wall of the room, its white rectangular bulk echoing the shape of the bed I lay in. I remembered lying miserably awake in that small bed thinking that if I were a bolder person, I would find a way to repay all Hellman's strictures and stridor: maybe lacing her beloved, fussed-over wine bottles with vinegar, or switching her medicines, or rearranging her furniture in the middle of the night so that she, nearly blinded by glaucoma, would become mazed in her own living room.

At the time I wasn't in the least aware that such malevolent thoughts might be harmful to my soul or that they reflected a frustration and vindictiveness that bespoke only my own unhappiness, but I was painfully conscious of it now, and amid the confusion of emotions I felt that afternoon—the embarrassment of sharp recollections, the relief and anger, the annoyance with myself at feeling any of these things—I was most bemused by my feeling of sorrow.

At seventeen I was woefully ill suited to the housekeeping job Lillian Hellman had given me, but at the time I thought that was beside the point; it wasn't about housekeeping. The youngest of seven children, I was, I think, a young seventeen. Though I wouldn't have admitted it, I could still feel mournful disappointment that Santa Claus was a myth and was still keenly attracted to the garish trappings of Halloween. I loved sledding. I was deeply attached to my mother. I loathed dresses and makeup and the time-consuming efforts women and girls made toward improving their appearance, made no attempt to improve mine, yet was uncomfortable with how I looked. I was shy and gregarious in equal measure, self-conscious but also cavalier, thick-skinned and hypersensitive. Outwardly I was convivial and light, but all of my efforts at sociability were calculated to hide my inwardly somber, sober self. I was a relatively popular girl with the heart of an unpopular one and the mind of an outcast. Every quality I possessed had its polar opposite, and each was a way of counterbalancing the other. I was defensive, competitive, reactive, suspicious, skeptical, mistrustful, and if you had told me I was any of those things, I would have denied it roundly and resented the presumptuous attempt to define me.

I was athletic but interested in books. I had plenty of friends, and my brothers and sisters were about as close in age as seven siblings can feasibly be, but I was deeply lonely. I turned to reading whenever I had the chance and had begun writing short stories when I was nine or ten. I liked it that when you were reading a book or writing a story the dreary, earthbound room you were sitting in disappeared temporarily, that you were liberated from the ongoing need to prove and protect yourself, from having to act, that in the complex and brightly colored world suspended between two covers you didn't have to think about the troubling complications of your own messy life; you could control the pace of time, attach your own pictures to the words before you, and the words, piled together as the were, became more real, more touching, more palatable than reality.

On summer evenings when I was eight years old, soon after my father died, I often lay across the foot of my mother's bed, silently studying her left leg. The leg, paralyzed by polio six years before I was born, was soft and smooth and utterly limp, darker in hue than her healthy leg, near-crimson because of poor circulation and warmer, gently radiating heat like a baked potato cooling on a dinner plate. The thigh was notably thin and had no muscle definition, the ankle was swollen to the point of seeming boneless, and the foot was puffy, shiny, and pink, like a doll's satin pillow. I was drawn by the softness and shape of the five paralyzed toes. Unmoving and com-pacted by their daily encounter with a stiff leather shoe, they had adopted a crescentlike curve and fitted perfectly together like little Brazil nuts. The knee was plump and dimpled, foolish as a baby's. Indeed, I saw my mother's leg the way I saw any infant: it could not be expected to do anything on its own, though one always hoped it might. The leg had to be cosseted and carried gingerly about; in its helplessness it compelled a regretful, self-consoling sort of love.

Those evenings, thankful when my brothers and sisters had found ways to occupy themselves in other parts of the house, I lay on my side with one ear pressed into the cool bed sheet and the other absorbing the parched bleating of the katydids beyond the darkening window screens, and while my mother read, I stared at her leg a long time in case it moved suddenly. It never moved. I tried to persuade it to move. I drummed my fingers on its shin and murmured silently to it in my head. I held the leg gently by the calf and bent the knee to see how it looked in that unaccustomed position. It looked comical, phony, the way it did whenever my mother crossed her legs or her ankles or arranged the leg in any quasi-offhand posture of repose. This leg was perpetually in repose; to push it into an attitude of coltish leisure was somehow perverse. Lowering the leg again, I would take my mother's foot gently by the toes and pump it back and forth in a coaxing fashion, whispering, *Like this, go like this.*

Before long, bored with these experiments, I sat up and tried to cajole my mother into making the leg work, requesting that she bend the knee just once for the fun of it, or move the foot, or wiggle the toes, at least, as though all these years the paralysis had been a mere ruse. She, in her nightgown and propped up on pillows, would lower the library book she was lost in, raise her half-smoked Lucky Strike heedlessly close to the lace-edged lampshade by her shoulder, and tip her head downward to look at me. I waited for her reading glasses— horn-rimmed, tortoiseshell, heavy as hardware—to slip toward the tip of her nose until her eyes were unframed and her cheekbones weirdly magnified. Peering over the top of the glasses at me, brown eyes narrowing slightly, her mouth going slack with amused interest, my mother reminded me with no trace of self-pity that she was quite unable to move her leg.

"Try," I would say.

"I wish I could, Rose, but I can't." She spoke softly and cast her leg a rueful glance for my benefit.

"When will you be able to move it?" I asked.

"Never."

"But how come?"

I knew how come but never tired of asking, never tired of hearing her explain the effect the polio virus had had on her spinal cord, nor of fantasizing that one day my mother's leg might work again, though it had been paralyzed since 1955, during the last polio epidemic, when she was thirty-two and pregnant with her third child. I had never seen the leg work and would have been disoriented and not a little alarmed if suddenly my mother had jumped up unassisted by crutches and brace and skipped nimbly across her bedroom. She used to ski, she told me. And dance. And run up Boylston Street to work. And during the war she drove a forklift at the naval shipyard.

My mother explained to me why the messages from her brain failed to reach the muscles in her leg: they stopped dead at a damaged place in the spine and couldn't get through. I would touch her foot with my fingers and ask if she could feel my touch. Of course she could. The reply made my lungs tingle with a confusion of frustration and giddy relief. "If I stuck a pin in it, would it hurt?" Of course it would. The leg wasn't dead. There was nothing wrong with the leg. It was only the spinal cord that had been damaged, its course of electric messages occluded, like a garden hose blocked by a wayward marble. Once, during this exchange, a mosquito lit on my mother's left shin and inserted its needle into her flesh; when I slapped at it, it lay still, collapsed forlornly in the tangle of its own lash-like legs. My mother glanced at the rust-colored patch of blood smeared on her shin and said instructively, "And that will itch," which of course I already knew, but that never prevented me from saying, "It will?" I wanted to hear again and again how a thing could be both dead and alive, passive and reactive, sensitive and not.

"It will," my mother said smartly, and, thumbing her glasses back into place, she returned to her book and pretended not to notice me staring at her. Her straight, black, chin-length hair curved gently around her face, partially blocking the lamplight from her features.

I thought my mother was pretty and smart, and I recognized even then that she had an ability to engage people. She had an arsenal of words and humorous stories. She had unusual notions, a point-blank manner, unexpected comments, a vivid imagination. Her words were high theater. She charmed people with metaphors: things were always like other things—she could make you see a picture before you when there was no picture, could make the ironing of a blouse a great adventure. When she described an elephant crashing through a fence, and her brown eyes widened and her fists stirred the air and she talked about his huge feet like clanking fire buckets and his snout breathing steam, you could see the elephant and were terrified. She never just said, "The man grinned." Instead it was, "The man grinned and his nose and chin seemed to meet in greasy consort."

I shifted my seat on the bed and watched my mother raise her cigarette to her lips. She had lost weight recently from worry and anxiety, and her high cheekbones and gently pointed chin seemed finer than they had before. Her cigarette smoke had turned the lacy white lampshade by her shoulder the gently burnished brown of a baked meringue. I watched fingers of smoke hanging in the yellow light above my mother's head, could see the words in their orderly black lines on the page before her reflected in the lenses of her glasses. The glasses were not my mother's; they were my father's, but he was dead now, and so everything that had once been his was now hers, including the alligator-skin physician's bag that stood on her bureau, the hematology books in boxes in the cellar, the brown Jeep in the driveway. Because my mother's reading glasses were always disappearing under the heaps of papers on her desk, my father's were often called upon to fill in—I was heartened to see them sitting squarely on her face, for it gave me the feeling that my father was helping her from his grave in Milton Cemetery.

I was sorry my father had died, was baffled and strangely embarrassed by his abrupt departure, and had an overpowering sense that I should not mention him, but I did not yet miss him. I missed only the completeness his presence had lent to what I thought of as my mother's house, and I had a creeping fear that his death would damage my mother's confidence and disrupt the already tenuous order of my family. With anxious foreboding I watched his side of my mother's bed, not three months after his death, disappearing under a rising tide of library books, magazines, folded newspapers and the clear plastic sleeves they arrived in, slippery piles of unopened mail—overdue bills and letters of condolence—a white telephone, scissors with their legs recklessly spread wide, a hairy ball of twine, several half-completed scholarship applications, lesson plans, a tannin-varnished teacup, a spoon pocked and chewed by the electric disposal in the kitchen sink. Like the square-shouldered Gilbey's gin bottle that had begun appearing that summer on the kitchen counter and the transmogrifying effect its contents occasionally had on my mother, this lumpy, tinkling clutter that she suddenly seemed unable to sort and properly place or dispose of was, to me, a sign of turbulence and worry to come. I thought that if it worsened, and if the world beyond our crowded yellow house could see it, they would pity me. More, they would pity my mother. Now and then I saw fleeting pictures of myself in the fast-approaching future defending my mother with explanations that this was not who she really was, not who I really was. We were not pitiable, despite what anyone might think.

To walk, my mother wore a metal long-leg brace that locked at the knee and kept her leg straight. Without it she could walk with crutches, but poorly. A man called Buschenfeldt had made the brace and attached it to the left of a pair of stolid orthopedic shoes. (I recall Buschenfeldt as a short figure in a graying undershirt standing behind a counter in Stoughton, Massachusetts—a town six miles south of ours that struck me as uncharted woods—his bald head sweating under a dim fluorescent tube and his thick arms lifting the newly repaired brace off a hook on the wall; he was somber and wordless and utterly unresponsive to my mother's charming persiflage: an odd choice, I thought, for my witty mother to have made in a man whose services were so intimately connected to her life.) The straps, shin cuff, knee cap, and thigh cuff of the brace were fashioned from leather, a deep chocolate color and hand sewn, like saddlery. There were locks on either side of the knee where the aluminum thigh bars and shin bars met, small knuckles of bright metal that slid down and locked the bars into place once they were straightened. Hugging the sides of my mother's leg, the metal bars were slender and highly polished; with their shapely taper and gently knobbed ends they suggested human bones.

I liked to watch my mother sitting on the edge of her bed in her slip, buckling her brace on in the morning and removing it at night. There was something involuntary in the way she did it. In the morning, with her face lifted skeptically at the black-and-white television near her bed, where Barbara Walters talked with dewy earnestness from her seat on the *Today* show, my mother absently fastened her brace on and talked back. "For God's sake, Barbara, will you shut up? Let Garagiola talk." In his munching way Garagiola talked, and then my mother turned her scrutiny on him. "His face is like a catcher's mitt," she said. "A padded pie-face. Look at it, Rose. See?" And all the while, in steady accompaniment to this parrying chatter, my mother's diligently undistracted fingers ran up and down her leg, spurring the brace buckles into place with a barely audible slap and clink.

Now and then my mother practiced putting her brace on and taking it off at high speed, testing herself in anticipation of some catastrophe in which the brace would be her only key to escape or, far from being a help, would be a deadly hindrance. Sitting on the edge of her bed, she shut her eyes and pretended she was on a sinking ship in the middle of a dark night, hurrying to get the brace off before she was tossed into the sea and dragged to the icy depths by its metal weight. Desperate for her survival, I sat beside her, watching her long fingers fly reflexively over the locks and straps, racing time and the sickening tilt of the ship. Listing toward my mother in the imagined darkness, I stifled the frenzied shriek, that swelled in my throat and clasped my hands tight in my lap to keep them from shooting out and clawing the brace off for her. How quickly she unlaced her shoe and pulled her foot out! And how relieved I was when finally she was free and both of us were treading water lightly on her bed. Immediately she practiced the reverse: waking up in a hotel afire, flames gobbling the curtains and licking the doorknob, smoke advancing in a bleeding creep toward her nostrils and mouth; how quickly could she reach for the brace, buckle it on, and get out? If I was able to stay moderately calm during these imagined disasters, I would time my mother on the little red-faced watch she had given me for Christmas, whose tiny golden hands I had only recently learned to read. Thirty seconds on, twenty seconds off: fast enough, we concluded cheerfully, that she wouldn't drown or burn.

Swimming was one physical activity my mother could do well; in water's uplifting embrace she was graceful and quick, if still unable to control her lame leg, which had a habit of floating to the surface, like a log adrift. To enter the ocean my mother would venture thigh-deep into the water with her crutches, then direct one of us to take the crutches from her, whereupon she had no choice but to fall down or dive in. We were to leave the crutches on the sand until she was ready to come out. My mother often says that as a very small child I stood alone at the waves' edge, my bare feet firmly in the sand, intently watching her swim, while my brothers and sisters played nearby or ran off down the beach. When my mother beckoned me to join her in the water, solemnly I shook my head *no,* aware that if I met with trouble in the waves, my mother could not save me. She was not easily able to lift me or any of her children into her arms, a fact that remained true even in the steadying agency of water. Her balance was so delicate a matter that the wriggling thirty-pound weight of a child could irretrievably tip the scales. I had seen my mother fall often enough, thwarted by the slightest mischance—a wrinkle in a rug, a slick string bean beneath a crutch tip, a wet leaf, a Lincoln Log underfoot—to feel that when she swam, I should stay out of the water. It may be that, as my mother believes, I stood at the water's edge out of fear for my own survival; but I know that it was also out of fear for hers, for if I drowned or was swept away, who would be there to help her? There were, of course, my brothers and sisters, but, childishly eager as I was for order and protection, it seemed to me that only I could be counted on. So I watched and waited, and with my very presence I believed I kept my mother afloat.

On my sixteenth birthday I received from my mother the gift of a typewriter. It was a small, squarish machine with a gray carrying case, a white plastic body, and intestines of glistening steel; it had impressive chattering teeth that bit the page with a satisfying *tch.* I was at boarding school then, at St. Paul's in the woods of Concord, New Hampshire, and my room at this wealthy school came puzzlingly unequipped with a desk. With no steady surface upon which to put the typewriter, I pulled out the bottom drawer of my dresser, laid a small board across it, placed the typewriter on the board, sat Indian-style on the floor with my knees tucked into the foot and a half of space beneath the drawer, and typed. From time to time, when I advanced the carriage too vigorously, the machine slid off the board and onto the floor with the ponderous thump of a dropped pumpkin. I wrote stories when I should have been reading history or math. The only class I looked forward to was my writing class, because I was reasonably good at it. One day, with a copy of a story I had written in his long-fingered hands, the teacher, Mr. Carlisle, went out of his way to praise my work to the class and then, settling his eyeglasses more comfortably on his nose, read the story aloud. I was both mortified and delighted. The assignment had been to write a short story in the style of an established writer—I chose James Joyce. That seemed possible to me simply because I was related to people not unlike the ones in his stories. I wrote stories in the style of all manner of writers, flailing desperately about for a voice. I had volumes lodged in my heart that I wanted to express and no real way to express them. I never trusted my own puny voice.

One winter weekend in 1977, Alan Paton came to St. Paul's to deliver a lecture. I had read *Cry, the Beloved Country* and liked it. While Paton was on the school campus, I saw him picking his way gingerly along a muddy path in a beige raincoat and was fascinated and enchanted by the sight of him. He was a small man with a large head, a lot of very white hair, and feet so fine he seemed to be walking on tiptoe, like a billy goat. Later that day he delivered a lecture to the entire school. He was too short for the podium and again looked as though he were balancing on his toes, stretching to get his toothy mouth up to the microphone. That evening he gave an informal reading in a room so overcrowded that many of us had to sit on the floor. I wanted to see Paton up close; I liked his voice and his strange accent. He had an odd, thrusting lower lip that bulged firmly, as though a row of pebbles had been tucked inside it. The lip made him look slightly annoyed. He read for us a short story called "The Gift," about a very shy, young South African boy who betrays his mother in the presence of his schoolmates by denying ownership of a basket of warm food that the mother, whom he loves, has prepared and had delivered to him in the schoolyard, courtesy of the family servant. Already that day the boy has received some unpleasant attention when his shoes, clearly chosen for him by his mother, are mercilessly judged by the other boys to be girl's shoes. By refusing his mother's gift, the boy for the first time takes a solitary step into the world. At the story's end the mother learns of the boy's renunciation of her gift and chooses to keep silent about it. "I have no doubt that she kept it in her heart," Paton read. "And so would any mother keep it in her heart. For this was one for whom she fears, going forward and retreating, now confident, now afraid, making his way from her womb into the world."

Hearing those lines I was gripped with sadness and began to cry. I was thankful that I was sitting on the floor because I could lift my knees and rest my forehead against them without anyone suspecting tears. I remember the drops falling onto the black slate floor in glistening spots like motor oil in the space between my sneakered feet. I was ashamed of the tears in front of my friends, but I was crying because renouncing your beloved mother was a thing I knew I, too, was capable of, a thing that seemed inevitable. It was clear that the boy in the story was Paton himself, and it seemed to me tremendous that he was able to say on paper that he had done a tragic thing.

Later that year, in a course called Women in History, I read Lillian Hellman's memoirs, which had a similarly strong effect on me. I was dazzled by her depiction of boat trips across the ocean, train trips across Europe, terrifying flights across Siberia, Nazis and Fascists,

Communists and Stalinists, Hemingway and Faulkner, epigrammatic conversations in which the wise and moral Lillian was always slamming some ruthless yet simple-minded dupe smartly into place with a withering retort. The people in Hellman's books had a way of saying ominously prophetic things like "If you don't understand now, you never will," or "Someday, if you're willing, you'll know the answer," or "I've treated you harshly today for your own good." When Hellman wrote about her smallest experiences, they had the feel of epic adventures with epiphanic endings. Her conversations were contentious and tantalizing. When she was in a bad mood, she didn't mind saying so; to the contrary, Lillian Hellman glorified bad moods, gave them a glamorous edge, brought them to the level of art. This was a revelation and a boon to a girl who had an abundance of bad moods of her own. Hellman's relationships with people moved fast, unlike mine, which seemed juvenile and repetitive, locked as they were within the endless regimen of boarding school: breakfast, chapel, classes, lunch, sports, dinner, library, homework, bed. Her life, even in its smallest details, meant something; it was guided by honesty and courage, while mine seemed fearful and tainted and dishonest somehow. She lived her life; I merely walked along beside mine, keeping an eye on it, reining it in. As a teenager Lillian Hellman smoked and snooped and had cops on the street grabbing her by the arm and saying, "Hey, young lady." She was always telling adults what to do, or telling them that their morals were bad, their language was bad, they cared too much about the wrong thing. I couldn't have done that. I wasn't daring, and it wasn't entirely clear to me what morals actually were. I had only a vague understanding of politics and what it was for. Instead of saying what I thought, I stewed and fretted in silence. Lillian Hellman slept with people. I didn't. She vomited in a dramatic way when she was upset. Such an imaginative response wouldn't have occurred to me. If I was upset, I hid it. Lillian Hellman was in control. I wanted to be in control that way, instead of how I was: naive and prideful, with no control over anything but my handed-down clothes, my books, my crookedly woven braid, my dark and deskless dorm room with its one window and its blunt view of some towering white pines that wept sap in a melancholy way.

When I saw the movie *Julia*, based on a story in Hellman's *Pentimento*, I was filled with envy and longing. Lillian Hellman got to sit at a typewriter and smoke and write a play and have a smart famous guy who loved her tell her the play was no good, which instead of making her cry and give up made her work harder. She was brave and strong and full of noble ideals. She had risked her life to help a friend, to support what she believed in. That she could tell stories about her life this way, that she had a life like this, seemed marvelous. It filled me with wonder that the person in her stories was a real person in the world. And when she wrote in *An Unfinished Woman* that she was "overproud, oversensitive, overdaring" because she was shy and frightened, I wanted to see her, have a look at her, and let her have a look at me, for surely she would recognize similar traits in me.

I needed a job that summer, but my only real option was to return home to Milton, Massachusetts, and work as a waitress at the Howard Johnson's on Route 138 up in the spooky Blue Hills, where the manager, who knew my mother, was willing to give me a job. Sitting on the bed in my dorm room that winter, I couldn't imagine myself going home to this particular job, for that Howard Johnson's was where my mother went to drink martinis. In the late afternoon, with a clutch of stamped letters and bills sticking out of her handbag, she would say to anyone who happened to be at home, "I'm going to the post office," and two hours later she would come home drunk. She sat alone in the air-conditioned restaurant in a big orange vinyl booth and had two or three dry martinis with a twist of lemon, then barely managed to drive the two mercifully straight miles home. After an arduous passage from the car to the house—two steps forward, one step back—she came unsteadily through the front door, sometimes with the letters still in her handbag. The letters brushed against the doorjamb with a papery scrape, like dried cornhusks. I pictured myself on hot afternoons to come, wearing a hairnet and a prim Howard Johnson's uniform, waiting on the table next to my mother's, while she talked drunkenly at me across the booth divider, or crowed like a rooster, or barked like a poodle, or offered a running critique on the other customers, or sassed the other waitresses, a cigarette smoldering in her hand. I imagined myself putting down a tray of hot dogs and fried clams, untying my apron, picking up my mother's gray metal crutches, cold now in the air-conditioned dining room, and ending the spectacle by driving her safely home from my place of work.

I loved my mother. Nothing could change that. But it was plain to me that when she drank she wanted to leave behind the life she was in. This filled me with anxiety, for the life my mother was in included me. At home I spent my days waiting for my mother's drunken surprises, and when they came I was never truly surprised, just grimly watchful. I couldn't imagine yet another sullen summer at home, mowing the lawn, doing the shopping for my mother, fetching her eyeglasses, steering her toward her bed when she was drunk, cleaning the house, then getting into bed at night in my humid box of a room, with brittle wasp carcasses cobwebbed in the window well and Homosote walls papered with scenes from America's colonial history: George Washington's Delaware Crossing, Benjamin Franklin's Experiment, Penn's Treaty with the Indians, Paul Revere's Midnight Ride.

Despairing over my tiny life, eager for an adventure, for change, I told my mother I didn't want the job at Howard Johnson's. When she asked me what I really wanted to do, I said, "I really want to work for Lillian Hellman," then laughed to show it was only a joke. Thoughtfully my mother studied my face. "Why don't you write to her?" she said. I waved the idea away saying, "She'll never take me."

"Maybe she will, Rose," my mother said. "You won't know until you try."

I sat at my little typewriter and wrote Lillian Hellman a letter. I knew that Hellman spent her summers on Martha's Vineyard, where two of my sisters, Ellen and Elizabeth, spent theirs. I addressed the envelope to Lillian Hellman, Vineyard Haven, Mass. 02568, certain that it would find her. In the letter I said I had read her books and asked whether she needed me to work for her in any capacity. She wrote back and said she needed a part-time live-in housekeeper for the summer months and asked if I could cook. Ecstatic, I wrote again and lied about the cooking. I knew nothing about cooking. The very sight of a kitchen bored and irritated me, but I was so eager to be in the same room with Lillian Hellman that I said, yes, of course I could cook, without any thought for the possible ramifications of this false-hood. I wasn't domestic. I hated setting the table. I knew very well how to clean a house and didn't actually mind it, was even good at it when I put my mind to it, but meticulous things like cooking and sewing, wrapping gifts and arranging flowers frustrated me to distraction. I had no attention span for these exacting tasks. I was involved in my own thoughts and was impractical. I wanted to read and write and dream all summer. Employment was the farthest thing from my mind, and when I applied for the job I was thinking only of how Lillian Hellman and I would become great friends. She would be so pleased by me, my interests, my personality, that she would forget about all those petty things I didn't know how—or didn't want—to do. I pictured us sitting at her table together, smoking cigarettes and making toasts to this and that with upraised glasses of a glowing amber drink (never mind that I had had only a few disastrous experiences with smoking and drinking), laughing sagely and discussing books and people and the world and life. She would ask to see something I had written, and I would demur, saying that anything I had written was terrible, and she would persist until I gave in and said, "If you insist," and later she would proclaim that my work was not terrible, my work was terrific.

No, she wouldn't use the word "terrific," she would use the word *fine,* it was an inspiration, a *fine* one. Then, naturally, she would reveal all her secrets and problems to me. I thought she must have known something about me, either actually or psychically, to have picked me out of all the people who were certainly as eager as I to work for her. I felt that this meeting with Lillian Hellman was a natural step in my destiny, proof that I was, as I sometimes dared to suspect in the darkness and safety of my bed, special. The moment I received Hellman's letter, school suddenly seemed inconsequential, provincial. I felt elevated, elated, freer, on a level with my teachers, who, when they heard of my good fortune seemed genuinely impressed, congratulating me and inevitably adding, "They say she's a pretty tough dame."

The tougher the dame the better, I answered jauntily.

Several times a day I went to my dorm room and unfolded Hellman's letter, holding it under my lamp, studying it, looking for meaning in the slanting signature, the date, the hue of the typed ink, the stately stationery that read 630 Park Avenue, New York, N.Y., elegantly centered in its upper margin. She had said that if I took the job with her on the Vineyard, I would be living in "a very pretty room." Endlessly I imagined the very pretty room (light and large, with flower-patterned wallpaper, a fireplace, Persian rugs), and me in it (composed, at a desk, no braids, clothing I didn't recognize), and

Lillian in the doorway (smiling), solicitously catering to *me*. With Lillian Hellman I would finally be touched by the world at large, and the world would have a chance to be touched by me.

My first meeting with Lillian Hellman was something of a shock. I had gone down to the Vineyard from Boston because Hellman wanted to have a look at me before she hired me. We met at her house. She was small and remarkably frail, a sliver of a person, when I had been expecting a tall, broad-shouldered statue. At seventy-three she was many years older than I had realized, and nearly blind. Her first words to me were oddly intimate: "My eyesight is bad now," and at the sound of her voice I had an overwhelming urge to curtsy. Her voice was a frog's bark, the weathered voice of a cigar-chewing man. She had a fox's thin wrists, and her hands, too, had the fine-boned, trowel-like delicacy of paws. She wore a housedress and slippers and walked in a laborious shuffle, carrying—rather than relying on—a wooden cane, which banged against the doorjambs and the legs of furniture as we moved through the house and into the living room. Following her, I was tempted to respond the way one might to a toddler: with humoring deference, loud slow speech, a hand ready to shoot out and prevent a fall.

We sat in her living room, a pleasant yellow room with a bar in the corner—a small round table forested with bottles—a fireplace, a built-in bookshelf, an ornate winged sofa, a flowered couch, two armchairs, and a wall of windows that looked east onto a deck and garden and beyond to a pale strip of grassy beach and Vineyard Haven Harbor. It was a hot, humid June day, the kind that made my long hair thicken and stick to my neck and fall in clumps on my shoulders. Beneath a hazy sun the sea threw off the muffled metallic glint of aged silver coins. Muggy salt air rolled through the open windows and settled like silt on the furniture. When I rested my damp forearm on the wooden table beside my chair, it adhered slightly and made a faint kissing sound when I moved it.

I had dressed, out of deference for this meeting, in the sky-blue skirt and white blouse I always wore when respectful dress was required, a skirt and blouse I had employed since the eighth grade, and sitting now in front of Lillian Hellman the outfit suddenly seemed pathetically wrong. My bare legs and sockless ankles felt pale and vulgar, and for the first time in my life I had the revelation that there was something clownish about wearing basketball sneakers with a skirt; I was certain that I looked like a child and that this fact would fertilize the skepticism and doubt that Lillian Hellman had surely reserved in her mind for me. I felt naked in front of her.

Through the furry veil of my nervousness I noted how Hellman sat in her chair, her slippered heels just reaching the floor, how she laid one bone-thin arm across the convex bowl of her belly while the other lifted a cigarette to her lips. She smoked in a thoughtful, nibbling way, and when she paused to carry the cigarette to her mouth, her chin rose in preparation, as though someone else's hand were feeding it to her. She looked vulnerable and girlish sitting there. She had large, flat thumbnails. I stared at her; no Eskimo icon could be more imposing. She blew smoke into the air and looked back at me, her cloudy eyes not seeing me clearly, as was obvious by the tilt of her head and the amused expression on her face, which I came to learn was not amusement at all but strain. The way her mouth settled when she was thinking, she seemed to be tasting her own large teeth, gauging their size and shape with her tongue. Her mouth was a wide, thin-lipped line that turned down slightly at its corners. Her face was a pattern of downward-slanting flesh, like cake batter running down the side of a mixing bowl, and that day her skin, like the furniture and the wood floors, glistened in the humidity. Her eyes had a faintly Asian slant that made her look almost seductive. Her face was narrower, longer, than it had seemed in pictures, and her nose in profile was colossal and angled in the middle. She had a broad and rather handsome forehead graced with the faintest suggestion of a widow's peak. But the most remarkable thing about her, aside from the complicated pattern of wrinkles, was her hair: it was beautiful, thick and soft and wavy and tinted a summery wheaten color. It was the hair of a girlish young woman, the sort of rich pelt that on an older woman inevitably prompts the observer to think *wig*. It wasn't a wig.

Eventually, getting around to business, Hellman told me she thought I would be quite comfortable in her house, that I could use the car she had leased for the summer if I needed it, I could use her beach, I could eat what I liked, and if there was ever anything I wanted, I should let her know. It seemed that I had the job. We arranged my schedule, which would be part-time to start with, agreed on a salary of seventy-five dollars per week, and set my first day on the job as July 28. I would return on the twenty-seventh to talk briefly with her again.

Hellman stretched out her arm and, without taking her eyes off me or looking for the object she wanted, let her hand fall gently onto a small box on the table beside her. She lifted the box toward me. It held lumps of crystallized ginger candy, which I hated. I stared at it, uncertain whether to be polite and take a piece or decline the offer.

Hellman seemed to be looking just to the left of me, vaguely out the window, and tasting her teeth. "You don't like it?" she said.

"Excuse me?"

"The candy. You don't care for it."

Her tone was neither kind nor unkind, neither accusing nor apologetic, but more a distant observation. Clearly her eyesight was good enough that she knew I wasn't delightedly stuffing the candy into my mouth.

"No, I care for it very much," I said. I took a lump of the

loathsome sticky ginger, put it on my tongue, and smiled at her. It was rubbery and spicy. It seared the roof of my mouth.

"It's an unusual sort of sweet," she said. "Smokers like it. You don't smoke."

"Sometimes I smoke," I lied.

"You shouldn't. It's a terrible habit. I smoke."

"Yes," I said.

"You understand it isn't my custom to hire high school girls. My summer help are usually in college. But . . ." She dipped her head an inch or two and motioned abruptly with her cigarette hand, as if shooing a fruitfly. ". . . be that as it may."

We chatted for a few more minutes. Hellman asked me some polite questions about myself, my school, my parents, and I answered nervously and without elaboration. I went to a boarding school in New Hampshire called St. Paul's. My father was dead. My mother had been a newspaper editor but was now an English teacher. I had three older brothers and three older sisters. This struck me as a noisy detail, and as soon as I said it the room seemed to fill up with the shrieking seven of us. These were the barest facts I could offer. I was awed by Hellman's presence, found it difficult to say anything with assurance, and as I left the house on foot, down Vineyard Haven's main street, I felt changed and dazed, as if my life had taken a sharp and very serious turn.

When I returned to Hellman's house on July 27, we sat again in the same chairs and for a few minutes resumed our idle chat, polite questions, polite answers, picking up where we had left off. When Hellman asked about my trip from Boston, I thanked her for asking, said the trip was very nice, that my mother had driven me this time, and didn't mention that all the way down Route 3 to Woods Hole that morning I had fought bitterly with my sister over the volume of the radio in the car. I wanted it off so I could think clearly about how I would behave in front of Hellman when I arrived; Sheila wanted it on so she could listen to "Disco Inferno" and dance in her seat with her bare feet planted firmly on the dashboard while she ran an Afro pick through her long blond hair and tanned her right arm out the window. My mother had decided to turn this trip into a little vacation for herself, taking her station wagon across on the ferry to Vineyard Haven and staying in a guesthouse for a few days, and at the last minute Sheila had signed on. I would be staying in the guesthouse with them that night and then was to move my bags and bicycle to Hellman's house and officially begin my job.

I told Hellman the trip was fine and didn't mention that while my sister went, still barefoot, up onto the crowded deck during the voyage across Vineyard Sound and spat over the railing and talked freely and brusquely to strangers and threw French fries at the hysterical gulls, I had remained below in the car in the belly of the ship with my mother in case the ship began to sink and my mother needed my help.

With her book cradled in the steering wheel, my mother read *The Women's Room,* her damp fingers sticking to the waxy plastic cover in which the Milton Public Library swaddled all of its books. There was something diaperlike in those library covers, fussily tucked and taped and thickly impervious. I stared at the New York license plate of the Jeep in front of us and listened to the humming of the ferry's engine and the occasional ticking of my bicycle wheel spinning idly in the back of the car. In my mother's benevolent presence I made no effort to hide my discomfort. I had exhausted myself with anticipation of this day and now, filled with fear and apprehension, I wished the boat trip would never end. I thought about the job and was glad it was part-time—there would be time to ride my bike and go to the beach and have fun with my sisters in Edgartown. I studied my hands. I bit my nails. I twisted the rear-view mirror toward me and checked my face: it was round. It was very round, and the nose was detectably crooked, broken by a flying hockey stick. As if she knew what I was thinking, my mother looked up sardonically from her book and said what I knew she would say: "I begged you to wear a face mask on the ice. But you said, *'No! If the boys don't, I don't!'* " And she captured the petulance in my autocratic voice with such eerie precision that although she had said this a million times, I smiled. She was right. It had been foolish not to wear a mask, but I was the only girl on the team at the time; that was enough oddness— I wasn't going to be the only one wearing a mask besides. I slapped the mirror back approximately into place and watched my mother reading. The faintest echo of the words on the page twitched on her lips. She liked this book, I knew; it agreed with what was in her mind.

From time to time I got out of the car and put my head through an open porthole and watched the mergansers and the black ducks flapping out of the way of the ferry, their lazily dragging feet tearing at the glossy surface of the sea. They flapped halfheartedly, as if they knew this plodding Steamship Authority vessel was harmless, in no way predatory. As we approached Vineyard Haven I could see black cans and red nuns bobbing at an indolent tilt in the greasy water, the cylindrical West Chop lighthouse, its shape startlingly like a huge baby bottle standing blandly among the trees, and the belt of white sand around the island, stitched now and then with poky wooden docks and black pilings. When I went upstairs to get my mother some lemonade, I caught a glimpse of my sister stretched out on a bench, sunning herself, with her eyes closed, her mouth open, her skirt hiked up high on her thighs, and her blouse unbuttoned down to her sternum. Her hair had slipped through the slats of the bench and dangled loosely beneath her in blond spears, sweeping the gum-speckled deck. Six years older than I, Sheila had been married once, had lived in France and Greece and California. She treated the world like her bedroom.

Hellman's hand moved out over the table between us and began patting its surface in a gentle, rotating motion; she was searching for her glasses. "My eyesight is very bad now," she said. The hand lit on the glasses, and she fitted them onto her face, accidentally stabbing herself once in the cheek with the end of an earpiece. She took up a pad of paper and pen and began writing my schedule out for me, and when it was done she handed the pad and pen to me and asked me to copy it over in large letters because she couldn't read her own handwriting.

To my surprise, the schedule she had drawn up had me working nearly twice as many hours as we had agreed on. Mutely I began to copy it out, and Hellman went on to tell me exactly what I would be doing for her this summer. I would be occupied for the next two months as her chauffeur, her housecleaner, valet, butler, messenger, kitchen girl, answering service, and laundress. In short, I would be her servant. She would pay me ninety dollars per week. I listened, becoming uneasy as the list of duties grew. It seemed I would be working full-time, around the clock in fact. I would hardly have time to think. When I gathered my wits and politely reminded Hellman that this didn't seem quite the schedule and salary we had worked out, she said quickly, as though she had been anticipating an objection, "Oh, it is. We spoke on the telephone about these changes."

"We did?" If such a phone conversation had taken place I was sure I would have remembered it. "It wasn't twenty-five hours a week? And seventy-five dollars?"

"No, I'm certain this is what we finally agreed on," she said, with a conviction that made me think she must be right, though I had no recollection of any conversation in which I had agreed to work these hours. "You must have forgotten," she said.

Confidently, firmly, she moved on with the business at hand. "Now, on Friday and Saturday nights I usually have guests for dinner and on those nights you'll have to prepare dinner with Donna." Donna, she explained, was a college girl who helped her part-time with the cooking. "By the way, those pieces of tape on the floor"— she was looking not at the tape but at me—"mark the places the furniture should be returned to after you've moved it for vacuuming. You must be sure to return each piece of furniture to its exact place, or I'll get confused and hurt myself. I don't see well anymore. And anything that you move when you're dusting should go back exactly where it was so I can find it."

I nodded and looked at the tiny bits of masking tape laid down around the feet of Hellman's dinner table by the window, like markings on an airport runway. My mind raced: *Move furniture. Vacuum. What telephone conversation? Chauffeur. Ninety hours per week. Ninety dollars. Terrible habit. Dust right.*

At last Hellman said, "And when you're working you'll wear a uniform."

I stared at her hair, afraid to look into her eyes, afraid she would glimpse my galloping apprehension. "Uniform?"

"Like Marta's," she said.

Marta was Hellman's present housekeeper, who the next day would be returning home to Guatemala. I had met Marta earlier in the kitchen and had noted her uniform and pitied her for it. It was a mock-Victorian servant's costume, a slate-gray cotton dress with a Peter Pan collar and a starchy vestige of an apron the size of a hankie. A person might use an apron like this to cry into, but certainly not to protect herself from kitchen stains and furniture polish. There may even have been a little cap involved, with a nunlike, nurselike twist of a wimple. The outfit was like a costume from a play, and its absurdity offended me. It was like the uniforms at Howard Johnson's. More distressing, it was a dress, which to me was the equivalent of prison stripes, and the thought of having to wear it for the rest of the summer horrified me. The words that twitched on my tongue were "I quit," but I swallowed them and nodded my head in a limp imitation of enthusiasm as Hellman spoke.

Later, Marta showed me around the kitchen, explaining the various appliances in her heavy Spanish accent, and when Hellman went out of the room she turned to me, wide-eyed, her hands up to her throat, and whispered furtively, "Hellman is no nice lady. You look out."

I was so surprised and confused that I wasn't certain what Marta had said, but I knew it wasn't good. From the way she stepped closer to me, whispering and peering over her shoulder through the kitchen door, it was clear that Marta was frightened of Lillian Hellman. Marta's English was difficult to understand, but she managed to tell me a sketchy story, something about how Hellman had hidden her own pocketbook and accused Marta of stealing it, then threatened to call the police if Marta didn't agree to do whatever unreasonable thing it was that Hellman wanted her to do. Hellman, Marta said, had a terrible temper, lied and yelled and insulted her. Marta lifted her small hands and clapped them briskly, an expression of Hellman's personality, I guessed. Her teeth and the whites of her eyes seemed to grow whiter in her pretty brown face, and her eyes widened at me, as though she had frightened herself with her own words. She went to the ironing board and, vigorously pressing pillowcases, told me how many times she had called her poor brother in tears *("Teng tines!")* and how she was happy to be getting away from this no-good shitty house and no-good shit island. She looked scared and sad, and her skin was moist and yellow in the heat.

"I fee sorry you, girl," she said, rolling her eyes and spraying starch in the general direction of the board, slapping at the pillowcase with the puffing steam iron, and when Hellman's voice eventually called to her from upstairs, she skittered and skated across the kitchen floor, muttering and twisting her apron strings around her fingers as she went.

I stood in that small kitchen in utter confusion. I stared at the wooden cabinets, the color of old pennies, and the little shoulder-level oven in the wall and thought that I must have simply misunderstood Marta, or that Marta at the very least must have misunderstood Hellman; she couldn't read English or speak it well enough to have understood her. I stared at the ironing board, at the seething iron, trying to collect my thoughts and pondering the schedule, the uniform, Marta. Something unpleasant had happened to Marta, something she had surely brought upon herself, something that wouldn't happen to me.

Hellman, through with Marta, came into the kitchen and asked me to wait for her while Donna took her shopping and to the hospital. "You can hang the laundry on the line while I'm gone," she said.

I stared at her. This was meant only to be a preliminary meeting; I wasn't to begin work until the next day, and since we had completed our visit, I felt I should take my leave. "How long do you want me to stay?" I asked, thinking anxiously of my mother and sister, waiting for me at the beach.

Hellman's face grew longer with unmistakable irritation, and she pressed her lips together over her teeth and raised a paw slightly before her, as if to silence me. She seemed to be shaking her head at me in a tiny, vehement way—a kind of refusal.

"You don't ask that question," she snapped. "That is entirely up to me to determine."

I winced, and the room appeared to tilt in a sudden, jarring way. My face tingled in the aftermath of this verbal slap, my scalp seemed to shrink tight around my skull. Eventually I managed to say, "But, I

. . . I thought I wasn't supposed to begin working until tomorrow."

Hellman's upper lip stretched flat against her teeth. Her face radiated anger, like the sharp dry heat from a coal fire. She turned to go back up the stairs and said, with no effort to conceal her annoyance, "Well, for God's sake, if you want to go and come back tomorrow at nine A.M. that's just fine with me!"

I watched her disappear slowly up the stairs, her tiny ankles rhythmically ascending, her slippered toes rising and warily searching for the next tread.

Reeling with surprise, embarrassment, and anger, I made my way out of the house, stumbling heavily on the outside stairs. I climbed onto my bicycle and raced through the streets of Vineyard Haven, heading for the beach my mother and sisters were on.

My mother says she remembers even now the terrifying sight of me marching toward her across State Beach, my heels furiously churning up sand, my long hair flying out behind me, the tears streaming down my hot cheeks, and the way I flopped to my knees in front of her and sobbed, "I quit!" And I, in turn, remember the look on my mother's face, the confusion and dismay, the wounded alarm as she felt the pain I was experiencing seconds before she even knew what had caused it.

TWO

I returned to Hellman's house at nine o'clock the next morning, telling myself again and again in a kind of incantatory mantra what my mother had told me: I should not be afraid of Lillian Hellman, I should instead have patience and compassion for her because she was old and unwell and going blind. I should say what I thought. I should discuss with her whatever problems might arise. I rehearsed the things my mother had urged me to say about the confused schedule, all the well-reasoned, level-headed, self-respecting assertions we had constructed the night before about what my expectations were for the summer. If Lillian Hellman had a right to her expectations, why shouldn't I? Everyone, however big or small, could have expectations. It made no difference that these businesslike and unsentimental statements I recited in my head bore no resemblance whatsoever to the fantastical desires I harbored in my heart.

I allowed my mother to drive me and my bag and my bicycle up Main Street from the guesthouse, but before we even set off I forbade her to drive too far down Hellman's driveway. I was nervous and irritable and didn't want Hellman to catch sight of my mother. I wanted to seem like an independent young woman, capable, self-possessed, and in control.

The previous night, crowded with my mother and sister into a small room in the Crocker guesthouse off Main Street, a few blocks from Lillian Hellman's house, I had felt miserable and bereft. When I stepped out of the shower, Sheila had enthusiastically admired the color of my pubic hair, and I had snapped, "Will you shut up?"

because I was in no mood for Sheila's airy prurience. Sheila could toss out, "Nice pubic hair!" the way other people said, "Nice hat you're wearing," with the same dramatic covetousness and glad flattery. Bodily form and function were what captured Sheila's interest, were her idea of fun, and while her attitude offended my somewhat more prudish view of the world (I was always bracing myself for whatever ribald thing Sheila might say next, horrible in all its embarrassing truth), it also made me slightly envious: a whole naked universe was open to her.

Later I had lain awake in the bed I shared with my mother, tossing, blinking into the hot darkness, feeling small and wrong. Did Lillian Hellman think ill of me? Had I made a mistake? Before turning out the lights, I had sat on the edge of the bed with my mother while she removed her brace, and she had coached me. "Don't worry, Ra. Just be a real person. Just be yourself. Go back tomorrow and say what you feel. It'll be all right. You'll see."

I stared, glum and silent now, through the windshield of the car; a parking ticket we had drawn the day before in Woods Hole flapped and ticked annoyingly under the thin black arm of the wiper like an identifying tag. My mother's crutches rested upright against the seat in their usual place between us, their round rubber feet positioned beside mine like two dainty hooves; when we turned a corner, one of the crutches slid cold against my arm—I gave it a shove and it clattered dumbly against its mate. My mother shot me an inquisitive look, and then I wanted to apologize to her, to beg her for last-minute advice, to clutch pleadingly at her warm, sunburned arm and shout, "*You* go in and talk to her *for* me!" But I didn't do that. Instead, as we rolled up Main Street and my mother said, "Is this the driveway, Rose?" I snapped, "No, this is not the driveway, Nona. It's the next one. Still right across from the library, just where it was yesterday."

As we swung into Hellman's driveway I directed my mother to keep her head down and take off as soon as I got out.

"Take heart, Rose," my mother said as I yanked my things out of the car, and at the sound of these kind words that always managed to present themselves in the face of my unkind ones, I wanted to cry. To prevent that from happening I said, "Just go." At the sight of her station wagon heading away toward Main Street, I felt a sharp pang of loneliness and remorse. My bare feet had begun to sweat in my sneakers, which made a rubbery squeaking noise with each step I took down Hellman's sloping driveway, wheeling my bike and lugging a duffle bag after me. I had slept poorly the night before and felt seedy-eyed and heavy. My hair was gathered in a long braid down my back; its tapered tip curved and came to a point like an artist's wet brush. On this warm day I wore white cotton trousers and a navy blue wool sweater with a little collar that fell in a tubular curve around my neck. My neck, too, was sweating.

From the top of the driveway, Lillian Hellman's house, sitting in a crevice at the bottom of a steep hill, seemed to be hiding its face in the hill's scrubby cheek. From above, the flat-roofed board-and-batten structure looked like a fancy chimneyed boxcar protected by shrubbery, but from the bottom of the hill—the sea side—the house was taller, whiter, with many tall windows that offered a generous view of the ocean. Its configuration of windows and railed balconies gave it the cheerful air of a riverboat. The yard was a square patch of grass, a small garden, and a few brushes. Above the house, on the hill, were several rows of corn. A long steep staircase that clung to the side of the house carried you down the hill, from the bottom of which you could look up and see the Mill House, the first house Lillian Hellman had bought in Martha's Vineyard and had long since sold, a pretty, stately, shingled Cape with a tower that resembled an octagonal windmill, a house that suited its colonial surroundings far better than the new one did. To the right and at the top of a high hill was Hedge Lee, John Hersey's enormous white cube of a house with a red pantiled roof and prancing statuary in the yard.

I sensed that I shouldn't use Hellman's front door, which was upstairs and led onto the bedroom level, so I made my way down the steep staircase to the back of the house, my heart rapping dreadfully at my ribs, my feet squeaking. Marta met me at the kitchen door and said breathlessly, "Hi, girl. You come back?"

"Yeah," I said, smiling.

She shrugged and lifted her eyebrows at me in resignation, then drew me in by the elbow. "She upstair. Tole me say you go up."

I found Hellman in her bedroom, sitting at her desk near the floor-to-ceiling windows, the natural light coming in on her at a soft, pleasant angle. An electric typewriter on the desk had a piece of paper rolled into it with a few thick lines typed across the top entirely in uppercase letters. A lamp with an articulated arm threw a circle of bright yellow light on her work. A magnifying glass lay on the desk beside several blank sheets and others that had been typed on and corrected by hand.

I envied Hellman this pretty place to work, envied her this kind of work. She looked tired, eyes still slanted with sleep. Her inability to see was disconcerting; it gave her a bored, blank look, robbed her of quick facial expression. Her face fascinated me; it was enormous. The lenses of her glasses were as thick as a car windshield. They looked bulletproof. I tried not to look at her too closely. When she began telling me what I should do that day, I asked if I could speak to her for a moment about my schedule before I began working. She nodded, said, "Yes," reluctantly, and I spoke. My voice sounded high and ventriloquial, shaky, and at the same time edgy; nervousness always gave me an odd defiance. My mother's words and phrases flew awry in my head. I told Hellman that I'd been taken a bit by surprise the day before by the schedule she'd drawn up, that I had thought the job was to be part-time.

Hellman listened quietly, blinking behind her glasses, raising the cigarette to her lips, nudging an overburdened ashtray an inch to the left with her elbow, and when I had finished she explained in a measured, businesslike way that she needed someone with her every day, insisted that we had discussed that, and she was positive that we had agreed I would be paid for my work starting yesterday and not today. Her voice was even, deep, assured, like a voice on a radio broadcast, and she had the manner of a person speaking to a small crowd hushed in appreciation. I pointed out that if I made myself available to work during all the hours that Donna was unavailable, Hellman would always have someone with her.

We both paused there. The silence was heavy, broken only by the keening of the herring gulls that wheeled over the beach below the house, idle melancholy cries like the sound of a rusty-chained swing being pumped by a plump child. As I stared at her desk I realized that the ashtray was actually a big porcelain soup plate; the brown butts stood crookedly upright in a bed of ashes, like rotting teeth slanting and snaggled in a sour black mouth.

Eventually Hellman consented and wrote up a schedule in which I would fill all of Donna's vacancies.

Donna had worked for Lillian Hellman for some time, didn't live in the house, was a junior in college. She was planning to leave the Island earlier in the summer than Hellman, and I agreed to begin working full-time when Donna left. I couldn't tell whether Hellman was aware that she had revised my schedule the day before or whether she really had no recollection of it. I feared that she planned to take advantage of me. It wasn't the money. It wasn't even the hours; I wouldn't have minded working full-time if that was what we had agreed on. I couldn't stand the idea of someone tricking me, controlling me, but at the same time I hated confrontation and I hated being wrong. The uniform she had mentioned the day before disturbed me now mostly because it seemed that if I wore it, she would win something, defeat me somehow.

I looked down at my sneakers. "And also," I said fearfully, "also I have been thinking. . . . I have thought once or twice about the uniform."

"Yes?"

"Well, I wonder . . . do I really . . . is it exactly necessary?"

Hellman peered strenuously through her glasses, as if through a cloudy sheet of ice. Her forehead was like the end of shoebox, flat and square. The silent way she looked at me made me think I should keep talking. Perhaps, like me, she was beginning to wonder what she had got herself into. My hands felt clammy and dirty. Desperately I blurted, "I was only wondering if a uniform is really necessary. I mean, it seems as though maybe I would find it easier to work in my own clothes."

More practical and more comfortable was what my mother had said.

"More practical and more comfortable," I said.

It may have been here that the niggling little struggle that would spread and flourish between us throughout the summer began, a struggle that meant a great deal to me and surely meant very little to her. I had said I wanted something—or didn't want something—that controverted Hellman's wishes.

My heart fluttered crazily, like a finch trapped in a small room. My throat felt thick and tight, as though lined with hot cotton wadding. It was awful and somehow strangely exciting. Hellman lit a fresh cigarette; her exhalation was weary, nearly vocal. Smoke seemed to atomize over her desk in a light blue cloud and settle onto the square shoulders of her typewriter. She considered my request, shifting her lower teeth slightly and tapping them against the upper ones. Then, with a mild expression of pity or resignation or disbelief, she said, "All right. No uniform," and got up and began showing me the things she wanted me to do for her.

Hellman's bedroom was at the top of stairs. It was L-shaped, with the bed just inside the door, hidden away from the bright windows that faced the sea. In the morning, this corner of the room was shadowy. On her bedside table was a pitcher of water and a clutch of cylindrical medicine bottles. Hellman stood by the table and picked slowly through them, holding them up one by one to read their labels, putting them down again, until she found the one she was looking for. She held the bottle to her eyeglasses and said, "This one needs to be on ice. The rest don't."

Her hands trembled with age, and when she put the bottle down again, she knocked several others onto the floor. I bent and picked them up, hyperconscious that I was making myself useful, that this was why I was here. I felt myself watching me do my job.

"Dust and vacuum and change the sheets once a week," Hellman said, moving out of the room. "Empty the wastebaskets and make sure the bath mat is off the bathroom floor so that I don't trip on it."

I followed as she proceeded through the house in her slow, shuffling way, showing me the various rooms and where things were. She had the gait of a wind-up doll and walked with her hands raised slightly before her to fend off what she couldn't see. My mind wandered wildly as she talked. I was so lightheaded at our rocky beginning, so elated that it seemed to have been resolved without undue violence, and that here I was, finally, treading three feet behind Lillian Hellman and looking at the back of her wheat-colored head, that I couldn't take in much of what she was saying. She spoke clearly, and I heard her words, but they didn't register, and whenever she stopped suddenly in her tracks to point something out to me, I was in grave danger of plowing distractedly into her from behind. This was the person who thirty years before had stood up to the House Committee on Un-American Activities, who had had daring and defiant adventures as a scrappy young girl in New Orleans, had stuck up for a black woman whom she loved at a time when white people didn't stick up for blacks. For over a year she had taken up residence in my imagination, and now here she was talking to me about the vacuum cleaner, the oven, the toilets. My hands and the backs of my knees were sweating.

Downstairs she showed me a pair of mousetraps in the kitchen, saying, "There's a horribly persistent little mouse here." She showed me the liquor closet beneath the stairs and told me how many bottles of wine should be available at any given time.

"Always make sure to put fresh water and ice on the bar in the late afternoon," she said, and I nodded and said, "Yes, Miss Hellman." She told me how to set the table, which, after years of setting the table for nine and then eight people at home, I was dead certain I already knew how to do. Soup plates, salt and pepper, dessert spoons, napkin rings. Her mouth moved at me, and I stood unhearing, fascinated by her thin lips. There was something fishlike about her face. When she brought objects close to her big glasses to inspect them, her gaze, the set of her toothy mouth, and the tilt of her head were fishlike too. She held a tiny long-handled bell in her hand and said, "This bell should always be on the table. During meals when I want something, I will ring it to call you."

I looked at the bell and at the age spots on the backs of her hands. I looked at the denseness of her bosom, large for such a small woman. Her breasts were like sloping cushions stuffed into her dress. "Yes," I said. "I see. You'll ring it. The bell."

When the instructions had ended, Hellman asked me to run some errands for her, and I brightened at the prospect, relieved at the opportunity to get out of the house and collect myself. In Hellman's car, a disappointingly dowdy American four-door, I went to Leslie's Drugstore in Vineyard Haven to pick up a prescription to treat what she called her low marrow level, then up Main Street to the yacht club to retrieve the cane she had left there the day before. When I proudly asked for Lillian Hellman's cane, a brisk, square-chinned woman in shorts and dock shoes hurried into a side room to get it, said, "There you go," with a wink, and "Give my best to Miss Hellman," and "Bye, now. Thanks a whole bunch," and thus dismissed me.

I put the cane gently and respectfully into the car, as if it had some great value, as if it were a frail person sitting on the seat beside me, and went back down Main Street. I drove self-consciously, checking my pocket for my driver's license, which I had only recently acquired, and in my frenzied effort to be careful I drove too fast, grabbing at the hot steering wheel, eyes trained on the cracked yellow line, tires whimpering as I turned corners a bit too sharply, fearing that at any moment I was going to be pulled over and asked to explain myself. That would have been difficult. I didn't know who I was in my new position; it all seemed to have happened too suddenly. All of my movements—each bend of the knee, each extension of my arm—felt strange and unaccustomed.

Explaining myself was difficult even before I arrived in Martha's Vineyard. I rarely knew what I was doing in those days or, more accurately, why I was doing it. I was a tough girl and capable, but increasingly my toughness and capabilities had begun to serve as a mask laid over other things I felt but had no name for. The face I offered the world was strong, confident, and happy, but it was heavily shadowed and mocked by a different reality: I was afraid. My soul was in a panic. At school, when I stepped out of my dorm room in the morning, the grinning mask slid down to cover my vulnerable features. I felt like a mere visitor to the campus. I suspected I was not entirely worthy, that I was occupying borrowed space and would never find a way to be grateful enough for the scholarship the school had given me. The students here were wealthy and privileged and more worldly than I, and if they weren't smarter, they were more sophisticated. They had expensive clothes; they had checking accounts; they spent their vacations in France and Chile and the Dominican Republic. They were descended from the people who had gotten here first, who seemed to have stepped confidently off the *Mayflower* with their mansions on their backs, knowing exactly where to plunk them down to best advantage. They had tidy, reasonable families in which there was never any fighting or swearing or strife. Their fathers bought them sailboats and skis and, later, cars. When I went to the school bookstore to buy books for my classes, I looked at the prices scribbled in pencil on the inside flaps and worried. I saw my mother receiving the bill and wondering, with her thumbnail fitted between her two front teeth, how she'd scrape the dollars together out of her teaching salary and what remained of my father's life insurance and the Social Security checks the government sent her because I was a fatherless dependent still in school. We were not destitute; we had shoes and plenty of food and there was always just enough money for whatever was deemed necessary, but my mother, sitting at her desk with her glasses slipping down her nose and her huge adding machine belching out a paper snake of printed figures, worried about the bills, and the thought of my mother worrying made me weak with homesickness. Most of my classmates would never really have to worry, I thought. This was their world. The very campus of the school, with its bone-white birch trees and Gothic buildings, felt privileged. Even the school pond had a heavy, ancient, bottomless look, the water weighted with years of study and tradition. Each day, by the time I finished breakfast I was already tired. I had traded what seemed like my real life at home, with its anxieties and warmth and jumbled familiarity, for this slightly unreal one.

I labored to keep my two lives separate. I never invited friends home. Since the fourth grade I had not invited a single classmate to my house. I was afraid to, for who could predict what brand of disorder they would witness there? My brothers fighting, tumbling down the back stairs locked in a tangled knot, or the dirty dishes shoved under the armchairs in the living room, or the upstairs toilet overflowing, as it regularly did, or the weedy lawn, the broken front step, the nimbus of fingerprints smeared around every light switch, the automotive junk under the back porch, the chaotic playroom, its walls scarred by flying ski poles, slap-shot hockey pucks, shoes hurled in tearful fury, the unmade beds in our little rooms upstairs, the shouting, the hysterical laughing, the tarnished strands of spaghetti stuck to the kitchen ceiling, flung there in some giddy test, the torn screens and peeling paint, my sister Sheila drying her marijuana plants in the oven (she grew them in the back yard next to the swing set), the dog-chewed armchair upholstery, the blue rug in the living room marbled with cat pee (I scrubbed the rug with dishwashing liquid, but it made no difference), and, worst of all, my mother lying on the kitchen floor, passed out, with her crutches skewed around her like abandoned oars. My mother on the floor was what every-thing else pointed to and what everything else stemmed from.

I made elaborate excuses about why it wouldn't be convenient for my friends to come to my house. My lies were imaginative and plausible; they sounded almost true. At school I pretended that my life was smooth and ordinary, that I had no fear, that I was happy, and the knowledge that these things were untrue made me feel false, like a person hiding out, an impostor sitting anxiously on the banks of her life instead of living it. I felt obliged to tell people what I thought they wanted to hear. For several years after his death, when people called on the telephone for Dr. Mahoney, I said into the receiver, "I'm sorry, he's not home right now," and dutifully wrote down the name and number they asked me to pass along to him. As soon as they hung up, I threw the note away. I did the same when people called for my mother when she was drunk. I felt that if I said

"He's dead" or "She's drunk," there would be no end to what else I might say. I might begin to explain that my father's death seemed like the cause of great misery among the people I loved, and that I knew there was no going back. If you said this to people, they might turn away. So I said nothing.

In the class above me at school was a girl I'll call Helena Anderson, who was brilliant and strange and slightly feral in her mannerisms. She was the goalie for the girls' soccer team, and when she made a mistake on the field she ripped furiously at her hair and pounded her knobby fists on the goal posts and snarled in a guttural way at our opponents, baring her teeth at them like a dog defending his dinner. When Helena Anderson flew off the handle this way, my teammates and I tried to placate her. She had to be approached gingerly. Helena had a feline habit of raising her hands at you in two falciform claws if she didn't like what you were saying, and sometimes even if she did, and then she would grin to show she was only kidding. The grin was unconvincing. Helena wasn't much of a goalie, but no one dared tell her that. She came from Mississippi and had a retarded brother there whom she referred to as "It," which made me wince with its callous indifference. She was skinny and wiry, had long, drooping brown hair, boxy shoulders, a pointed white nose, and a southern accent that in the boreal woods of New Hampshire sounded oddly supercilious and judgmental. Her little face was pretty in an Appalachian way, and her legs were spindly and pale; on the playing field her kneesocks sometimes slipped down around her ankles like lumpy bandages.

Helena's immense intelligence made her somehow more dangerous than her gawky, gloomy figure implied. It was rumored that once, in a fury, she slammed her desk drawer shut on her fingers because she had received a mere 99.5 on a Latin test instead of a full 100. She was known to bang her head deliberately against her dorm room wall in febrile fits of angst or frustration, and with such force that the pictures on the wall of the girl next door jarred loose and crashed to the floor. On the door to her room Helena had taped a cartoon by George Booth. It made sense to me that she liked this artist: all those scraggly hicks sitting on run-down porches in the middle of some bog with a light bulb dangling from a frayed wire and rabid dogs scratching at their mange and grinning maniacally at the reader. Everyone in these drawings looked slightly electrified, and when Helena went to the door and peered through her wire-rim glasses at her beloved cartoon and snickered softly at its aberrant humor, she looked to me like one of them.

At some point during my time at St. Paul's, Helena Anderson took briefly to following me, waiting for me outside the dining room after breakfast, showing up after my piano lesson, shadowing me. I'd be on my way to chapel in the morning and suddenly she'd appear, a white-faced haunt lurking behind me, hair hanging like black icicles, shoulders hunched, walking in that stiffly coiled way of hers, deliberately bringing her face within inches of the nape of my neck, forcing me to notice her. Sometimes she stood outside my room waiting for me to return from class. She wanted something from me, but I never knew what. One day when she scowled and muttered and lifted her claws at me, I asked her what was wrong. She said, "If you don't know, you don't care," which irritated as much as frightened me, for how had I come to be responsible for the welfare of this strange girl?

I talked with Helena whenever she seemed to want me to, yet when a friend of mine made wisecracking comments about the time I spent on her, I made light of it, laughed and rolled my eyes and jeered, "I know it," and pretended I thought it was a foolish waste. I didn't think it was a waste and I didn't feel like laughing. I was interested in Helena's oddness and the odd things she said about astronomy. She was an expert at Latin and Greek and everything else, which I admired in spite of the rest. Her academic ability was dazzling, and I remember being astonished when I learned that she played the flute, sweetly and quite well. I sensed there was something unusual about the home she came from, but I knew that no matter how psychologically complex it was, her family would not have surprised or scared me. As frightening as Helena was, I saw the insecurity and desperate need that lay barely veiled beneath her mean exterior. Her discomfort was obvious, and she was able to say, *You don't care.* She was able to say what she wanted. Whereas I, smiling and glib, evasive and appeasing, was not.

What Helena Anderson wanted from me I didn't know. I can only suspect that she saw something in me that answered something in herself. And in this crabbed and wounded character I, in turn, must have seen the same.

When I got back to the house, Marta was washing dishes at the kitchen sink. As she rinsed a large platter with a cradling motion, water ran in a clinging ribbon up her forearms and fell in drops from her elbows. She dried her hands on a dishtowel, took the cane and the medicine from me, and informed me that Miss Hellman wanted her to show me how to change the bed sheets.

I stared at her. I knew how to change sheets. Any idiot knew. And even if you didn't, it wasn't something that had to be taught. If you found yourself in front of a naked bed with a pile of clean sheets in your arms, you would figure it out, no matter how dim you were. Marta knew what I was thinking, I could tell from the way she stared back at me; like me, she thought a lesson in changing sheets was an annoying waste of time, an exercise that could have been cooked up only by somebody who didn't have to change her own sheets.

I followed Marta out of the kitchen. She moved through the house with the doleful look of a hound cowering beneath a brusquely raised hand. I watched her, knew I was replacing her, was being exchanged for her, but I couldn't quite put myself in her position. I felt sorry for her, the ridiculous uniform she was forced to wear, the white shoes, the nylon stockings on this hot day, her lack of English, her obvious fear, her loneliness, her unending days of labor directed at making another person's life easier than her own. She was smart, I could see that in her eyes and in her watchful silence, but what opportunities did such a woman have? Marta had taken this job for the money; she was forced to take jobs like this one. Cooking, cleaning, shopping—these were her marketable skills, this was her life. For Marta it was employment; for me it was a brief adventure that I had chosen of my own free will. But as I stood at the foot of the bed dumping pillows out of their cases, I had a faltering feeling—exactly what sort of adventure was this? Changing sheets was still changing sheets, no matter how many Lillian Hellman books you had read. It was work that people with money didn't want to do and didn't have to do.

Marta sighed and muttered gently and furtively in Spanish and punctuated my work with, "Hi, girl. No like thas, like thees. She no like peelows on de floor."

If I felt sorry for Marta, she surely felt sorry for me. It must have been eminently clear to her that I wasn't cut out for this, that I was in for a surprise. I picked up the pillows and tucked my little hospital corners with great care and concentration, trying to wring some excitement out of the task, trying to infuse it with the feel of adventure. I pictured Lillian Hellman pulling back the blankets and climbing into bed—her skinny legs and tiny feet sliding down between the very sheets I had smoothed with my hand—and experiencing some sort of satisfaction and pleasure, however transitory, at how amazingly well her bed had been made. But as I bent over the bed, tugging and fitting and tucking, I had to ask myself, How exactly was I different from Marta?

Later Hellman asked me to pick up her mail at the post office and then go to the market. She slippered into the kitchen to re-trieve the shopping list she had written out, held the list up to her glasses, and spent a long time checking it, crossing one thing out and adding another. Her handwriting was cuneiform—her let-ters had a kind of hieratic angularity, a masculine slant that I liked. I stuffed the list into my pocket, said "Yes, Miss Hellman" for the twentieth time that day, and decided that with the heavy traffic and the dearth of parking in Vineyard Haven, it would be easier to walk.

Down Main Street I went, past the Vineyard Haven Public Li-brary, a small structure that reminded me of an information house at a highway rest stop. It was shingled, orderly, and as simple as a cottage; it looked nothing like a library to me, nothing, at least, like Milton's Palladian public library or the dense, columned library at school. I walked down the weedy sidewalks, past the white Colonial houses with their green shutters, the bandstand on the grassy slope of Owen Park. Out in the harbor, white triangles of sail leaned and tilted their way slowly across the flat, sun-beaten sound. An elderly woman in a straw hat ploddingly pedaled her three-speed Raleigh up the Main Street incline smiling thinly under the strain of the exercise. Red zinnias trembled delicately in the wicker basket attached to her handlebars; harassed as she was, she rang her thumb bell at me in a coquettish little greeting.

The side streets branching off Main Street were mostly one-way, and heavy summer traffic snaked its vaporous way up and down them, Jeeps and Saabs and VWs wheeling by with a sandy hiss. Occa-sionally a Buick or a Cadillac with Florida plates came floating up the street looking gangsterish and out of place in this genteel village. There were white picket fences here and inviting gates with well-oiled metal latches. Flowers grew in abundance around the fronts of the houses, purple impatiens and pink phlox, lilies and pansies growing seemingly at random, which simply illustrated the thoughtfulness and determination of the leisured homeowners who had planted them. A lawn mower droned somewhere up Woodlawn Ave; the lawns were rich and plush, like golf course grass, and so green that in the shade they looked nearly black. Shirtless college boys painting the pillars of a porch kept themselves company with a radio balanced on the railing—its tiny broadcast came to me in warped snatches, buffeted and thinned by the slow breeze. The caterwauling of the Bee Gees.

I hurried down the street and hoped I wouldn't see anyone I knew. In Martha's Vineyard I was always running into people, people I went to school with, or their brothers or parents, or friends of my brothers and sisters, and whenever I met these people I felt trapped, as if they had caught me somehow. I was good at spotting familiar faces two blocks away, good at ducking down a side street to avoid the paralyzing small talk I knew would ensue if we came face to face. But sometimes I turned a corner and there, not a foot from me, stood some wholesome long-haired friend of my sister's in torn jeans and a Mexican peasant blouse, with four earrings running up the rim of one ear and a bracelet of elephant hair on her bony wrist—Anne Garfield or Polly Little or Kate Wentworth—exclaiming with incomprehensible glee and a show of big white teeth, "Hey! Rosie Mahoney! What are *you* doing here? How's Baba? Where's Stephen these days?" And sometimes, if Sheila had been up to something particularly profane, "And my *God,* I *heard* about *Sheila!*" These girls always looked pretty, despite their efforts to mimic the wasted, tortured, hollow-eyed vagrancy of Grace Slick and Patti Smith. I hated these encounters. I felt like a Girl Scout in billowing bloomers next to them. I felt inspected and pumped for information, and like I never had the proper response. I wanted to move through the world anonymously, but having so many brothers and sisters was like having sixteen soup cans tied to your ankles with ribbons, dragging down the street going clinkety-clank.

Under the oak trees the air was cool on my face and neck. I pulled the shopping list out of my pocket and read over what I was to pick up: Kale. Okra. One lb tongue. Cigarettes. *N.Y. Times.* Cream. Soap. Tripe. Medaglia D'Oro espresso.

These items looked sinister and slightly foreign to me. They looked like nothing edible.

Cronig's was a small family market on the corner of Main and Spring, a cramped and crowded shop with a great confidence that allowed it to charge comically high prices for its gourmet oddities. It didn't offer much variety, but it catered to the tastes of wealthy summer people and therefore one could buy all manner of unexpected delicacies there: hearts of palm, pickled water chestnuts, pigs' feet, kippered herring, kalamata olive paste, three kinds of mushrooms, raspberry jam from France. The customers in Cronig's had deep tans and golden retrievers, Tretorn tennis shoes, tiny tennis skirts, strings of pearls, big diamond rings, bracelets of knotted gold, and red Volvo station wagons whose rear windows were plastered with the names of boarding schools and Ivy League colleges. The women were always politely, delicately complaining about something and sending corrective messages to the "man in back" who had put too much spice in this, or mistakenly deboned that, or sold them beef that wasn't fresh, or sent them lamb chops instead of the rack they had ordered.

The man in back never had a name. I felt something like him. I was the palest person in the market that day, for even the girls who worked there were richly tanned. As I passed through the door I heard a girl at the cash register saying to somebody laboring behind a stack of boxes, "I finally went sailing yesterday. It sucked. He promised he'd sail me to Cape Pogue, but we get to the boat and he goes, 'It's blowin' the wrong way. We can only go north.' "

I gathered up the tongue and kale and espresso, had to ask an attendant what okra was, pushed my cart nervously up and down the tiny aisles, squeezing past tight-faced women with veiny hands peering through their half-moon reading glasses at the fine print on packages and labels, and finally I approached the checkout counter. When the cashier began ringing up the items, I asked her to charge them to the account of Lillian Hellman.

The man bagging the groceries lifted his face at me and said, "Lillian?" His voice was soft and high and he spoke slowly, as though he were slipping off to sleep. He looked at me with shy curiosity, flapped open another paper bag. "You friends with Lillian?"

There was a momentary thrill in the possibility that I might seem like a friend of Lillian Hellman, a houseguest perhaps, a visitor who had flown in from New York or Washington or Los Angeles. I wanted to say, "Best friends." I paused, let the feeling settle and die. "Well, not really," I said. "I work for her."

Even reporting that I worked for Hellman carried with it some kind of badge, some honor, some status that was strange and new to me, and decidedly adult.

The cashier let out a long low whistle of surprise, and the man said, "Wow," and dropped two bars of soap into the bag and four packs of cigarettes.

The man's name was Thomas Palmer, I knew, because on other visits to the Vineyard I had heard people calling him that. He was little and black, a career grocery man who had been at Cronig's for years. His hair seemed to me unnaturally dark, the color of licorice; it was fluffy and smooth and combed back lovingly in a wave. He had a jutting chin like the heel of an adze and a set of perfect teeth that glowed when he smiled. He was bashful. He moved with the wiggly, jerky motions of a marionette, hemming and shrugging and never quite looking you in the eye, as though the light you gave off as a human being was too bright for him. Sometimes when he had finished stacking boxes in the freezer he would come to the front of the store wearing white gloves, which gave him the faintly urbane air of a magician—idle at his sides, the gloved hands took on the numinous curves of Easter lilies. He wore a green apron with *Cronig's* embroidered across its front in white cursive script, and his clothes were always fresh and pressed. He would carry bags of groceries to people's houses if they asked him to and lived close enough and were nice to him. He was ageless. Summer people seemed proud to be acquainted with Thomas, carefully and deliberately using his name because it showed they were familiar with the local people and somehow had more right to be here than those marginal unfortunates who were here only fleetingly.

"You work in Lillian's house or something like that for her?" he said.

"Today's my first day."

Thomas put a hand on his hip, and it may have been my imagination, but his inquisitive expression seemed to melt into one of sympathy as he considered my position. "Gosh, well, how d'ya *like* it?" he asked finally.

"OK so far, I guess."

A young woman idly sweeping sawdust around at the end of an aisle raised her head to look at us. She was skinny, her small face splattered with tiny chocolatey freckles like the backspray from a paint roller, and though it was only one o'clock she looked exhausted. She straightened her back and walked slowly toward us with the broom slung over her shoulder—a hunter heading home after a long day's disappointment. She seemed glad of the interruption and eager to talk. "Lillian?" she said, with a wary squint.

Thomas giggled in a puzzling way, covered his mouth with his hand, nodded his head at the girl. His chestnut skin glistened in the dirty white light of the store. I liked him.

The girl stared at me, narrowing her big eyes, sizing me up. "Well," she said thoughtfully, as though I had asked her a question, "see, there are nice people in the world and not-nice people in the world. Lillian happens to fall into the category of the not-nice. As a matter of fact . . ." She stood the broom on its prickly head and leaned heavily on it, making the straw bristles crunch beneath her. "As a matter of fact, Lillian's nasty. Why? Beats me. But she makes you feel like a nickel sometimes. For no reason. She makes you feel like you did somethin' wrong half the time. Which I don't even know why. Because you didn't do anythin' wrong. If you go to her, 'Oh, hi, Mrs. Hellman. How's everything today?' she goes, 'Get out of my frickin' face.' "

She gazed at me. She seemed to be waiting for me to agree, to add some piece of affirming evidence. She pushed at her bangs with her tiny fingers, and I saw that the backs of her hands were covered with scratches, as though she'd had a scuffle with an angry raccoon. Suddenly she tipped her head back, drew her lips into a grim line, made a heavy-lidded, slit-eyes face that I understood was an approximation of Hellman's, bent her kness slightly, and padded flat-footed across the linoleum floor, like a baby learning to walk. Her long ponytail swiped across her back as she swayed. She gave a stray shopping cart a vicious jab with the end of the broomstick and croaked, "Where the hell are my cigarettes?!"

The girl ringing up my purchases let out a shriek of laughter so loud it made Thomas jump. "Ha ha! Yep, Judy, that's Lillian!" she crowed, and she pulled her own slit-eyed version of the sour face. "Ha! God, I love it!" She took a quick swig from a can of Tab parked atop the register, swallowed with a spluttering cough, and laughed some more, slapping her thigh and showing a mouthful of thorny metal braces and a wad of chewing gum perched on a back tooth. A shoal of bright pimples bristled on her chin.

The girl with the broom said, "A couple days ago Lillian came in and was really gettin' on my nerves."

The cashier stared and chewed her gum in a grinding, ruminant, concurring way. She looked deeply affronted. "And if sometimes you try to be nice and help her with her groceries she goes 'Don't fuck with my shit.'"

One side of Thomas's mouth hitched upward, a reluctant smile of recognition.

"Jesus, Judy, remember the time Lillian came in and reamed Betty out for—"

Thomas lifted the plastic-wrapped cow's tongue from the conveyer belt and said softly, "Now, now, girls."

Clarisse shrugged, rolled her eyes, sighed heavily. She ripped a coil of receipts from her cash register and dropped it into a wastebasket by her feet, then cracked a roll of pennies on the edge of the cash drawer and let them slither in a copper blur into their well. She folded the snail-gray wad of gum between her grisly front teeth and poked at it with a fingernail. "Ho-hum," she said, to show how bored she was. She slumped over her register, her body settling into inertia with instinctive ease, and stared vacantly out of the window. "Jesus, when I get outta here tonight . . ."

In a prompting way Thomas said, "Clarisse? The customer?" and Clarisse's wandering thoughts swerved toward me again. She stared at me, trying to focus. "Oh, yeah," she said soberly, "Lillian." She pulled a charge slip out of her drawer and scribbled HELLMAN on it. "It comes to twelve-twenty," she said, handing me the slip. "Sign here. So, what happened to the other one?"

"What other one?"

"The Mexican lady that worked for Lillian."

"She's leaving today," I said, pleased that I knew something.

"Lucky thing. Seemed like she was getting kind of a nervous breakdown off Lillian. Huh, Tom?"

Thomas hadn't been listening; he was distracted by the cow's tongue lying heavily in his hand. Its pinkness bristled with bumpy taste buds. He looked up at us vaguely. "What say, ladies?"

"Nervous breakdown. The Mexican. Off Lillian."

They called her Lillian freely, which I didn't. I called her Miss Hellman.

"She's not Mexican," I said.

Why did I care whether they knew what Marta was? They were like motley members of a casual club. They were safe in their store, each assigned a specific task, a role. They knew what they should be doing at every moment. They were friendly only because they had to work together and watch the same parade of people going by day after day. There was general commiserating jocular agreement among them about everyone who came into the store. They had bright sunlight streaming through the big front windows and piles of colorful fruit in the produce section and pleasingly tidy stacks of boxes and cans. They had air conditioning and the smell of bananas and pineapples, and roast chickens in the deli section. They could see the gleaming traffic out on Main Street. I envied their community.

The cashier shrugged at me. "Mexican. Cuban. Puerto Rico. Whatever. We all know the lady I mean. Lillian almost seems like there's a different worker every summer."

The girl with the broom said, "No shit," and frowned, as if recalling every persecuted char that had ever stumbled under the asperity of Hellman's demands.

I handed the charge slip back to the cashier, and she looked at it and read my name out loud. "Rosemary Mahoney."

Judy's eyes lit up. She was suddenly infused with a brilliant idea. "Guess what! Rosemary Clooney!"

"Rosemary's Baby," Clarisse said, delighted with herself.

They grinned at me, waiting for me to laugh, and when I didn't laugh Judy hefted her broom and said, "Hey, it's OK. I wouldn't laugh either if I was you."

Thomas dropped the rest of the groceries into the bag and carefully wiped his hands on the front of his apron. He put the bag into my arms, gave an apologetic little wave of his hand, and called out with something like sympathy in his voice, "Good luck, now," as I went through the door, as though I might never be heard from again.

I walked slowly up Main Street, sure that this job would be different for me.

THREE

Back at the house, Marta was standing alone in the shadowy hallway waiting for a cab to take her to the airport. Her little vinyl suitcase was parked by her feet. She was leaving the island for good. I put the bag of groceries down on the kitchen table and went to say goodbye to her. Her sorrow was palpable, as was her relief at leaving. Dressed in her own clothes now—brown pumps, a white blouse buttoned up to her throat, a crucifix on a silver chain around her neck, a gray cotton skirt, and, on this sunny day, a navy blue raincoat too long for her short frame—she looked somber and gray-faced and faintly holy, like a harried missionary escaping a war-torn land. I wondered whether Hellman had said goodbye to her. She had put on lipstick and powdered her face, and the powder made the fine hairs on her cheek stand out in the window light. She looked middle-aged to me, although she must have been in her late twenties. Her mouth was set in a grim line, but when she saw me coming toward her with my hand extended to shake hers, she smiled weakly and lifted her right hand and said softly, "Welcome," as though greeting me at a cocktail party. Her hand was tiny and cool, her handshake limp. I felt enormous next to her, and clumsy, and as if my hands were thick and coarse. I felt that my presence in the house was already erasing Marta's. We shook hands awkwardly and for a long time. Finally Marta must have seen that I was wondering where Hellman was, for she said, "She go feesheen," and indicated fishing by raising her arm and pretending to cast a line down the dark hallway. Her raincoat rustled and whispered with the sudden motion. "She tell me say you she come back fie o'clock."

When Marta was gone I was left alone in the house to unpack my bags and settle into the room she had just vacated. I felt nervous and self-conscious; every sound I made seemed to ring out loudly in empty house. As I hung my clothes in the closet, I imagined what the fishing expedition would be like and tried not to allow myself to feel left behind. I would have liked fishing, but, I reasoned, it was unlikely that Hellman would invite me, at least so soon in my tenure here. Maybe another time she would.

I unpacked my bags slowly and without relish. My room was behind the kitchen, with a door from the pantry and a windowed double door to the outside. It felt like a room designed for a house-maid, a child, or a burdensome lesser guest, segregated from the rest of the house, an afterthought squeezed in near the washer and dryer and the storage room. Nevertheless, it was clean and freshly painted and full of light, and the door to the yard and the generous eastward-looking windows and the sight of the ocean made it feel less con-fined. I could vaguely see why Hellman had called it pretty. The view at least was pretty, and the heavy-headed pink roses that grew along the front of the house wagged in front of my windows. The room smelled like Marta's soapy perfume. In her haste to get out, Marta had left some small possessions behind, a cotton hankie, a box of Ritz crackers, a hairnet, stockings, bobby pins in a Robinson's 5 & 10 bag in the drawer, a greeting card in Spanish that depicted a leering, sawtoothed kitten with a clutch of pastel balloons hooked in its paw. The sight of these things depressed me. I threw them away. That Marta had made a small space of her own at the edge of a place that was adamantly not hers touched me and made me sad.

When I had finished unpacking I skulked uneasily around the

empty house, staring in wonder at everything I saw. I stood in front
of Hellman's bathtub and stared at the soap, the dripping faucet in
the sink, the rustrimmed drain, her toothbrush, her furry washcloth
hanging on a towel bar. Lillian Hellman's washcloth. I stared at the
long line of beautiful dresses in the closet in the hallway; the dresses
smelled of her perfume, musky tea rose. I stared at the neatly made
twin beds in one of the guest rooms and the small night table between them—it looked, I thought, like a room in a nice hotel. The
bedspreads matched, and some of the pink roses from the garden
stood in a vase on the table. I went into the living room and stared at
the high-back wicker chair she sat in at the head of the dinner table:
the woven back of the chair fanned out wide in an elegant way; it
was like a throne, like the chair Morticia Addams sat in, with her
long black hair falling over her breasts and into her lap. I sat down in
the chair, rested my head against the stiff wicker, and pretended I was
a rich person entertaining a large group of people, saying, Too true!
Too true!—smiling and nodding my head and waving my hand. In
my peripheral vision I saw my own plump pink fingers oscillating in
the air. They didn't look right.

Self-consciously I got up and glanced around the still room to see
if anyone was there, half expecting a figure to jump up from behind
an armchair. I studied the pictures on the walls and shelves: sharp-
nosed Dashiell Hammett in repose; a younger, sturdier Lillian with a
fish, sunglasses, and a cigarette; a large shingled house in the country;
a block-headed dog; Lillian as a young child with the black nurse that
I knew from her books was named Sophronia; pen-and-ink drawings
of medieval—or maybe they were biblical—figures in sepia brown.
The wooden floor creaked now and then as I traveled over it. I stood
in the stairwell and listened to the house. The only thing I could hear
was a soft buzzing in the kitchen, an appliance or a clock, something
greedily sucking up electrical current. There was a smell to this
house, like spice or wood or cooking or new carpet.

I wandered, daydreaming my way from room to room, imagining the Lillian Hellman I had read about. Her mother's name was Julia. My grandmother's name was Julia. She had broken her nose jumping out of a tree. I had broken my nose playing hockey. Lillian killed turtles and shot ducks and skinned rabbits and camped out. She planted trees and drank hooch and defied people. She was famous. In the kitchen I opened the refrigerator and saw jars of pickles, a carton of cream, butter, white paper packages of different sizes sealed with butcher's yellow masking tape. There were string beans in a drawer, half a tomato wrapped in plastic, three kinds of mustard, half a home-made pie, a bottle of capers, plates and bowls of leftover food covered in foil. The telephone rang as I stood there, and I was so startled that I jumped, and a choking sound came out of my mouth. I slammed the refrigerator door shut and spun around to stare at the phone. It kept ringing, shrilly, piercing the dead solitude of the house. Not knowing whether it was part of my job to answer Lillian Hellman's telephone, I left it alone. As soon as it stopped ringing, I was convinced it was Hellman herself calling to tell me something important, calling me to duty. I stared at the mousetraps planted under the overhang of the cabinets, the little pieces of orange cheese cleverly balanced on the treadles, and went back into the living room, thinking up what I would say if she asked me why I hadn't answered. I looked at the dark rows of books without touching them—Dostoyevsky, Chekhov, Hawthorne—books I hadn't read but wished I had. And then, at a loss to know what to do, I walked down to the beach.

The sandy path from the house to the shore passed through clumps of long, tough grass that sawed at my bare ankles, and though the air was cool I could feel through the soles of my sneakers how warm the sand was. At the water's edge I sat down on a pile of limpets; there were thousands of them in this crescent-shaped cove, little slipper shells of brown, white, and mauve spilled two inches thick across the sand. They crunched under my feet like hardened snow. I watched the undressed sailboats bobbing at their moorings—their masts tipped and jigged in the gentle chop—and the gulls and mallards facing into the breeze. A catbird in a bush mewed like a creaky floorboard. A light bulb had washed up on the beach and, a little farther down, a baby bottle and a swollen, rotting grapefruit as white as an autumn gourd. Tiny silvery waves lapped lovingly at the limpets on the gently sloping shore, and I could smell the hairy clumps of seaweed stewing sulfurously in the sun on the rocks of the jetty. This was a town beach, with the rough sights of commerce and industry nearby, the gas tanks at the marina and the freight ferry carrying eighteen-wheeled tankers full of oil, but it was pretty in its way. It felt old and relaxed and prosperous, warmed for eons by the same faithful sun.

I turned around and looked at Hellman's house. If I were building a house, I thought, it wouldn't be like that, but it was passable because it was practically sitting on the beach. It was Lilian Hellman's house and I lived there now, could go in and out of it freely. The thought thrilled me and made me anxious.

I walked down the beach the two hundred yards to the ferry landing, and when I saw the strange black woman sitting in the sand near the huge tarry pilings of the pier, I stopped in my tracks and pretended to be looking across the harbor to East Chop. This woman fascinated me. I had seen her here several times before on visits to the island. She was tall, with a figure like a Zulu woman's—long erect neck, long arms and legs that tapered at the wrists and ankles. Her strong cheekbones gave her a noble, stately air. She couldn't have been more than thirty. Her wiry hair was pulled up into a sort of cone on her head, twisted into a knot and held in place with pins and sometimes with a broken chopstick stabbed through it. She spent hours sitting straight-backed in the dusty sand, with her legs stretched out before her and her arms crossed, looking soberly out at

the glinting harbor, or at the pilings, or at the people going by. Her
expression rarely changed: it was the expression of privilege and
pride, as though she owned all of Vineyard Haven and had been kind
enough to allow these tawdry visitors streaming off the ferry to use
it. And when it wasn't that expression, it was the fiercely concentrated expression of a person thinking hard, a person trying to visu-
ally untie a barrel knot. Her eyes held a wild intensity. Now and then
she waded into the water up to her thighs, scratched herself distractedly as she peered about, took her hair down and immediately
put it up again, then came striding importantly out of the water on
the roiling spume her powerful legs whipped up, water tumbling
from her thighs in strings of tinsel, and flopped her big wet body
back onto the hot sand. Her damp flesh was always covered in dust,
like Turkish delight in its sickening coat of powdered sugar. Sometimes, with her legs buried completely in the sand, she looked like a
limbless torso. When the spaghetti straps of her soiled halter top
slipped down off her shoulders, I could see that this already dark
woman had a deep tan line from sitting all day in the sun. Her thighs
and upper arms bore an intricate pattern of fine white stretch marks
that branched and zigzagged like the hairy roots of weeds. Some days
that summer when I came upon her, she had a sticky plastic bag of
trash and bottles by her side, but I never saw her rummaging fever-
ishly through it in the usual transient's manner, and though sometimes she talked softly to herself, she rarely muttered or shouted.
Mostly she said nothing at all. What interested me was that despite
her dirty clothes, the intense look in her eye, the way she lay her wet
body in the gritty sand with no apparent discomfort, and the fact that
she was always in this spot, she seemed nearly ordinary. Today she sat
serenely reading an old issue of the *Vineyard Gazette,* chin raised and
a pair of glasses perched on her nose, and seeing her this way I half
expected her to get up and jump into one of the Volvos parked in the
lot behind the steamship office and head off toward East Chop or

Chilmark. The first time I had seen her she was strolling regally up and down outside the Steamship Authority ticket office in her flattened flip-flops, walking with the purposeful stride of a woman on an important errand. She caught me staring at her and turned her high cheekbones toward me and stared boldly, stonily back, as though I had defiled her sidewalk, and she kept staring, spaghetti straps hanging off her shoulders like the ears of a hound, until I retreated. Her eyes were yellowish green, the color of tiny leaf sprouts. I always pretended that my staring had been an accident. She scared me a little, and made me curious. I made a wide berth around her when I saw her, but I was drawn to her. Today, after watching her out of the corner of my eye, I walked slowly back to the house.

While Hellman was out, a short, elderly man named Albert Hackett stopped by to see her. He wore his rust-colored pants pulled up high and belted tight around his thickening waist. He was clean-shaven, and gray-haired, and his soft pink cheeks gave him an innocent babyish look. But for the wicker basket dangling from his forearm by its ropy handle, like an Easter basket, he looked like a classics professor. He looked foggy and nervous. He was either bringing something from his garden to Hellman, or hoping to take something from hers, it wasn't clear. I told him Miss Hellman wasn't at home just now but he could come back later, she probably wouldn't mind, and as soon as I said it I thought it was the wrong thing to say. It was already becoming obvious to me that I had no idea at all what Lillian Hellman minded and didn't mind. She was unpredictable.

Hackett shifted his weight in his boat shoes, settled the basket more comfortably on his arm, clasped his smooth hands together, and made an affable noise in his throat that meant either that he agreed or that he would think about it. He went off with the basket rocking against his hip.

———

At five o'clock Hellman returned. I heard the door bang open and went to meet her. She was dressed in trousers that bagged at the knees and crotch, a windbreaker, and thin-soled sneakers with pointed toes. A wide-brimmed straw hat was tied under her chin with a ribbon. She stood in the hallway struggling to undo the knotted ribbon, her clawlike fingers plucking randomly at it. She held a lit cigarette between her lips and made an irritable sound. "Can't get this damn thing," she muttered in her slightly nasal way, talking into her knuckles, trying to see over her own chin. She stood with her feet apart, for balance. I approached her from the far end of the hallway and said, "I think I might be able to untie it for you."

She lifted her head and peered at me, surprised at the sound of my voice, her fingers frozen in the air beneath her chin. She had been expecting Marta, I could see, and for a moment she seemed to be reminding herself who I was. She took a short puff of her cigarette and tipped her head back. "Oh," she said. "Did Marta go?" Smoke dribbled from her mouth as she talked.

"A few hours ago," I said.

"That's fine. Fine. Yes." She made a gesture with the knot, a sign to me to come and help her with it. I stood in front of her, and as I lifted my hands they brushed against hers. Our faces were close, I could hear her breathing, could feel her warm tarry breath on my wrists. As I worked, she raised the cigarette to her lips, then moved it away, thinking better of it. The tip of it glowed near my eye. My knuckles grazed the warm loose bags of flesh under her chin as I picked at the knot, and each time I tugged on the ribbon her head jerked toward me slightly and her eyes blinked with the jolt. It embarrassed me, this closeness, the physical control I had over her while the ribbon was in my hands. The thought slashed through my mind that I could, if I wanted to, yank hard on the ribbon and knock Hellman face down, like a rag doll hurled to a playroom floor. Hellman seemed like a child to me, vulnerable, patiently waiting, lips pressed together, breathing heavily through her nose, hands hovering helplessly near mine. The ridiculous hat and the pointed sneakers reminded me that she had described herself in some story as "child-happy" whenever she was sitting in a boat. And still, she was a powerful presence, a person who deferred to no one, didn't want to be bothered, had no time to waste.

Nervously I said, "Catch any fish?" The question sounded moronic as soon as I heard it. *Catch any fish?* It was boring and lame, an obvious stab at a conversational start. It was like saying, *Have any hobbies?*

"Nothing," she said disgustedly, her voice low and gruff. "Not a thing. I don't know what the hell's the matter. It isn't what it used to be. Too many boats now. Too much traffic. Too many people. The Vineyard, you see, has become terribly popular."

I plucked the knot loose and made a sound of agreement. Her answer made me think she was used to having people ask her questions, and I wished I could say that I fished, wished I could talk about it, describing hooks and lures and lines and techniques, maybe tell her something that would be familiar to her, something about chum or gills or bait, but all I could say was, "One time I fished," which was true. Once, when my father was alive, he took my sisters and me out on a jetty near Falmouth and showed us how to fish with a hand-held line with a red bobber attached to it. I didn't catch any fish.

"Oh?" Hellman said. She didn't care whether I fished. "Hooking a fish is a thrill," she said, and she thanked me for untying the knot, then headed for her bedroom to dress for dinner. She was going out with the Herseys, she said, her neighbors. As she hashed her way slowly down the hall in her sneakers, one hand lightly touching the wall to steady herself, she added over her shoulder, "He's a writer."

I was the child now. *"Hiroshima,"* I said, to show that I knew.

"You've read him," she said with mild approval.

I hadn't read him, I had only heard about him. "Yeah," I bluffed.

"Really great." I followed her down the hallway, cringing at my own words, and hoping she wouldn't ask me anything about it. I stopped at the threshold to her bedroom. She sat down on the bed with her feet dangling and the straw hat on her head and the kinked legs of the ribbon hanging around her face like two strips of burnt bacon. She looked tiny, like a refugee sitting on a fence. Slowly she unzipped her windbreaker and struggled to get her arms out of the sleeves, her fingers clutching at the slippery material, eyes narrowing with deter- mination. "Will you go, please, to the closet," she said without looking at me, "and find the blue silk dress there?"

I went to the closet and flipped through the harvest of dresses. There were scores of them, and more than one could be classified as blue silk. Her clothes were beautiful, satiny, richly colored, expen- sive, like costumes, like a doll's clothes. I picked out three blue dresses and carried them to her. She was standing in the bathroom now, hat removed, unbuttoning her blouse while the bathwater cas- caded at full canter into the tub. I hesitated in the doorway. "Excuse me, Miss Hellman," I said, "is it one of these dresses?"

She shuffled toward me, her bra and the flesh of her belly plainly visible beneath her open blouse. I tried not to look at her body and focused instead on her flattened hair and the red indentation her hat rim had left across her boxy forehead. She leaned forward, frowning at the dresses, rubbing the material between her fingers. She was slow in everything she did, finicky and encumbered. "This one," she said, giving one of the dresses a little yank, and before I could turn away she shrugged off her blouse and let it fall to the bathroom floor. I tried to hide my surprise, but she didn't care that she was standing in front of me in her bra. It was as though I simply wasn't there. Her wrinkled yellow flesh hung loosely from her bones, and her shoul- ders were skinny and knobby. There was a sere, leathery quality to her skin that made me think of Egypt, of mummies and papyrus and the desert. She reached out, tugged briskly at a second dress, and added instructively, "This one isn't silk." Then she bent and fiddled with the bathtub faucet with one hand and began tugging her trousers down with the other.

Her comment, unnecessary as it was, had the effect of making me think I had failed her somehow, or disobeyed her. I hated being wrong, hated not knowing things, hated not being good at my job. More than that, I hated that she didn't seem to really notice me. I laid her dress on the bed and returned the rejects to the closet, staring at the one that wasn't silk, trying to determine why it wasn't silk. I looked at the label: *100% silk.*

When she had finished her bath, I zipped the dress for her, brought her a glass of water, found the shoes she wanted, and thought to myself that being around her was like being around a baby—you dressed it, propped it up, made it comfortable, moved it from one place to another, and sometimes talked to it. My impulse was to say, "That dress *was so* silk," but I didn't say it. I kept quiet. I could still hear her saying, *You don't ask that question!* I hadn't been with her long enough to sense her mood, and it wasn't worth protesting. As though she had read my mind she said instructively, "Rayon, you know, feels very much like silk. Remarkably like it. Yet it's synthetic. Give me your hand, will you? I need to go downstairs."

I put out my hand in surrender.

When John Hersey came to the door, Hellman introduced us. Hersey was tall, white-haired, gentle and had a big forehead and an enormous nose that managed, on him, to look handsome. He shook my hand and looked me in the eye and said, "Hello, Rosemary." He was graceful and slim; his smile was friendly. He had the look of a person who understood other people, who wanted to hear what they had to say. He said he was very happy to meet me. I felt that he saw me as a person, and after that, whenever he saw me he remembered my name, which impressed and pleased me. The sight of him made me feel safe.

Later that night, alone in the house and bored, I sat on my new bed and looked at the reflection of my room in the dark windows. I looked small sitting on the bed, the whole room looked small. I could see the ferry coming into Vineyard Haven just beyond Hellman's beach, its light like a searching eye going across the stone jetty. I felt strange in the house and unsure of my purpose here; I realized I hadn't done a lot of work that day or even seen Lillian Hellman much. She hadn't really told me to do anything. And it was strange to be sitting on a bed in the house of a person you hardly knew, strange to call the bed yours. I lay down, feeling as far away from Lillian Hellman as I ever had. I picked up the book I was reading, *The American,* which I was close to finishing. I liked Henry James, the fancy language and the puzzled people trying to figure out the best thing to do. I heard crickets in the bushes outside my window, the hum of the freezer, and then the ferry's horn blast droning out its excessive warning; what skipper, however stupid, could fail to notice the approach of that huge, glowing boat? I opened the book and stared at the words on the page—*What a horrible rubbish heap of iniquity to fumble in!*—but I was distracted and couldn't take them in, and finally I let the paperback fall onto my pillow.

I thought about my mother, missed her, wondered what was she doing that night, and the thought of her possibly thinking of me, wondering what I was doing, made me feel sadder. I hoped she was all right. My brothers and sisters were all away now, and I wondered how my mother would get by on her own. What if she fell down and couldn't get up? What if she was lonely? What if she got drunk and went out in the car?

With a familiar hollow feeling, I pictured the way my mother's face looked when she was drunk and remembered the first time I saw it that way: a warm afternoon in late May. I was eight years old. Our kitchen freezer was still crowded with casseroles and cakes that sympathetic people had brought in response to my father's death. I was outside playing roofball with my brothers. The grass of our front lawn was overgrown, utterly still that day, and pimpled with dandelions that gave off a lurid phosphorescent light. The sounds of Dino, Desi & Billy came thinly through Sheila's bedroom window at the top of the house. (Sheila didn't play roofball; she wasn't athletic, was too mature. She spent her time listening to music and reading *Zap* comics with her bare feet up on a table in the living room, or studying her split ends, or getting ready with dramatic sweeps of lipstick and eyeshadow to meet her friends in Harvard Square. When a voice on the radio sang about a stoned soul picnic, Sheila knew what that was.) Through the open front door of the house I could see the lamp in the hallway burning. From where I stood in the blinding white heat of the sun, its light seemed muffled and amber and lonesome. If my mother had been at home that afternoon, the light would not have been on, the screen door would have been shut against the insects, and we would probably not have been playing roofball, set instead to various tasks around the yard: trimming shrubs, mowing the grass, weeding, picking up sticks.

Long-legged wasps hovered and lurched under the eaves of the porch. Our dog, lay under the bushes, nibbling determinedly at his paw. My oldest brother, James, threw a tennis ball up to the rough, glittering shingles of the roof and called out Stephen's name, which meant that Stephen, loping back and forth between two yew trees, his face lifted anxiously to the yellow sky, was required to catch the falling ball before it hit the ground. The white rubber rims of Stephen's sneakers were stained lime green from mowing other people's grass for money. Damp blades of grass clung to his bare ankles. He raised his long, thin arms.

My mother's huge station wagon bounded into the driveway, its chrome bumpers flashing in the leaden sunlight, tires spitting up gravel. I ran to greet her, as I always did the moment she returned safely home, for few things could fill me with as much joy as the sight of my mother returning home.

The car door did not open. Through its window I could see my mother staring at the center disk of the steering wheel, her head tipped slightly forward. Her crutches lay beside her. She looked gloomy and alone, like a glass-encased figure in a humid mausoleum. She wore that day my favorite of her dresses—pretty white silk patterned with blue and pink flowers. I opened the car door, and slowly my mother turned to look at me. Her face seemed to sag. Her eyes were hooded like a great horned owl's. At the sight of me she smiled in appreciation, but when she spoke, her voice was flaccid and loud.

"Hi, Rose," she cried; it sounded maudlin. It didn't sound like her.

Behind me my brothers waited, looking on, their bare arms dangling by their sides. I remember Johnny's scabby shins and Stephen's puzzled brown eyes, the tablets of his buck teeth luminously white between his slightly parted lips. With excessive deliberation my mother got out of the car, tipped backward against the door frame for a moment, and began making her way up the brick path in a halting fashion, her crutch tips landing heavily, as though she had no idea where the ground was. I stood on the hot grass with my brothers, off the path and out of her way. Each step my mother took had the awkward, uncertain quality of that last unnecessary step mistakenly taken on an utterly dark staircase. The path seemed to rise up and smack her crutches long before she expected it to. She stepped, then steadied herself, stepped, then steadied. She sighed heavily in an overtly physical and sorrowing way. The tip of her dead shoe hitched on an unlevel brick in the walkway, and there followed a familiar breath-stopping pause of imbalance until slowly she readjusted her weight and flicked the shoe free. She held the hand grips of her crutches so fearfully that her knuckles went yellow-white, like bone. Her diamond ring caught the hard sunlight and threw it off again.

Halfway to the house my mother stopped and stood staring at the ground, swaying. Her lame leg was heavy and swollen. Her cheeks and chin were shiny with perspiration; she looked sick; her eyes were clouded. James tried to talk to her, and she interrupted him with mumbling nonsense. She stamped her good foot, cawed like a crow at dusk, then turned her eyes toward me and mocked the baffled look on my face in a cruel way. I didn't recognize anything of my mother in this. With enormous effort she made it into the cool hallway. She stood before the table and its weakly burning lamp and the mirror on the wall behind it and blinked and swayed. The temperature in the hallway seemed to drop suddenly, the air grew thinner. I felt dizzy. I watched my mother's face in the mirror; her expression hadn't wavered from blank somnolence. She didn't seem to see any of us. One crutch dangled from her forearm by its hinged metal cuff as she held onto the hall table, maintaining her balance. Without a word she weaved her way up the hallway to her bedroom and fell into a blank sleep.

In the hallway James stood silently looking at me. There was scorn and disgust on his face. Before he could speak I said to him, "Shut up."

I sat at the foot of my mother's bed and watched over her, my heart full of fear and dread, my ears ringing. I stared a long time at my mother. Without her I had nothing. I had no choice but to stand as a helpless witness to this stuporous disappearance. I sat until the room grew dark, and then I undressed her, untangling the limp arms and legs, unzipping the girdle, unhooking the bra, unbuckling the brace, untying the shoes, and when it was done I went out and turned off the hall lamp.

I woke a few hours later to the sound of Hellman coming into the house and to a dry, brownish, dusty smell—the pulpy pages of my book pressed against my nose. The light by my bed was still on, and the small room looked overbright, and when I saw the unfamiliar furniture and realized where I was, my heart sank a little. I heard voices on the stairs and determined that Hellman was with a man. He spoke loudly and emphatically. I thought I heard him say, "Chinchilla." I was sure it wasn't nice John Hersey. They sat in the living room and had a drink, and I listened to their voices, bold, carefree, bright, studded with sudden bursts of self-satisfied laughter.

I lay awake a long time in my clothes with the light on, staring at the white ceiling, the curving shadow of the lampshade making an obtuse shadow on the wall, smelling the book and Marta's perfume. Later, when it had grown quiet and the man was clearly gone, I wondered if Lillian Hellman would come and say goodnight to me, but a long time passed and she didn't, and I felt silly for thinking she might have. I turned the light off and put my head down on the pillow and thought to myself, "You idiot," but it was unclear who I meant, Hellman or me.

The next morning, when I emerged from my room at eight to report for work, Hellman was sitting in the living room in a bathrobe and slippers, smoking and reading a book, her bare legs crossed at the ankles. Her narrow shins were paper-white. Although tall columns of bright sunlight filled the room, she had switched on the lamp on the table beside her and was holding the book under it, frowning with the effort of making out the words. The book looked enormous in her little hands, and she appeared to be exerting a tremendous amount of energy just to hold it upright. She looked pale in the morning light, her face the grayish yellow of an artichoke heart, and her paleness intensified the glow of her red lipstick. Her lips were pressed together in a solid line across her teeth, which made her look prim. She stuck the cigarette in her mouth to free her hand and plucked at the corner of a page with her fingernail, turning it slowly, as though it were extremely fragile.

I said, "Good morning, Miss Hellman."

She lowered the book, raised her chin, said it back, and asked me to bring her a cup of coffee. As I turned to go out of the room, she said, "You know where everything is?"

"I think so," I said.

"Marta showed you?"

"Yes, she did."

"That's fine, then."

I hurried to the kitchen and labored over the cup of coffee, my thoughts rushing in my head now that I had finally been called on to do something useful, to prove myself. How many of the yellow plastic coffee scoops did Marta say I should use? There was a mixture involved—some parts espresso to some parts regular coffee. How many parts? Well, boil some water anyway. Boil it in what? Where was the kettle? I didn't see any kettle. Maybe a saucepan would do just as well.

I paced fretfully between the refrigerator and the oven, my sneakers slapping the linoleum floor. I opened and shut numerous cupboards, peered for no reason into the billowing fog of the freezer, plucked a rattling clutch of aluminum measuring spoons out of a drawer, gathered together on the countertop a cup, a pot, sugar, paper filters, a carton of cream, and a serving spoon, then stood there staring at them. Finally, somehow, I managed to make the coffee.

Steaming in its pot, it looked toxic. It was sludge-brown and oily, with a faint rainbow of color eddying on its surface and a bitter, rusty smell. I put it on a tray, the way Marta had showed me, with a flowered coffee cup and a pretty little napkin embroidered with Hellman's initials. I checked the tray three times, hovering over it, trying to remember the things Marta had said and whether she had told me to say something particular in the morning, something servants usually said to their employers. Finally I lifted the tray, carried it into the living room, and put it down on the table beside Hellman, thanking God that she had not also requested an egg.

Hellman turned toward the tray, reaching for the coffee cup and breathing in a soft but deliberate way, like a ventilating machine. I hesitated a moment, thinking she might ask me to sit down and talk. She lifted the cup to her lips, realized that I was still standing there, tipped her big glasses up at me, blinked once, and murmured, "Thank you," which I understood meant that I could go now.

I went. I cleaned her bedroom and the bathroom near the kitchen, scrubbing, straightening, flushing. I did the laundry and hung the wet clothes on a line strung up in the back yard—stringy brown stockings and slips and heavy white bras with cups so copious and solid they reminded me of quahog shells. Most of that morning Hellman said very little to me, seemed indifferent to my presence. She sat all morning hunched at her typewriter in her room under the yellow glow of a lamp, leaning toward the machine, cloaked in a shroud of cigarette smoke, coughing richly and filling an ashtray with crumpled butts, and when she was finished with her work she got up and moved slowly around the house as though through a dense fog, making phone calls, shuffling papers, taking books two-handedly down from shelves, tilting her head at the things she wanted to see, looking minutely at them, as if through a loupe. Her poor eyesight made me feel invisible, and fearing that she would snap at me for no reason, I stayed out of her way, trying not to do anything abruptly or incorrectly. I waited for her to call me, but she ignored me, and it seemed there wasn't much for me to do.

I felt otiose and awkward, idle and a bit useless, deflated some-how. I couldn't help overhearing her telephone conversations, which both embarrassed and fascinated me. She called the liquor store, carefully fitting a fingernail into the holes of the rotary dial and ripping it around with swift little jerks. She waited, with her hand on her hip and the receiver pressed to her ear and her head tipped slightly to one side—the posture of a woman skeptically interrogating a disobedient child. Rudely she said, "Let me speak to Mister Ben-David! Right away! Tell him it's Lillian Hellman! No you won't! I can't wait all day!" and when Ben-David came on, she said, "How are *you*, Mister Ben-David?" in a sweet voice. She ordered a case of beer, a case of wine, and some bottles of hard liquor and hung the receiver up with a rattling bang. She called the beauty salon and barked for an appointment, she called a couple of friends and barked at them too, but in a coarsely festive way. She said *fucking* and *shitty, faggot* and *kike,* with cheery abandon, and she laughed and coughed uproariously. Her laugh, a crashing watery wheeze, made the din of pie tins clattering to the floor. It was the embodiment of mirth and was itself entertaining—it made me smile in spite of myself. Her foul language startled me. I liked it and didn't at the same time. I had expected her to be somehow more proper.

At noon a woman named Rose Styron picked her up and took her out to lunch, and when they returned, the two of them sat down in the living room to play Scrabble. Hellman had explained to me that Mrs. Styron was the wife of William Styron, the novelist, but I had figured out already who she was; my sisters were acquainted with some of the Styrons' children, and I knew about his books, at least one of them anyway, the one about Nat Turner, the slave. The Styrons lived not far up Main Street. Rose Styron was pretty and friendly, with round hips, burnished skin, a wide white smile, and a pleasant voice. She and Hellman looked to me like mother and daughter, sitting at the dinner table in front of the big windows, talking and leaning over the Scrabble board, Hellman leaning particularly close so she could see better. By their elbows stood the tall glasses of iced tea I had prepared for them with sprigs of mint from the garden. When Rose got a good long word, Hellman congratulated her and pretended to be pleased, but I could tell by the look on her face, the heated slant of her eyes, the way she sniffed, rubbed her fingertips together as if ridding them of crumbs, and the prim set of her mouth that she was bugged and threatened. She smiled with her lips together, took a tiny sip of her drink and said, "Touché, Rose," with false indifference. When Rose went out of the room I saw Hellman peeking at her letters. Hellman was competitive. So was I. I envied them the game. I loved Scrabble. I loved the little wooden tablets that clicked onto the squares in their definite way, the pink and blue and gray of the board. I wanted to be asked questions about words, but no one asked me any questions. When I brought more tea into the room, I tried to see what words they'd constructed, see if there were any good ones, any words I didn't know. Hellman had made the word *hepatic,* and though I didn't know what it meant, I saw that she could have gotten a few more points by making it *pathetic* instead. Later, I snuck into the living room and looked *hepatic* up in the dictionary, and when I saw its meaning I was surprised that I hadn't known the word.

"Come out to the garden with me, will you?" Hellman said when Rose Styron had left. "I want to make sorrel soup."

She shuffled across the kitchen to the back door, and I followed her out. The sun had passed over the roof and was beginning its descent, pressing the blocky shadow of the house onto the wooden deck and out to the edge of the garden. As I followed Hellman through the door I thought about the New York way she talked. She said *godden* and *remockable*. She said *vey* for very and *feefle* for people, and she formed her words in a faintly slurry way, as though her tongue were too big for her mouth. Her upper lip rarely moved when she talked—it looked stiff, as though shot full of Novocain. She said *abslooly,* and her words seemed to blow around her big teeth. Sometimes, when she wasn't under pressure, she mumbled and trimmed articles and objects from her sentences, extraneous monosyllabic words that nevertheless left their shadow behind.

"Like sorrel soup?" she said as she struggled across the lawn with a basket in her hand, taking small shuffling steps in her stiff sneakers, as though her feet hurt. *Sarrel.* She was asking me a question.

"Oh, yes, I do," I said. I had never tasted sorrel, never even heard of it.

"Delicious," she said. "Very easy to make."

"Is it?" I tried to sound deeply interested.

"You like cooking?"

I was afraid to say no. I had told her I knew how to cook, and that seemed the same as saying I liked cooking. Furthermore, I knew she liked cooking and didn't want to get trapped by a debate about it. "I like spinach salad," I blurted, hoping we could talk about the food we liked to eat instead of how we liked cooking it.

"Spinach." Hellman was breathless with the effort of getting across the lawn, teetering and working her arms, gripping the handle of the basket, the pointed sneakers dividing the grass like two tiny plows. The yellow cotton sundress she wore hung loosely from her shoulders like a Roman tunic, and her pumping knees punched weakly at its hem. I could see the lace edge of her underslip and her hairless armpits. The rumpled tissue she'd tucked under her watchband looked like a bandage stanching a small wound. Squinting in the sunlight, she had the dazed aspect of a small child just up from a nap. Her hair needed washing—stiff fingers of it hung down the back of her neck and scraped at the collar of her dress. "Never had such a salad. How do you make it?"

I didn't make it; my mother did. I pictured the salad in the brown wooden bowl on our kitchen table at home, tried to envision the ingredients. A fat bee nuzzled my hot cheek in a drunken dance, and I flapped it away. "Bacon. I think. And almonds. A boiled egg, if you like that. Cut up. Mushrooms. And those tiny little oranges. The little Chinese ones."

She said, "Hmph," in approval. "Sounds good."

It was a positive, encouraging reaction to something I had said; still, I feared saying anything else.

Hellman stumbled on a grassy tuft and her hands flew up in counterbalance. I offered her my forearm, and she groped for it and curled her fingers around it; her fingers were cold and smooth and firm, like a blood-pressure cuff. It was a familiar feeling—when my mother didn't have her crutches nearby she held my arm in the same way or curled her fingers around the back of my neck in a way that I loved and leaned on me as she walked, using me as a cane. I liked that. It made me feel important, and as if my mother were guiding me as much as I was her.

We stood at the edge of the garden, the toes of our sneakers in the hoed-up earth. The sight of Hellman's clawlike hand gripping my arm was strange; her skin was dark and rough next to mine, her knuckles bony. My skin was pink and freckled and my bones were padded in a layer of baby fat.

"Now," Hellman said blandly. "Let me see." She stood in front of the neatly planted herbs with her feet apart and a hand on her hip, staring into the rows of greenery. She stared a long time, with her eyes pinched to slits in the sunlight, baring her teeth and screwing up her eyebrows. Quasars of light glanced off the lenses of her glasses. She couldn't see anything. I stared, too, waiting for her to make a decision and tell me what to do next. I could see tomatoes, basil, a pea trellis, dill, zinnias, radishes, foxgloves, lettuce, a few things I couldn't name, and three plump black-bibbed house sparrows crouching and twittering in the dusty earth, fluttering their wings as though they were bathing. I could smell the bitter leaves of the big potted geraniums on the patio. The spidery canopy of the oak trees hissed and rattled in the breeze. There was a big gas grill in the yard cloaked in a canvas cover, like an expensive sports car.

Hellman leaned forward and began rubbing the leaves of things between her fingers, judging, checking, determining what was what. Sometimes she plucked off a leaf and smelled it, held it up to her glasses, or put it in her mouth and tasted it, ripping it with her teeth and making little smacking noises, keen with concentration. Then she said, "No, no, that isn't it," with a dismissive shake of her head.

When she found the sorrel, I knelt down and picked bunches of it for her, and she checked each bunch to make sure that it was, indeed, sorrel. She was fussy. She wouldn't just take my word for it. She stuffed what she accepted into the basket, like a bank teller pragmatically stuffing money into a sack. Down on my knees with the sun roasting my hair, handing the hot, broken plants up to her, fitting them into her brittle fingers, I could feel myself growing impatient. I waited, obeyed, did what she said, and began to see that going to the garden with her was like going to the garden with my mother—slow and dull. I had to keep an eye out that my mother didn't fall or get hurt. I followed her and pulled up the weeds she wanted pulled up because it was difficult for her to bend over and do it herself. I was always way ahead of her, but she was the one giving orders. "Not that one," my mother would say from behind, leaning forward on her crutches to have a better look. "That's a zinnia. The little green thing next to it. Give it a yank." When my mother needed help, she needed arms and legs to perform the functions she couldn't perform for herself. In those moments I was a tool, useful and visible, but unseen. With my mother I accepted it. She was my mother; I wanted to please her. But with Hellman this familiar role annoyed me. She had the power and the free will. I had nothing. I followed dumbly behind. I lifted leaves up at her. She rejected some of them; too old, she said, not old enough, a goddam rabbit had chewed them.

How could she see all that?

"No, no, this one isn't sorrel." She was sniffing and frowning at what I had just handed her.

"It isn't?"

"No, it isn't."

I took it from her. I stared at it. It was sorrel. No different from what I'd been handing her all along. "I'm sure it's sorrel," I said, looking from the leaves to her ankles, which were only slightly thicker than her wrists and had the bluish tint I recognized as poor circulation.

"Forgive me, it isn't." Her voice was stern, and tight with impatience.

Stung, I ducked my head and blinked at the reticulated leaves. A jay screeched crankily in a tree behind us. Was she joking?

"Mint," she said. "The sorrel is next to it." She put out her hand, scraping at the air for the next bunch, indicating that I should move along.

"But I'm sure this is the same thing I just—"

"Let's don't argue." Her fingers wiggled near my face.

Don't argue meant *you're wrong.* It was a rebuke. I hated it. I dropped the leaves and picked some more—more of the same—and handed them to her. She squeezed them, sniffed them, patted them. "Yes," she said and opened her hand for another bunch. "You'll learn."

You'll learn meant *You're young.*

———

Silently I stood at the sink, tearing sorrel greens from their stalks and rinsing them, while Hellman padded softly about behind me on her flat feet, taking things out of cupboards, lighting a cigarette, locating her ashtray. "Put the light on, Rosemary, will you?" she said, blowing smoke. "I can't see what I'm doing."

I flipped the light switch, and a fluorescent wand on the ceiling rudely blanched the sleepy afternoon shadows of the kitchen with a thin blue light insipid as skim milk. Hellman tugged a Cuisinart out from its spot in the corner of the counter. It was new, she told me. Someone had given it to her as a gift. It was a terribly fancy gadget. She hadn't used it much. Its blades were terribly, terribly sharp. We must use extreme caution. She fussed over the plastic machine, removing fittings and containers and putting them on again, feeling their shapes with her fingers, bending over to inspect the handle, the electrical cord. Her long fingernails clicked on the hard plastic, and her hands hovered gingerly over the pieces, as though the machine were a fancy pipe bomb.

"Before you use it you must always check to see is it plugged in." Her voice sounded doubtful. "Is it plugged in?"

"I don't think . . ."

"You must always leave it unplugged until you're ready to use it. Otherwise it could be extremely dangerous, cause a terrible accident. Is it plugged in now?"

"No, Miss Hellman, it isn't."

"It's a very powerful machine with very sharp blades. You really must be careful with this at all times."

The way she used the word *must* interested and irritated me. It issued from her as from the highest authority, as though she were quoting from a Cuisinart manual she herself had written. It was bossy and regally imperative and meant that whatever happened, whatever I did, she was in charge. Even the way she pronounced the word *must* seemed imperious to me. She dropped the *u* and pushed the consonants together. You *mst* do this, you *mstn't* do that. It was a scolding sound, like *tsk* and *shush*.

"You can put the leaves in it now. Careful pushing it down. Watch your fingers."

I stuffed the sorrel leaves into the cylindrical bowl of the Cuisinart, and Hellman added butter, cream, chicken stock, and an egg yolk, her hand wobbling, her cigarette sending up noxious garlands of lavender smoke. She tried to fit the top onto the bowl, failed, and asked me to do it for her.

"Where's the switch?" she mumbled, pawing at the base of the machine. I took her arid hand and put her fingertips on the switch, peeking at her out of the corner of my eye. A sizable flap of chewed sorrel stuck to her eyetooth, nearly covering it, making her look slovenly and a bit sinister, like a jeering pirate. Why couldn't she just step aside and let me turn the machine on?

"I'm going to turn it on now, so would you step back, please?"

Her arm swung out like a gate and pressed against my chest, holding me back. This overbearing caution seemed comical to me, operatic, and the fearfulness it carried surprised me. She stabbed at the switch, and when the machine ran with a whining whir, she winced and hopped backward a few inches in deference. She had raised her arms slightly, as if to fend off anything that might come whizzing off the horribly spinning machine. The sorrel was violently slashed into bits—like grass clippings against the white of the milk—and very quickly it lightened and became a uniform pale green liquid. Hellman peered at it with her mouth open, her face looking severe. "Look OK?" she shouted over the noise.

"It looks very pretty," I said.

"Puréed yet, though?"

"Maybe a little longer." I watched the thrashing green potion. I had no idea what sorrel soup should look like.

"Think?"

"I think so."

"Minute or two?"

"That sounds about right."

She thought she was asking someone who knew. Her face was heavy with seriousness; she was thoroughly engrossed in the project. The two pouches of flesh under her eyes looked stuffed and weighty, like little sacs full of liquid mercury. Our shouting sounded coarse and crude to me, and I wondered whether our conversations would ever go further than this meaningless honking back and forth about nothing.

When the soup was done and we'd poured it into a big bowl, Hellman asked me to remove the Cuisinart blade and wash up. "It's so sharp," she warned me. "Be careful."

I held on to the knob of the blade and pulled upward, but it didn't come off. I shifted around to the other side of the machine and pulled on the knob again; it wouldn't budge. I twisted the knob clockwise, pushed down on it and then up again, hard enough that the entire machine lifted an inch off the counter. The blade was stuck fast. I leaned down on the machine with one hand and gave the knob a yank with the other; still it wouldn't come off. I was embarrassed; I should have been able to do this with ease. That was my job. And she was watching me. I knew that if I didn't hurry up and get it off, she'd brush me aside and try to do it herself. I tried again, twisting as I pulled, and suddenly, with a powerful release that was more like an explosive push, my hand flew up into the air, the blade shot free of my fingers, rocketed upward over our heads, and clattered noisily against a wooden cupboard. For a nightmarish second the blade appeared to stand perfectly still in the milky white air while, agape, I stared, and then in a fast-forward blur it arched outward a few degrees and came squarely down on Lillian Hellman's sneakered foot.

If she hadn't seen it, she had certainly felt it. Her head tipped forward, seemed to wobble on her neck. "Oh! Oh! Jesus Christ!" she yelped. Magnified through her eyeglasses, her lashes fluttered wildly, her face a map of tension and fear. "Oh, my God! Jesus Christ!" she gasped. "Am I all right?" Her lips trembled and she clutched at her own hands and stared down at her green-stained sneaker. She took a tiny step, a kind of test to see if her foot was still there. She looked up at me. "Are you all right?"

"Oh, fine," I said. My heart pounded with confusion and fear. I saw no blood on the floor or on either one of us, so I concluded aloud again that we were both all right. I picked up the Cuisinart blade by its little knobbed handle and held it up for Hellman to see, perhaps hoping that the sight of it in my hand would provide further evidence that we were not hurt.

"See?" I said, smiling. "Here it is. It's all right. Nobody got hurt. It was just a little accident. The blade got stuck and then, gosh, it just went zipping up like that." I gestured at the cabinet above us. Sorrel soup dribbled down the wooden door like a leggy green squid. I grabbed a sponge and swiped it off, hopping off the floor to reach the upper parts of the cabinet, and then I bent to wipe Hellman's sneaker. I feared she might smack my head for this transgression, or at least say something fierce. My cheeks burned with embarrassment. My armpits were hot.

"Jesus Christ. It nearly took my head off." Her mouth hung open in fright. Her lips trembled. "My God, that fuckin' thing is a menace. I've got to have Melvin take a look at it."

She went to the table, stabbed her cigarette into the ashtray, snatched up a pack of cigarettes, fished a fresh one out with trembling fingers, fitted it into her mouth, and lit it with her palm cupped protectively around the match, as if the room were subject to a howling wind.

Beyond the window the shadow of the house covered the garden now like a huge blue tarpaulin, and the purply sky was beginning to deepen and ripen to a royal maroon. Over East Chop a spill of high, ladderlike clouds had begun to appear, like ripples in water. Crows were settling in the trees. Hellman set her teeth together, tasting them. Her mouth, which had a life of its own, was the most interesting feature of her face. She plucked the tissue from her watchband and touched it to her nostrils. I went to the sink and began washing up with my back to her, certain that she would offer some kind of admonishment.

"I warned you you must *must* be careful with that machine," she said presently, her voice quavering.

I frowned into the sink. I hated nothing more than being dressed down or corrected. The opprobrium in her voice fell heavily over my head, like a lead-lined X-ray apron.

"It's just too dangerous. In the future, I'll deal with it."

When I turned around, she was staring at her stained sneaker, thinking, pressing a knuckle to the side of her nose. The fright had altered her face—she seemed to be smiling at her foot, but she wasn't smiling; it was that same strained grimace. With fluttering fingers she reached for the spiky clumps of hair at the back of her neck and smoothed it. I was certain she was wondering whether to fire me. She sighed heavily, and the phone rang. "Will you get that, please, Rosemary?" she said.

I hurried across the kitchen, wiping my soapy hands on my shirtsleeves and thinking about the way she said *Rosemarry*. When I picked up the receiver it slipped away from me like a frightened codfish and klunked onto the counter. I grabbed it, fumbled, said, "Hello."

A man's voice shouted loudly, "Lillian, my dear!"

"No, sorry. This isn't Lillian."

Hellman whispered roughly, *"See who it is!"*

I said, "May I ask who's calling, please?"

A guy named Joe with a fey voice and a fancy accent, an American, clearly, but an American who wished he were English.

I looked at Hellman. "It's Joe," I said.

She scowled and tapped her lips frantically with an index finger, a sign to me to keep my voice down, and indicated with her hands that I should cover the mouthpiece. *"Joe who?"* she whispered sharply, leaning forward, inching toward me with her hands raised in the air.

I lifted the receiver to my face. "I'm sorry, but Joe who?"

I could hear liquid being poured into a glass on his end of the line, its ghostly timbre dancing up a muffled scale, and then a match being struck and the deep, ragged inhalation of cigarette smoke. The man said, *Heh-heh,* and cleared his throat regally. *Joe Alsop.*

I covered the mouthpiece and turned toward Hellman. "Joe Alsop."

Hellman grimaced and her hand rushed to the side of her head, as though she had been struck by a rock. The look in her eyes said, *Oh, shit.* She stood still for a second, considering her options. She looked trapped. Tiny spots of green soup had landed on the left lens of her glasses, making her look even more blind. She pushed a plume of smoke sideways out of her mouth, tapped the ash from her cigarette into a potted plant on the windowsill, and raised her fingers to her mouth again, plotting. She lifted her hands at me and said in a clumsy rasp intended as a whisper, *"Tell him . . . tell him I'm not here right now!"*

I looked at her to see if she was serious. This scratching bleat could have been heard up on Main Street. Her mouth was set, lips pressed grimly together around the brown filter of her cigarette. She was serious. She wanted me to lie to the guy. I knew how to do that. I straightened my back and raised the phone to my face. "I'm sorry, Miss Hellman is not here right—"

Hellman shuffled closer, shaking her head, and tapped my shoulder with a bony finger. *"No, no, just a minute. Tell him . . . tell him . . ."*

She was putting a great deal of energy into this ruse. It ignited her, made her excited. She had her cigarette hand raised to the side of her mouth, the cigarette tweezered between two fingers stiff as the legs of a clothespin. She seemed to think her tiny hand might muffle her booming whisper. *"Say I'm . . . I'm on a boat. A boat!"*

The man would have to be stone deaf not to hear all this frantic rustling chatter.

"She's, um . . . really not here right now," I said, "because she's out on a boat."

Hellman waved her hands at me in a prompting manner. *"On the sea. Tell him I'm on the sea!"*

"She's out on the sea in a boat," I said.

"So I can't be reached."

"So she can't be reached."

The hands flapped and hacked at the air. *"You'll take a message."*

"I'd be happy to take a message, if you like."

Hellman didn't seem to see how absurd this was. *She's on a boat right now . . .* It was embarrassing.

Alsop harrumphed and repeated what I'd said about the boat and the sea. He believed it. "A message won't be necessary," he said. I heard the stubble of his five o'clock shadow scrubbing the mouthpiece, crackling like static. "I'll ring again."

I hung up the phone and faced Hellman. "He said he'd call you back."

"Good!" She rearranged the glasses on her nose, scraped at her cheek with a thumbnail, scowled, and snorted two long chopsticks of smoke through her nostrils. She turned toward the refrigerator, and I heard her mutter to herself, "Jesus Christ, I nearly had my throat slit by that Cuisinart. The last thing I want to do just now is chat with that fop." And then, as if remembering that I could hear her, she said, "Oh, he's a good man, really. A good writer and a friend, but a bit pompous. You know who he is, of course."

I didn't know who he was, but I knew she would tell me. It interested me that she would put a friend off like that. Why couldn't she just answer the phone and say, *I'm busy now. Call me back.*

Hellman sighed, still ruffled, trying to calm herself. Her smoke floated in large lazy clouds toward the open windows, then was sucked abruptly through the screens in a precipitate rush.

FOUR

Quickly I learned the routine of Hellman's day, her habits, her wishes, her volatile moods. In the morning she sat at her typewriter while I cleaned the house and did the shopping. The days of my first week followed one after the other with an unnerving blend of anxiety and plodding tedium, filled with routine cleaning and ironing and fetching of things at the market or the drugstore. Sometimes I fetched the wrong item and had to go back to the store and exchange it for the right one. Some days I went down to town three or four times at Hellman's request, and each time she asked me to go out yet again, I watched her raise the lipstick end of her cigarette to her lips, the smoke curling up languidly into her face, and wondered why she couldn't just ask me to do all the errands at once. When she sucked on her cigarette, her lips squeaked and her eyes narrowed and the corners of her mouth turned down, as though she were tasting something bitter. She would eat lunch, take a nap in the afternoon, then read for a while and have a drink and go out to dinner or have a guest in for dinner. I drove her to the hairdresser, to the yacht club, to the Styrons' house or the Herseys', waited in the hot car, and drove her home again.

I spent hours waiting for her to come home from her lunch date or waiting for the next directive. The waiting made me uneasy. I felt that I should be occupied at all times, that I should be doing something useful in the idle minutes but wasn't perceptive enough to know what. Because I didn't want to look lazy, or as if I wasn't earning my pay, I was afraid to sit down. I took to wearing an apron all the time, to give myself the air of a person at work. I spent hours in the kitchen, standing around with the garlic and the onions and the strainers, waiting for Hellman to give me something to do. I was afraid she would come into the kitchen and catch me staring dumbly out the window. I began to sneak peeks at my new book—stories by Colette—at the kitchen table. I read standing up, spreading the pages with my fingers, like a priest reading a sacramentary on an altar, delving into Colette's cheerful childhood, and when I heard Hellman's feet whispering down the stairs, I'd flip the book shut, shove it aside, grab a pot or a wooden spoon and start across the kitchen with it, hoping to mimic the posture of domestic industry. I had no idea what I was doing or what I should be doing. The first few days in Hellman's house I was afraid to eat anything that wasn't expressly offered to me, so when I was hungry I would take a piece of bread and some butter or a cookie or an apple—or all of them— and sit on my bed and eat in great hurried gulps, stuffing the food into my mouth and wiping my lips on my sleeve. I was afraid to show I was human, afraid that was unacceptable. I knew I was flawed in countless ways and underqualified for this job, and I didn't want Lillian Hellman to see that. I didn't want to be asked to do something I didn't know how to do, I didn't want to look stupid or make a mistake.

When I stared out the window, which I did a lot, what I saw beyond the yard was tantalizing. People in shorts and bathing suits walked by on the beach or rowed dinghies out to their moored sailboats. Great black-backed gulls wheeled above the little cove against the blue sky and the ragged white scraps of clouds, their slate-smooth wings flapping languidly in the bright sun. The dark green sea grass and the glittering sand looked soft and warm. I leaned against the window jamb and stared out, the sun at midday falling just short of the kitchen windows. There was a gay pumpkin-colored umbrella over Hellman's deck table, and I wondered what it was like to sit under it. While the ticking of my Timex snipped loudly at the minutes, I daydreamed about being on the beach with my sisters in Edgartown—laughing and swimming, gossiping and singing songs, with the salt water drying in our eyebrows, making the hairs dusty and stiff. But my dreams were frayed and half-formed because of my constant awareness of Hellman in the house. I was always waiting for her to call me. The house was small, and if I coughed or sobbed or banged my shin on a footstool, she would certainly have heard me, regardless of where she was. Sometimes I stood at the window and looked out at the blinding sea and imagined what it would be like to really live in a place like this, what it was like to be an adult who owned a house and had money and a car and could do as she pleased.

I became accustomed to my job, but not to my place in the house, nor to the fact that this position, which I had so long been looking forward to and was so proud of having cleverly obtained for myself, so near the beach and my sisters, was proving to be dull and at times a little scary. My schedule was choppy, with many of the days broken up into morning and evening parts. The four or five free hours in between were not quite enough to make anything of beyond browsing in the library or riding my bike to the end of West Chop before I had to return to the house and begin helping with dinner. At first I was excited when Hellman finally had some task she wanted me to help her with directly, until I discovered how slowly her projects proceeded. I didn't mind hard work, but I hated more than anything having to wait for a person who was slower than I was. I hated having anyone stand over me reciting instructions, observing my work, and that was precisely what my job entailed. The slowness of everything Hellman did distressed me. Cooking with her was an excruciating exercise in fetching, stirring, measuring, waiting, obeying, and cleaning up. Her eyesight had a baffling fickleness. She had trouble pouring liquids from bottles and pitchers, sometimes missing entirely the waiting glass or bowl and splashing the milk or juice or

vodka directly onto the counter, yet the next moment she was reading the fine print in a stained and greasy old cookbook and distin-
guishing sugar from salt just by looking at the granules. When she
filled a measuring cup with milk or poured herself a glass of water,
she stuck a finger in the glass to feel the height of the burbling liquid.
I followed her around, handing her a towel to wipe her finger on,
wiping up what she spilled, putting pots away, picking up what she
knocked over, moving chairs out of her path, lifting boxes, taking
bottles down from shelves, emptying ashtrays full of crumpled butts.

All day long I answered the telephone, taking complicated messages from Art Buchwald and Mike Nichols, Claudette Colbert, Jules
Feiffer, William Styron, and a woman named Ruth Field, who had a
mannish, shouting voice, while Hellman stood nearby throwing se-
matic signals at me with her spindly arms. Whenever a soft-voiced
guy named Feibleman called from LA, she dropped whatever she was
doing to take the call. She hurried to the phone, unable to keep a
smile from creeping into her face, and said, "Peetuh." She talked to
him with real interest and warmth, sounding like the person I
thought she'd be. Softer, humorous, a little uncertain, pleasantly sar-
castic.

Each day I woke thinking maybe this will be the day that she talks
to me, or asks me who I am, or tells me something about myself. But
day after day, what she told me as we worked side by side on some
household project was incidental, trivial, fleeting, and always slightly
didactic, the kinds of things a stranger on a bus might tell you,
whether you wanted to hear them or not. It was never the run-on
prattle of a doddering old woman, but a series of small sentences that
slipped out over time as I chopped celery, or hooked her bra, or
opened the car door for her, or clipped zinnias for the living room,
or tied her shoelace, or scraped price tags from wine bottles with a
butter knife. After Dashiell Hammett died she built this new house;
she also owned a changing shed at the beach out in Gay Head; it was

her understanding that deadly nightshade and the tomato were related; Feibleman would be coming to visit; she was thinking of buy-
ing a fishing boat with Jack Koontz; Albert Hackett and his wife
were writers—something to do with Anne Frank. Alsop would be
coming to visit. He was a columnist for the *Washington Post*. He had
a writer brother, dead now. She had had a farm in New York but had
to sell it. She was sick of doctors, hated needles, was worried about a
possible eye operation coming up in August. Tommy Styron used to
be a disagreeble child, but now he was positively *chawming*. Her eyes
were getting worse. Her foot hurt. She didn't sleep well. She hoped
the corn Melvin Pachico, her handyman, had planted above the
house would be good this year. And Mike Nichols and his lovely
wife, Annabel, would be visiting this month.

What she said never involved me or required any particular response. At times she seemed to be talking just to fill the air with her
own voice. I wondered as she talked if she knew what I looked like,
if she could see my face, if she wondered anything about me. I
watched her shuffle through the house and thought about all the
amazing things she had done, the things she had written about in
Pentimento and *An Unfinished Woman*. She had smashed a desk chair
against Tallulah Bankhead's hotel room door. She had run through
the streets of Valencia while it was being bombed. James Thurber
once hurled a glass of whiskey at her. She had run away from home
for a night, and she was always sassing people. She had crazy fucked-
up relatives. With all my heart I wanted to be able to ask her questions. As I crawled under her bed to retrieve a fallen pinky ring, I
wanted to say, "Hey, what about that time when you were thirteen
and that old lady smacked you on the streetcar?" or "How about that
time you smashed up the soda fountain in LA because you were so
mad at Dashiell Hammett?" But some internal censor kept me from
it. It was fear of her volatility, her unfamiliarity, but more it was a
certain perverse pride, a need not to let her know that I cared, that I

wanted anything, that she had something I didn't have. If she was not going to show an interest in me, I would smother my interest in her. To let anyone know that I felt I didn't have everything I needed would be to give away too much.

On trash days I lugged the garbage cans up her driveway to the top of the hill for the trash men to pick up. I often ran to the Herseys' house to drop something off for her, to the Styrons' to pick something up, to the post office to buy stamps. When the liquor store made its delivery, I put the bottles away in the closet under the stairs, and when she told me to funnel a bottle of Jim's vodka, the cheapest brand available on the island, into the empty Smirnoff bottle in the living room, I did it. As I fitted the beak of the plastic funnel into the bottle's open mouth, poured and waited, poured and waited, while the quivering liquid pissed its way from one bottle to the other, the act seemed needlessly crafty to me. What was she saving by doing this? Surely she had enough money to buy whatever kind of vodka she wanted. Was she just stingy?

I cleaned the oven, washed windows, made lunch reservations for her at the Café du Port, dusted her desk and emptied the wastepaper basket beside it full of typed pages with lines crossed out and hand-written emendations. The pages looked like an epilogue to *Pentimento.* I saw the phrases *second cousin to Julia* and *guessed her identity* and *a phone call from Smith,* and I paused over the trash can, reading furtively for fear she'd catch me—it felt sneaky, like reading someone's diary. I had the same sly feeling when I glimpsed the names in the address book lying open on her desk. Woody Allen, Richard Avedon, Warren Beatty, Samuel Beckett, Dick Cavett, Ira Gershwin, Dustin Hoffman, Mrs. A. Onassis, Elizabeth Taylor. Penciled into a regular address book this way, the names were startlingly intimate. And there were phone numbers. If I picked up the phone and dialed Elizabeth Taylor's number, would her elegant voice answer *Hello?* That these people were so casually accessible to Hellman made her seem powerful to me. Her life was important, full of daring acts and important people, and looking at these big names and magical addresses, a sight that my own ordinary life would never have provided, was like peeping through a golden keyhole.

At night I ate my dinner alone at the kitchen table, a less ceremonial version of the same food she was eating alone at the dinner table in the living room. In the dark kitchen window the slurred reflection of my own arm lifting a fork or reaching for the pepper like a mocking puppet always spooked and distracted me. I was tense and couldn't really taste my food, knowing that Hellman was in the next room. Occasionally I could hear her fork meeting her plate, her watery cough, the base of her wineglass knicking the edge of her plate when she put it down, but except for these accidental noises the dinners were utterly silent. When she rang her little servant's bell, I dropped my fork with a start, spanked my mouth with a napkin, and jumped up to serve her, regularly banging my hip on the edge of the kitchen table in my haste. I turned her bed down for her, drew the curtains in her bedroom, put her eye medicine on ice, and retreated to sit nervously on my bed and think about my sisters and my mother and where I was and how I should act. Or I wrote in my journal, as my mother had urged me to do. I wrote letters to my friends, Nancy Weltchek, Corinne Zimmermann, Cynthia Colt, Shelley Robinson, cheerful messages full of bravado, stick-figure drawings, and cavalier remarks about my job. To my mother I wrote long letters with beginnings like *I haven't cried or anything like that yet.*

Some days, if guests were expected, at around four o'clock Donna would arrive to help me prepare dinner. Donna had strong arms, an athletic way of walking, and thick reddish blond hair that she wore gathered up in a ponytail like a sheaf of wheat. She was attractive and calm and knew a lot about the workings of this job. I liked her, and it was a relief to me that she, at least, was a good cook. She liked to laugh, but she was also conscientious about her work, loyal and deferential to Hellman in a way that made me think twice. If it hadn't been for Donna, I might have got myself into more trouble.

At dinnertime Hellman would carefully seat her guests and ring the little table bell for service, and I would scurry in—prompted and coached by Donna—to see what Hellman wanted. I learned to serve from the left and pick up from the right, to say *Would you care for more?* instead of *Seconds?* to point the handle of the serving spoon at the targeted guest as I lowered a platter, and never to remove a plate from the table without first asking whether it was needed further. These things weren't difficult, but I saw that Hellman was exceedingly particular about the dining process, formal in the workings of her table, and firm about the proper trappings and protocol; the pressure to perform well made me paranoid and forgetful. Her dinner table was like a table in a restaurant, and I was the waitress. I had never been a waitress before and was used to a much looser sort of table, one at which people jumped up and fetched for themselves, one that had no order of courses stiffly following each other but instead had all the food placed out at once in large quantities, to be passed around from hand to hand. Our food at home was good but hearty. Hellman's food was delicate and small, fanciful and always worked up from scratch. Cold gazpacho with sour cream, an absurd dish of raw hamburger that she called Steak Tartare, spaghetti with pesto made from her own basil, duck prepared on the outdoor grill, a meatloaf unlike any meatloaf I had ever tasted, bluefish done in an elaborate sauce or painstakingly smoked over carefully selected wood chips in a contraption like a file cabinet in the back yard. She spent what seemed like inordinate amounts of time planning meals, preparing food, preoccupied with getting the ingredients just right. It didn't make sense to me and made me impatient. I was baffled by the long minutes she spent plucking tomatoes from the vines in her garden, then dropping them into a pot of roiling water to break the skin and peeling them systematically before using them. I had never seen this done before, and while it improved undeniably the flavor of the tomatoes, the amount of time it took wore on my nerves. She had asked me to help her peel the cow's tongue I had picked up at Cronig's, a task not only tiresome but disgusting. Why not just open a can? What was wrong with a sandwich? This picky fussiness over food was tedious and mincing. It made me anxious.

I had no aptitude for cooking; it was as alien to me as chemistry. As soon as I learned something new in the kitchen, it left my head. Donna patiently taught me how to make lobster salad, yet the next time Hellman requested it, I didn't have the faintest idea how to make this simple dish. I helped Hellman make spaghetti sauce one afternoon, and when we were done she said, "Leave the sauce out." I was certain she meant she wanted me to leave it outside in the yard. I didn't want to ask why. I knew how little I knew and assumed this was a method chefs used to enhance the flavor of a sauce, some clever Italian trick. Later, as we were preparing dinner, she asked me to get the sauce, and when I walked out the back door and came back in carrying the lidded pot, she stared at me, put down her glass of wine, and stared again. She raised a hand to her chin. Her mouth opened. Her eyes seemed to swell a little, and she gazed at me with no expression, not certain what she was seeing. "Is . . . is that the sauce?" she asked finally. I told her it was. "Where'd it come from?" I told her the patio. She looked stumped, dumbfounded, too surprised to be annoyed. "But . . ." She lifted a hand, palm up, as if waiting to receive a clutch of coins. ". . . is there a reason?" Her voice was full of childlike curiosity.

"You said leave it out," I offered fearfully.

Her hand searched for her wineglass, blindly patting at the countertop until her fingernails clinked against its stem. She raised the glass slowly to her lips and sipped, stared thoughtfully into the glass as she swallowed, and sipped again. A smile began to grow on her wet lips, and I thanked God for the wine, which tended to dull the hatchet of her responses. She pointed her face at the ceiling and laughed and bared her grapy teeth. "That is funny."

Her laugh was inward and dry, solitary, as though inspired by the folly of an absent person. It was neither derisive nor cruel, it was as though I simply weren't in the room. I wanted to make Lillian Hellman laugh, but not like this, not at my own expense, not to my own exclusion. I wanted her to laugh at my witticisms, my jokes, the way I made my family and my classmates laugh, but I had no way of reaching her. I couldn't be funny. I couldn't think clearly, never mind cleverly. My tongue was tied in her presence. I was so embarrassed that night that I went to bed at nine, as soon as my duties were completed.

My tenth day on the Vineyard started out sweltering. I was awakened by a blinding yellow sheet of sunlight projected onto my bedroom wall. I smelled the heat before I felt it: hot dust, hot wood and paint, hot grass, and my own sneakers baking in the sunlight, giving off the salty stink of corn chips. My mouth was dry, my eyes were swollen shut with the heat, and my breath squeezed through my nostrils with a soft whistle. I stared at the ceiling and heard the springy drumming of bumblebees stumbling against the screens, their hot buzzing as they harried the roses. I felt lonesome, wished I was waking up in my own bed at home, with the crows coughing noisily in the oak trees above my mother's car and the woody smell of the attic drifting down through the ceiling. A bell clinked feebly on a buoy somewhere off the jetty, and a big ant twitched effortlessly up the wall. Where did he think he was going? What in his life would improve by his being on the ceiling?

It was six-thirty. I heard Hellman bumping around in the bathroom just off the kitchen, which had become, in a matter of a week, my bathroom. I heard the whir of the fan, the toilet flushing, water whispering into the sink. My body tensed. Would she knock on my door and get me up early to start working? Would she be in a good mood or a bad one? I held my breath so I could hear better. But the freezer clicked on and drowned out the sounds, and no knock came, no voice.

When I got up at seven-thirty I discovered that she had gone back to bed. I gathered my hair into a ponytail, stepped out into the yard in my bare feet, and was startled to see a sparrow lying dead in the grass near the door, his toothpick shins stiff in the air and the thorn of his beak gaping open, as if the heat had stunned and then suffocated him. The sight of him filled me with a woeful regret so heavy my throat seemed to close. This was the only chance a bird ever gave you to come close, to really see what he looked like, the only chance you'd have to hold him in your hand, and yet he was dead, his struggle to escape you was over. I thought of my mother; a dead bird always saddened her too, and whenever I saw one like this I felt my mother's presence very near, like a soft cap warming my scalp. I picked the bird up, laid him carefully in the shade under the trees, and made a plan to bury him later. I knew that if Hellman saw him on the grass, everything would come to a halt and she'd turn his removal into another hour-long project, complete with rubber gloves and surgical masks and sterilizing ammonia. And a running, know-it-all commentary on dead birds.

I stood on the lawn. The air and the sky were still and birdless, and the house gave off a pink light in the early morning heat. The heat had a noise—a steel brush buffing the surface of a snare drum. Everything looked enervated. East Chop was just a flat, exhausted strip of dark green land, the water a sheet of tinfoil. Far off across the water, the shore of the Cape had been stretched vertically by mist and heat into an illusion of white cliffs. I watched a fishing boat struggle slowly out of the calm, flat harbor, pushing against the shimmering heat. A voice spoke from its FM radio, small and intimate but startlingly clear across the slick expanse of water, like a buzzing whisper in my ear. And then came a tiny burst of merry music, the high-handed clarion of an advertisement.

At eight I went into the living room, where Hellman was sitting now, dressed in loose denim trousers and a white blouse, not reading, not doing anything but thinking with her legs crossed, smoking and looking hot and irritable and unwell, as though she hadn't slept. She was so thin that with one knee slung over the other, both feet still touched the floor. She had poured herself a glass of milk, which stood half empty on the table beside her. Her glasses were folded in her hand, and as she stared into space she seemed to be holding something disdainful in her mind, watching a scene unfold that she wasn't sure she liked. When she realized I was crossing the floor toward her, she turned her head quickly and said in a voice full of wet gravel, "You forgot to put my eyedrops on ice last night."

The sentence arced through the air in a wobbling rope, tightened around my neck like a lasso, and nearly jerked me off my feet. She was stunningly right. I had forgotten. The yellow air was heavy with her displeasure—it clung to my face, wrapping me in a sticky cocoon of dread. My fingers tingled. I crossed my arms and brought my sneakers together. "I'm sorry, Miss Hellman," I said. "I did forget."

"You mustn't forget, Rosemary. It's very, very important."

"I won't forget again."

"See that you don't. That medicine *must* be kept cold." Her voice was hard, and her creased upper lip stood dramatically still, a long blind of flesh over her teeth. "And the salt cellar needs refilling."

I peered over my shoulder at the salt cellar sitting cruelly empty on the sideboard by the dinner table and felt a hot blush tickling along my jawline. "It does?"

"Yes, it does, Rosemary. You should notice these things."

"Of course. I'm very sorry."

"The salt and pepper should be kept filled."

I nodded. "Very filled."

"Fill it, please."

"Right away."

Hellman breathed, looking personally offended, and smoothed the creases of her trousers. She brought her cigarette to her lips, thumb pad to cheek, knuckle to nostril, but before she could fit the filter into her mouth she began talking again, and the cigarette stayed poised, nudging at her lips, waiting for them to stop clapping in that obstructive way. This was a habit with her, a kind of tic, her need to smoke rivaling her need to speak. Clutching the cigarette, her hand appeared to have a will of its own. "Now, this morning," she said, dumping the words into the cupped palm of her hand, "I'll have an egg for breakfast. Boiled, please. And a piece of toast. Lightly buttered. And coffee." She looked up at me over the mask of her hand, her eyes scanning my features, as if figuring the depth and width of my face. Was she wondering if she could trust me to do it right? The cigarette pressed forward; she made it wait. "And a glass of ice water." Looking away, she puffed, and blue smoke leaked from her mouth as she said, "Please open these windows a bit wider. I need some air."

I went to the windows; they were the hinged, mullionless, crank-out sort. As I reached for one of the cranks, my elbow bumped the Scrabble lamp on the dinner table and it teetered crazily over the edge. I whirled around, my sneakers made a screeching bark on the hardwood floor, and my arms flew up to catch the lamp before it fell. Hellman lifted her head, aware of a disturbance, like a dog scenting another animal on the wind. She said nothing, lowered her head again. I was too far away and the light in the room was too bright for her to see what the stir was. I cranked the windows open, tiptoeing from one to the next, breathing shallowly, hoping she'd forget I was there, and when I was done I went silently out of the room, snatching up the salt cellar on my way.

The kitchen was filled with a distracting sunlight that made the room hard-edged and ugly. The sugar bowl on the table, the plants on the windowsill, and the knobs on the cabinets cast long purple spills of shadow, like warped reflections in a funhouse mirror. The floor looked dirty in this light. I made a note to wash it. I took the eggs and butter out of the refrigerator, and immediately the butter began to soften and the eggs to sweat. I hugged the stove, timing the egg on my watch, watching over it, while the rolling water pushed steam into my face. The toaster raged on the counter with a high-pitched hum, its metal slots glowing violently like two evil eyes. The egg scalded my fingers as I juggled it into an eggcup, and I whispered viciously at it, "Fuckface!" I filled a glass with tap water, got out the ice tray, and banged it over my knee, loosening cubes that were old and cloudy and smelled like chives. When I dropped three cubes into the glass they splintered loudly and slopped water onto the counter.

I carried the breakfast tray into the living room and put it on the table beside her. "And," Hellman said as I poured her coffee into a cup, "the kitchen floor is dirty. You must wash it today."

My mouth slipped open in surprise. How had she seen that? She was always on top of me, noticing every tiny detail, as though she had nothing better to think about than a few insignificant things I had forgotten to do. Hoping to make the best of it, I smiled, and, trying to sound lighthearted and jesting and snappily boggled by the coincidence, I said, "Say! How do you like *that!* Would you believe I was just making a note to do that?"

"I shouldn't have to point it out to you," she barked. "If you saw that it was dirty, it should be washed by now."

More words of apology and promised reform muttered up from my throat. My voice was weak, like damp air fluttering loose from the baggy mouth of a balloon.

"I have guests coming for dinner tonight and a lunch appointment this afternoon, so we have a great deal to do today."

Hellman touched her fingertips to her forehead, as if checking the progress of a headache, then picked up the glass of milk, put her nose into it, and began drinking with grim fastidiousness. From her throat came a squashing noise as she swallowed. Her hand shook. Her eyes were small, and in this insolent morning light they looked triangular and painful. The complicated big nose was made bigger through the bottom of the milk-glazed glass. Drying her lip with a finger, she held the empty glass out to me and without looking up said, "You can take this to the kitchen." She put on her glasses, pinched the cigarette between her lips, and reached for the egg with both hands. Like a gun moll, she grumbled crookedly around the cigarette. "Upside down. Pointed end goes up." She flipped the egg and began chiseling its top off with a knife. Cigarette smoke climbed up into her nostrils and choked her eyes as she worked; it didn't seem to bother her but made my eyes water just to see it. A white salamander of steam wriggled out of the egg as she pulled back its cap; she doused it with salt.

I hurried back to the kitchen and went to work on the floor, angrily shoving the string mop around in savage strokes, pushing its head into the bucket of hot water and slapping it back onto the linoleum. I danced the mop around the room in big steaming swaths, under the table, in front of the door, over by the refrigerator, mopping my own feet in the swampy fray. Why was she so mad? The medicine, the salt, this floor—they seemed like minor things to be so agitated about, they weren't going to kill her, yet something in her voice made me feel thoroughly defective and diminished, made me feel that she was right and I was a fool. What a moron I was for not knowing how the egg went! Fretting, burning with embarrassment, I jerked the mop this way and that, giving it every bit of my strength, and as I jammed it into the corner under the baseboard I managed to set off both mousetraps at once. With the stinging snap of firecrackers, the traps locked their wire jaws around the gray hair of the mop. One hardened piece of bait cheese shot up and clanged against the baseboard radiator, the other landed under the table. I lifted the mop with the traps clinging to it. I stared at the doorway and thought, *Please don't come in here.* I let the damp gray head of the mop fall against my shirt, and its lukewarm soup seeped through to my skin as I clawed the traps free. I hurried to get everything back into place, digging the cheese out of the refrigerator, cutting off a hunk, resetting the spring bar and copper trip wire. I crouched down with my chin against my knees and, breathless with exertion, carefully tried to reposition both traps under the baseboard, but each time I set them down they got jarred and snapped shut again with the same nasty suddenness. After several tries I got them to stay. As I moved to get up, I felt Hellman's voice shockingly near saying, "Rosemary, are you eating this cheese?"

At the edge of my left eye I glimpsed her rickety blue-jeaned legs stretching gingerly through a plank of sunlight across the wet floor, like a cautious circus performer on stilts. Her pants were too long, and when she stopped to look at me, their flared bottoms covered her shoes like two floppy bell jars.

"No, no. I'm not," I said, scooping up the old piece of cheese and slipping it into my pocket as I struggled up from the floor.

"Then put it away, please. The heat will spoil it. I want you to help me clean out the refrigerator. It's a mess."

When she turned, the toe of her shoe nicked the tin bucket, and her hands jerked in fright. *"Never* leave that bucket and mop in the middle of the floor like that, Rosemary. I could fall over it."

She went to the refrigerator and began removing its contents seriatim, inspecting each object, frowning in distaste, as though she had never seen these things before and wondered how they got here, as though the entire refrigerator were wrong, had landed in her house by some strange accident. She read the print on a jar of mustard, twisted the top off, sniffed it, then clapped it down on the counter in a way that meant this particular mustard had a hell of a nerve. I wondered if she would try to implicate me somehow in the annoying presence of all these encrusted jars and packages. I wanted to shriek, *I don't know anything about them!* I picked up the bucket and the mop and put them away, trying to think of something to say, something that would be interesting or nice or helpful. I stood near her, letting her know I was available. After a minute I said, "Was the egg OK?"

She took her head out of the refrigerator and gave me a blank look. She shifted a bottle of capers from right hand to left, staring absently at it. "Egg?" Her voice was thin with impatience. The struggle of focusing on two things at once showed behind her glasses; her eyes were clouded beneath the rapidly blinking lids. A second passed. I had no idea whether I was safe or whether she would lash out at me in a horrible way. She opened her mouth slightly and coughed once in a minute spasm like a door gently clicking shut. "Oh," she said, frowning, "the egg. Fine. Yes." And she bent toward the bottom shelf of the refrigerator, already on to the next thing.

There was no warmth, no easy dialogue with her, no acknowledgment of anything I had done except what I had done wrong. No appreciation of the few skills I had. As she handed things to me, instructing me to save them or throw them away, she paid no attention to me, didn't seem to realize that I had thoughts, that there were people in the world who cared about me. We worked this way for several minutes. The bottles and bowls she lifted up to me in her knotted sunlit hands were wet with humidity. *Rinse this,* she said. *Throw that away. See if those have spoiled. New milk in back, old milk in front. What in the world. I've never in my life seen. This should have been. How did that get. Good God, no. I have to be able to.*

When the refrigerator was finished, we began the preparations for that night's dinner: pot roast and snow peas and noodles and, for dessert, a pineapple ice that Donna had made. I did what she told me to do, slicing, mixing, stirring. For half an hour we worked side by side. I kept perfectly silent.

The air conditioning vents blew a tepid breeze onto our bare knees as we rolled slowly through the streets of Vineyard Haven in the roasting car, heading home after Hellman's lunch date. On the seat beside me she sat limply hunched against the car door in a sleeveless beige dress, like a cloth figure stitched around a skeleton of whittled sticks and twisted wire hangers, a piece of Peruvian handicraft. How tiny she was. In their dainty spareness, her delicate-heeled sandals emphasized that her ankles were only slightly thicker than her wrists. The gold-link chain around her neck hung to her waist. She stared blankly through the windshield. Her profile was solemn and still, sliding evenly across the white houses and thick tree trunks and colorful storefronts as they passed. Her lipstick was the color of dried blood. The lunch and the heat had made her sleepy. Her face looked immovable and slightly sinister, the big beaky face of a sea turtle at rest on the ocean floor, dreaming and digesting, with one dyspeptic eye half open in a sluggish scan for predators and perhaps more food. Her expensive purse lay on the seat beside her, her hands were curled into loose yellow fists on her narrow thighs. In a moment I expected her to begin snoring.

The pleasure of the hour and a half I had spent alone on her beach, while she had lunch with a laughing, red-faced man, on whose arm she had come out of the restaurant, and now the pleasure of driving the car had eased the embarrassment and anxiety the morning had choked me with. I loved to drive. When I was nine I started begging my mother to let me steer the car while she worked the accelerator and brake. Sometimes, when she drove me to ice hockey practice at six o'clock on dark winter mornings, her overcoat buttoned in haste over her nightgown, and the curious dog sitting upright in the back seat with his pointed mouth shut tight against the bitter cold, she let me do it. I could see the colorful stars needling the dark sky those cold mornings, a sky so dark and clear and cold that it was navy blue. I knew, because my brother James had told me, that some of the stars we saw weren't even there anymore, and that their beauty was an illusion, that up close the stars would be as horrible as our most fiery imaginings of hell. As we walked to the car, the dry snow creaked like Styrofoam under our feet and the air freezing in our nostrils smelled like stainless steel scissors. I could see the particular way my mother plucked out the cigarette lighter in her car, with the knob pinched between the knuckles of her first and second fingers because the thumb of her right hand was nearly useless, weakened by polio and worse in the cold, and the way the glowing lighter gave her a goatee of pink when she lifted it to her shadowy face. When the car began to warm up and she was halfway through her cigarette, my mother would sing "On the Street Where You Live," looking sweetly and comically through the dark at me as though I were the object of the song. I would lift her crutches from between us, slide over next to her on the bench seat until our hips touched and, with her consent, reach across her lap for the steering wheel and maneuver us through the streets of Milton and Dedham.

I liked the way that driving in a car you couldn't be caught by the things that passed by. It was like being apart from the rest of the world, like getting away with something rich and secretive and clever. I liked the long box of my mother's station wagon stretching out behind us like a massive prairie schooner and the way this hard rubber steering wheel, tugged so easily right or left, could bring us where we wanted to go. Sometimes she let me work the gas pedal and brake. The car was like a responsive animal, a horse, a friend. I remembered how our headlights yellowed the ragged snowbanks as we took the turns. One morning, in front of Dedham Courthouse, when I was hanging on to the steering wheel waiting for the light to change, we heard a tapping on my mother's window and looked up to see a pale-faced cop staring at us with his arms crossed on his chest and his belt hung with small, dark packages of leather: gun, walkie-talkie, ammunition, block of parking tickets, and one chiding eye-brow flung upward on his forehead in a look that said, *What the hell is this?!* When the light turned, my mother stepped on the gas, and the mischievously guilty look on her face glowed green in the fanlight of the speedometer. As we passed through the town she smiled slyly at me.

Thinking happily of my mother now, I inched to the end of a one-way street and stopped in line behind two other cars at a stop sign. As the cars in front of me proceeded through the intersection, I followed slowly behind. When we were nearly halfway through, Hellman's voice, like the sudden startling honking of a Canada goose, blared wildly out of her mouth, filling the car with an un-godly sound. "Jesus Christ, what the hell do you think you're do-ing?" she cried. "Stop! Stop! Stop this instant!"

I eased my foot off the gas pedal. Was she talking to me?

"Stop this car immediately! You have a *stop* sign!"

It was, indeed, me she was shouting at. We were in the middle of the intersection. A stream of cars had rolled up behind us, pressing us on in their hot current. I couldn't just stop now.

"That was a stop sign back there!" Her cheeks trembled with anger. Her left hand held her throat, while her right hand gripped the Naugahyde armrest, as if in anticipation of a head-on collision.

"I saw it," I said. "But we're third in line. It's okay to go through."

"It is certainly *not* okay to go through!" she snapped.

I stared at her, dumbfounded. "But . . . it *is*. The law says if you're second or third in a line that's already stopped, you can go through on the coattails of the first car."

She went rigid in her seat, and her two loose fists became hard balls punching at the air above her lap. "I *never* heard such a law!" she shouted.

Her anger struck me as thoroughly disproportionate, insane even, especially because she was wrong. "But . . . it *is* the law," I said.

"I never heard of it!"

"But this is Massachusetts."

"I know it's Massachusetts!" she said. "I never heard such a crazy law!"

Her hands flashed open and made an unsuccessful lunge at the dashboard. A surge of anger flooded upward through my chest. I could feel it in my throat, my mouth, my eyes, in my fingertips on the hot steering wheel, and when I realized that I had said *coattails,* my anger grew suddenly worse and I wished furiously that I hadn't said it. The word suggested stealth and cunning corruption, precisely the kind of spuriousness I was hoping to dispel. But I knew I was right. Massachusetts was my state. She was from New York. And for her to yell at me so rudely this way, persisting in telling me that I was wrong, was intolerable. Her voice banged against my ears like a hockey fan's coarse shouting at a Bruins' game. I couldn't let this go by.

"But, Miss Hellman, it really is the law!" I said.

"How do you know that?!"

"I took the Massachusetts driver's test six months ago! I passed it! I got my license! That's how I know it."

She raised her head, clutched up the strap of her handbag with both hands, like a buggy driver clutching leather reins. She appeared to be thinking of something to say, some snappy string of words to whip back with. A blistering silence ensued as we inched up Main

Street in front of the Bowl & Board. A blond family of five, looking like people I might know, stood on a corner in front of the Capawock Movie Theatre, squinting happily under the sharp blue sky in their shorts and flip-flops, pressing dripping ice cream cones to their lips. I wanted with all my heart to be one of them. Hellman tapped her lower teeth crookedly against upper, as if checking to see that the teeth were still there—a turtle sensing danger. I gripped the steering wheel, strangling its rubbery hardness with my fingers. I wanted to push the gas pedal to the floor and ram into the back of the car in front of us, or floor it up the sidewalk in front of the Vineyard Dry Goods Store, knocking off flower boxes and parked bicycles until she shut up.

"I got a ticket last year for going through a stop sign," she said. "I don't want you ever to do that again!"

"It was legal." The authority and resoluteness in my voice made me nervous.

She raised her hand between us to silence me. "Don't argue! And don't *ever* do it again! It was *dangerous!*"

I hated her. She could raise her hand like Jesus and say, "No," and that was it, that made it true and right. She was the winner no matter what. She could rattle her jowls and correct me, though she was the one who was wrong. Her defensiveness, her unwillingness to hear anything that didn't confirm her own ideas, infuriated me. She was famous and powerful and people waited to hear what she had to say, but that didn't mean she could change state laws. I could feel my face twist into a glowering scowl. It seemed to affect my vision. The sky looked blood-red, and the pavement disappearing under the hood of the car had a weird violet hue. Sunlight flashed in fractious platinum patches from the chrome and glass of the cars parked along Main Street. I felt I was on the verge of saying something irreparable, for my dread of making mistakes, of being wrong, of being wronged, was gaining on my fear of her wrath. I wanted to defend myself, to say, *Fuck you, you bony old bitch!* but that would surely be the end of this adventure, and I'd have to flee the Vineyard in disgrace.

My rage had pitched me into a dizzy confusion, and the heat was unbearable now. I reached for the fan switch in the bland pea-green dashboard, hit the radio knob instead, and an avalanche of between-station static thundered at us full-volume, like fanatic applause. I snapped the radio off. She gave me a snake-eyed look. She must have thought I was a complete dunce. Though she hadn't actually said it, I knew she wasn't delighted with my performance so far, but it wasn't entirely clear to me why. I was not a dunce. And some things I did well. I could drive, for example. That was one thing I could do. Hellman couldn't drive at all anymore, couldn't see over the steering wheel, couldn't see *period*. She needed me to do it. And I was good at it. I had had practice.

When I was ten, eleven, and twelve and my mother came to pick me up from school or a party and I gleaned just from the slant of her mouth that she had been drinking, I would climb quickly into the car so that no one would have a chance to come over and find out from her face and her slurred words that she was drunk. More than once as we sped down Route 128, her heavy lids would begin to slip shut over her eyes, her head would tip forward, and her hand would drop limply off the steering wheel and into her lap like a piece of heavy fruit. And then the car would begin to slide across the white lines toward the wobbling hubs of the eighteen-wheeler beside us until, in a fit of uncontrollable fright, I hit her arm and her head snapped up again. My fear of dying on this dull gray highway lined with stiff green pines was not greater than my fear at seeing my mother like this: limp-faced and inviting such danger. If she loved me and I loved her, why would she do it? Eventually terror would make me knock the crutches out of the way so I could slide over and put my hands on the steering wheel. I shoved her good foot aside with my own foot and pressed the gas pedal. I didn't ask her permission.

What would be the point? I knew how to do it. I knew from all the practice that I could keep us between the lines. I was glad I could do it. I would rather be there with my mother in that car, where I could help her when she was drunk, than be standing alone at a window at home worrying about her.

I knew that I could get us home without killing us, and now, as the sooty line of traffic slowed to a glinting stop, I pushed on the brakes a touch too hard, deliberately, and watched with a certain satisfaction as Hellman's head jerked forward and her fox's hands went up and her big breasts strained against her seat belt.

When we arrived home, Hellman changed her clothes and went to the beach for a swim, passing wordlessly through the kitchen in a beach dress and heading out the back door and down to the shore. I stood at the sink washing wineglasses and watched her cross the back yard to the beach path. Then I went into the living room, picked up the binoculars she kept on the table, carried them to the window, and trained them on her as she stumbled through the hot white sand. The binoculars rendered the world slightly two-dimensional—the sky and sea and sand, foreshortened, were stacked up like hazy stripes painted roughly on a wall. Warped ribbons of heat wriggled through the air around Hellman's face like a rippled pane of glass, and each time she turned her head I could see her great grimacing profile and the brown age spots on her temples. It gave me a thrilling sense of power to know she couldn't see me, that she had no idea how close I was to her, that my nose was pressed against hers through the dark tunnel the heavy lenses created. She dragged her ankles slowly through the glowing sand—a dromedary slogging across the desert.

When she reached the water's edge, she dropped her towel and pulled the loose beach dress over her head, and as the dress slid up her body I realized with a sudden shock that she had nothing on underneath it. She stood stark naked on the beach, a skeletal figure with two pendulous bosoms dangling from her rib cage like white leather wineskins two-thirds empty; her pruny arms and legs the color of butterscotch in the bright light. I was fascinated and frightened by the sight of her nakedness and astonished that she didn't care. On other days I had seen her go down to the beach in a black bathing suit. She waded jerkily into the water with her hands up, sank down suddenly to her shoulders, as though she'd bumbled into a deep hole, and sat there: a big yellow head floating on the thick, flat water. She climbed out again, glittering, the bladdery bags of her breasts swaying, the triangle between her legs a mossy blur. She bent down to pick up the towel, lost her balance, staggered slightly off course, and tried again, fingers reaching. She wrapped the towel around herself and stopped to rest with her hands on her hips. Her broad chest sparkled. Her mouth hung open in the sun like the entrance to a cave. She peered about. I knew she couldn't see a thing, and a look of uncertainty clouded her face, as though she didn't quite know what to do next.

She looked tiny in the deafening light, and I felt a sudden pang of sorrow. She was old and defenseless, standing there all alone like the blindfolded object of a firing squad, her chin held high, trying to determine what was near her. I knew she had no relatives to speak of, no children, no husband, no parents or siblings. She had friends, but I had a sense that she bothered them sometimes. She was always calling John Hersey and asking him questions and sending him things from her garden and asking him to come over to have a look at this or that, and I had the feeling he just wanted to be left alone so he could go back to his work. She was always fighting with the Styrons, always banging the phone down on people. Her lips moved slightly. As I worked the focus, the image trembled slightly in my eager hands. I could see she was muttering to herself, raising a hand in a kind of explaining gesture. And then the phone rang, and I jumped with a start and thunked the binoculars against the window pane, jabbing myself in the eye with the eyepiece. I hurried to the phone; the voice of some guy named Palevsky pulled me back to my job.

By late afternoon the kitchen had grown darker and softer, and Hellman moved through it, from table to counter to stove to refrigerator, with unwavering momentum, making last-minute adjustments to her dinner. The wine-ripe smell of pot roast filled the kitchen in dense wafts that crossed the hot current of her sour mood; the swim seemed to have worsened her displeasure. She tasted the gravy, standing over the stove and leaning forward until her lips bumped against the raised spoonful of sleek brown sauce. She put the spoon down, and with her mouth watering she peeled red onions, holding them to her chest and flicking at their crumbly mauve skins with her long fingernails. She made a vinaigrette dressing in a glass bowl, beating the viscous liquid slowly with a whisk, whipping up an important noise, like the soaked wings of a cormorant slapping at the surface of the sea. She picked up spoons and forks, jabbed into plates and pots with them, and laid them smartly down on the counter with a click, turning immediately to the next task. Standing over a pile of snow peas on the counter, she muttered, "We'll be six." Then she clutched up a handful of peas, dropped them into a bowl, and said, "That's enough for one." Her hand stretched across the counter, fingers scrabbling at the pile of smooth flat pods, raking up another handful. "That's two." She straightened her eyeglasses, snatched again, breathing through her nose. "Three."

The handfuls were stingy, and as she went along, counting in a cranky voice, they grew smaller still. By the time she was finished, there were enough pods in the bowl for two and a half people. I pictured the guests at the dinner table staring in perplexity at the two glistening pods I had laid on their plates. When she turned her back to measure out noodles from a box, I quickly shoveled up more peas with both hands and threw them into the bowl. And when she went out of the room, arms dangling, to find a gravy boat, I added many more noodles to the scanty pile she had apportioned. Didn't she know this wasn't enough food for six people? In fact, if you considered that I would have to eat dinner too, it was seven.

"You can slice these onions," she said, pointing at the purplish translucent spheres.

And you can sit on them and rotate, I thought.

I picked up a paring knife and went to the cutting board. I hated cutting onions. Slicing and mincing for hours, and for what? Who ever noticed anyway that there was any damn onion in the dish they were eating?

She stepped to the back door on her way to get some tomatoes from the garden, and as she opened the screen door an enormous figure in a baseball cap crowded the doorway, having come around the corner from the outside staircase. His huge and unexpected appearance startled Hellman and made her snap, "Who the hell are you?!"

The young man plucked the cap from his head and held it to his chest like a shield. "Victor Lynch from The Department."

Hellman's lip curled in wary confusion. "What?"

"The Sanitation."

"What is it?!"

"You called me."

"Like hell! I don't know anything about it. I can't be bothered like this." She made a move to shut the door on him, and he tipped his head to keep her in sight, stirring the air with the blue lump of his hat as if to fan her memory. "The trash men, ma'am. You called us."

"About what?!"

Dryly he said, "Your trash."

She looked at the swollen plinths of his sneakers through the open slit of the door. For a fleeting moment she was disarmed. A low, ingenuous *Oh* escaped her mouth, and then the door flew open and she took a step toward him and fixed him in her vision. "Well, why didn't you say so! Listen, I'm sick and tired of having those men tell me I must put my trash at the top of the hill. I do not understand why they can't come down here to my house and collect it, the way they do for every little shack on this island."

He shook his head. "They can't do that anymore, ma'am. Sorry. There was a near incident here last summer. The trucks are too heavy to come down this steep hill. It is highly dangerous."

"This isn't the goddamn Middle Ages. There are hills all over the Vineyard with trucks going down them. What's the matter with these men? They don't know how to drive?"

He closed his eyes for a second in a practiced way against her words. "It's an accident waiting to happen."

"It's a fucking travesty is what it is."

"It's dangerous."

"It is nonsense. It is silly. And you are silly."

The man stepped backward, like a person moving away from an automobile freshly aflame by the side of a highway. He waited. The steady look he gave her through the silence held neither injury nor anger but simply patient disappointment at such an uncharitable remark, and seeing his stillness, his unwillingness to bark back at her, Hellman lowered her voice. "I pay my taxes in this town," she said. "I'm entitled to the same services everybody else is entitled to. As a resident I have certain rights. I'll speak to your superior."

Her indignation was imperial now, professional, commanding.

The man leaned back on his heels, crushing the grass and the earth beneath him. Behind him the afternoon sky had begun to change, the blue to the east tainted faintly now with orange. He fingered a hankie out of his hip pocket and wiped his gleaming pink forehead in soft dabbing motions, pressing and lifting, as though stemming the flow from a cut. He thought about the problem. He winced at the hankie, folding it meticulously into a neat square.

"We'll help you as much as we can, ma'am, within the bounds of safety."

This lawfulness irked her. "Rotting uncollected garbage is unsafe!" she cried. "A young girl hauling heavy cans up the hill is unsafe." As an afterthought she waved her hand in my direction to show him which young girl.

The man looked at me in my apron hacking at the onions. He scratched the padded palms of his big hands, adjusted his glasses, and looked back at Hellman in a way that seemed to question the sincerity of her concern for me. "Four tons of garbage shooting down your chimney is unsafe."

I thought this was a very good thing to say.

Hellman inspected him, sizing him up, looking at the fat balloon of his belly, the pale expanse of his bare arms, the blue T-shirt damp with sweat stretched taut as a trampoline across his big bosoms. The bottom half of his face was mottled pigeon-blue with the powerful ghost of a beard. I feared she might snap something cruel at him. But instead, with surprising acquiescence, she said softly, "Well, you got me there."

She had seen that he was quick, and this caused the change in her tone, the shift in tactics. Her voice took on a wheedling, self-deprecating, self-pitying twist. She was suddenly his friend, they were in on this together, colluding, succeeding. It was almost sexy. "I know it's difficult for the men," she said, fingering a button on the front of her blouse. "I know it's dangerous. I understand your concerns. It means a great deal to me, however. You see, I suffer a physical disability at the moment." She brushed a hand daintily along her soft hairline at this personal revelation. "And to show my gratitude, I'll tip the men extra at the end of the summer."

I gathered up the disks of onion. She was shameless. She was sly. One minute yelling, the next minute appealing to his sympathies.

"Ma'am, I will see what we can do for you."

"What can you do for me?"

"Trust me."

"I don't even know you."

He sighed. "I will come down and get your trash cans my personal self."

"Fine." She leaned out the door and pointed toward the side of the house. "They're kept over there."

"Fine," he said, putting on his hat. "A pleasure meeting you."

Without saying goodbye, Hellman stepped back into the kitchen, muttering, "Christ, what a fatso," and headed for her gravy. She sniffed with delight. She stirred the gravy needlessly with a spoon, thinking, replaying the encounter in her mind, her elbow gently pumping and her hair shining in the warm light beneath the hood over the stove. I could see, from the slant of her shoulders, the incandescent web of folds on her cheek, the cozy set of her mouth, what great satisfaction this little triumph had brought her. The clock on the stove hummed. The smell of pot roast clung to my hair. My knife clicked regularly on the cutting board. She lifted a bowl in her hand and, without turning around, said, "Will you rinse this?"

I had rinsed that bowl a moment ago. I told her so.

"Well you didn't do a very good job. Rinse it again."

I put down my knife, took the bowl from her, and looked into it, trying to see what she saw. It looked clean; like her hair, it shone in the mellow light. Before I could move, she barked, "Rinse it again!" and with breathtaking hostility she shoved at the bowl to get me moving. My heart seemed to sink lower in my body. I felt she wanted to hit me. I couldn't look at her face. The bowl was clean, but I went to the sink and held it under the faucet anyway, a stupid little performance, an exercise in sheer subjugation. I was bound to her with chains. She moved from the stove to the counter and said, "Get me another spoon."

The spoons were in a drawer directly in front of her; when I tried to open the drawer to get one, she pressed her hip against it, pushing it shut. She stood firm, blocking the drawer while she peeled the waxy paper from a fresh stick of butter. "Wait a minute," she snapped. "Don't hurry me. And don't get in my way."

Her words came at me like a solid mass bouncing against my cheeks. Her anger filled the kitchen—the walls seemed to creak with the pressure of it. My face and ears burned. The only people in the world who ever treated me this way were my brothers and sisters, and they could be forgiven because I knew they loved me, and because I could treat them the same way back and be forgiven too. Being spoken to this way by a virtual stranger was like being hurled with great velocity into an unfamiliar dimension. I was struck dumb. I was defeated, and my failure paralyzed me. My head was suddenly empty. I felt the stinging pressure of tears building behind my eyes and turned away, determined not to let her see me cry. My nose tingled, my mouth watered, my eyes began to swim in their flooding sockets. The brown cabinets were a blur. I pressed my eyes hard with my knuckles to keep everything from spilling shamefully over and returned to the onions, dazed, unable to see the outlines of the cutting board. But my cheeks stayed dry. I vowed not to let her know anything about me.

In the slowly receding evening light I knelt beneath the trees and scraped at the ground with a serving spoon until I had formed a shallow bowl, a warm grave for the dead bird. His feathery jacket was a subtle design of camouflage colors, the reddish brown, the gray, the white and beige, the striped wingtips and the serried daubs of black on his head. The soft crescent of his belly was smooth and round and white as an egg. Already the black beads of his eyes had lost their hard shine, had begun to wither and sink and go gray. The slightest thing could kill a bird, yet bravely they flew huge distances, migrated through harsh storms, searched for food in dangerous places, built intricate nests with anything they could find—dental floss and straw and dollar bills and dust, and sometimes their own feathers.

The air was moist and salty, grainy with an auburn light, and the shadows beneath the trees were still hot. East Chop was aflame, reflecting the falling sun, its houses and rooftops brilliant orange squares across the gold-flecked water. Clouds of starlings flexed and twisted above the trees. The house and yard were quiet. Hellman was in bed with a sheet up to her neck, napping before her guests arrived. The slightly sandy earth felt warm against my fingertips at first; the deeper I dug the cooler it got. Earwigs emerged and shimmied away from me. My ponytail slipped forward over my shoulder and brushed against my chin as I worked. The ground beneath the trees was strewn with scree and gleaming white shells fallen from the beaks of gulls.

I laid the bird in his hole. It was terrible to put this pretty thing under the dirt, but not terrible for him. Death, I knew, was sad only to the people who got left behind, unbearable to those who remained because it was irreversible and final. My father was dead, that was one thing. We hadn't seen him for nine years. We would never see him again. No one ever said anything about that; we didn't talk about it. It wasn't a story. But my mother had told me stories about people in her family who had died, stories that made me so sad as a child that I begged her to retell them. Her family was sometimes more vivid in my mind than my own family because they were stories—they had beginnings, middles, endings. A few details and a few bright lines of dialogue made them more memorable and easier to digest and identify than the constantly running film of my own family, jumbled and unfocused, projected onto a screen too close to my face. I imagined the people my mother talked about and was drawn to them because they were gone and couldn't be reached and because I knew how much my mother loved them. I would sit with my sisters on my mother's bed and we'd listen to the stories until our lashes grew black and slick with tears. Though she tried hard not to get sucked into this bourgeois pool of sentimentality, even my oldest sister, Sheila, was affected by the words, and her face would grow long and stern and worried, and her blue eyes would dart nervously from face to face, as if something terrible were about to happen.

There was a story about Ellen, my mother's oldest sister, who was pretty and was the only one of the four Rohan girls who had blue eyes and curly hair. Ellen and her mother were best friends and went everywhere together. One Sunday on their way to Mass they saw a man going haltingly along Poplar Street on crutches with one leg dragging limply after him, and Ellen asked her mother, *Mama, will I ever be like that?* and her mother said, *Of course not, Ellen.* In July of 1927, Ellen made her first communion. A month later, walking home from Tenean Beach, Ellen said she didn't feel well. She was nauseated and weak. She had a fever. When they got home her mother crushed some aspirin into powder, mixed it with a little water, and fed it to Ellen in a spoon, but the little girl had trouble swallowing, and the liquid dribbled down the front of her navy blue bathing suit in stark white rivulets, like rain streaking a windowpane. Her mother put her to bed. In the night Ellen tried to get up to go to the bathroom, but she was too weak to walk. A doctor came to the house, examined her, wrapped her in a blanket, carried her down the front steps to his car, and rushed her to Children's Hospital, where it was determined that she had contracted polio. By the end of three days she was totally paralyzed. Her mother stayed by her side, holding her hand, talking to her, observing the progressive devastation of the virus. Finally, Ellen was unable to breathe well enough to stay alive, and when her mother realized that she was dying she said,

Ellen, which would you rather do, come home and play with the other kids or go up to heaven and see Jesus? And Ellen answered, *Heaven and see Jesus.* In the hospital bed Ellen wore a long-sleeved nightgown, and when my grandmother felt her hand growing cold, she pulled the sleeve of the nightgown down over the small hand and held on to it that way so she wouldn't have to feel the cold evidence that the life of her girl was gone.

The story made me so sad I couldn't see straight. I would stare at my hands resting at my mother's feet, embarrassed by my foolish grief over people I had never met. It made me think of the day my sisters and my mother would die, and just the thought of my mother with her eyes finally closed, unable to answer me, was so unbearable that I felt weak. The idea of being left behind was too terrible to contemplate. I had once asked my mother why Ellen chose Jesus over going back home with the kids, and I remember my mother staring at me, thinking hard about the answer, her mouth slightly open. After a long silence she said, "She must have known she had no choice."

I pushed the loose dirt into the hole, covering the bird's pretty feathers, and piled it up in a safe mound so nothing would get at it. Marking it with a small stone, I stood up, brushed the blades of grass off my knees, and headed for the house. I tiptoed up the stairs to see that Hellman was still sleeping: through the open door I could see her nose and cheek and one hand hanging slightly over the edge of the mattress. Then I went down to the kitchen telephone and dialed my mother's number. It rang a long time. I could see my mother's house at this hour—five o'clock, the sun rushing through the kitchen windows, lighting up the washer and dryer and the brick back stair-case. On the windowsill was an avocado pit skewered with tooth-picks, filling a glass of water with the pulpy white clot of its tangled roots, thin as rice noodles, and on the stove was the teakettle I stole for my mother when I was twelve. Talking dreamily on the phone

one morning, Sheila had burned the bottom out of the old one. I knew it upset my mother; the kettle was costly. A lot of things Sheila did upset my mother. When my mother said, *Sheila, you did that to my kettle?* Sheila slapped her way out of the kitchen on her big bare feet saying, *Power to the people, Nona,* and my mother shouted after her, *I am the people!* I went to Lechmere's and picked out a Revere Ware kettle with a copper bottom, put it under my arm, and walked out the door without looking over my shoulder. I don't know what my mother thought when I walked into the kitchen and clumped the kettle down on the stove. It was the brightest thing in the kitchen that day.

Finally I heard the receiver being lifted from its cradle, clunking clumsily, loudly, and the feeble sound of a TV in the background: Christopher Lydon divagating on Channel 2. I heard the muffled sound of the receiver being dragged across the bedspread, across magazines and papers, with telling slowness, fingernails tapping on the hard plastic, and I knew she'd been drinking. With a familiar sinking wave of disappointment and resentment, I hung up the phone before that thickly counterfeit voice could fill my ear.

FIVE

A Thursday arrived with a dark sky and a humid wind that disturbed the trees. The water in the toilets upstairs swayed gently, as if the earth itself were rocking in the wind. According to my schedule, Thursday was my day off. Somehow it had been arranged, against my better judgment, that even on my days off I would still prepare Hellman's breakfast. I did it, put the tray down before her in the living room, and asked if it would be all right to leave when Donna arrived at nine.

She squinted up at me from under the wide cutting board of her forehead. "Why would that be all right?" she said testily.

What now, I thought. What trick was she going to pull now? Perhaps she had simply forgotten my schedule, or perhaps the word *schedule* meant something different to her, something looser, more flexible, something she could stretch to accommodate her mood. "Maybe I'm wrong," I began, "maybe I got it wrong, but isn't this the day I don't work? I could be wrong."

"Don't work?" She took no pains to hide her skepticism. She struggled out of her chair and shuffled into the kitchen, where she brought her face up to the schedule taped to the wall over the telephone. Her mouth was stiffly fixed, lips corralling the big teeth as she strained to see the days and hours parceled out in my handwriting. I stood in the doorway, leaning on the jamb with my hands in my pockets, and watched her. These minutes were rightfully mine: knowing that gave me strength.

"Absolutely right," she murmured in astonishment. A faint glimmer of consternation flashed for a second across her battered features. She had forgotten. I narrowed my eyes at her in triumph, half-hoping she would notice.

"Of course," she said gently. "Of course. Go ahead."

I headed for the door.

"But before you go . . ." She cleared her throat with a raking noise.

I turned around.

"Before you go . . . I wonder would you mind just taking the spare tire in the trunk of the car to the garage and having it fixed?"

Was she out of her mind? Just have the tire fixed? That was a ninety-minute job. I was dying to leave, dying to be on my own finally and choose the course of the day for myself, and I dreaded the possibility that she would find a way to take this away from me. I had no great adventures to fill my time with that day, in fact, I had nowhere to go—my sisters were working, and it looked as if it would rain anyway, but it was the principle of it. But when I saw her looking at me through those shatterproof lenses, her hands joined at her chest in feeble defense—or was it supplication?—and her two dry yellow elbows pointing, waiting for my answer, I felt compelled to say, "Sure," resenting her request and myself for yielding to it.

She reached for her handbag hung on one of the kitchen chairs and said, "And I'll give you your paycheck now." A palliative gesture.

She scribbled with a felt-tipped pen, peeled the check from its block, and handed it to me complaisantly. "Thank you," she said. She paused, the knots of her cheeks seemed to loosen, and her eyes looked briefly puzzled. Then she said, "You did a very nice job last night."

Was she smiling, trying not to smile? I took the check.

"As a favor to you, I've made your check out to cash."

I looked at the check. Indeed, it said *Cash*. I looked back at her.

"For your taxes," she said.

What taxes? Did she think a person who made nine hundred dollars a year paid taxes? It seemed odd to me, but I folded the check, put it in my pocket, said, "Thank you," and went out the door.

The garage was a stall in Oak Bluffs with a gritty cement floor. A couple of used mufflers hung like grey hams against one wall. A guy in a colorless jump suit stiff with dirt was working on somebody else's flat tire, whistling a song and pausing in the melody to grunt each time he punched a stubborn lug nut with his wrench. Above him a light bulb in a tiny cage hung from a wire in the ceiling, shining so weakly it seemed to illuminate only itself. I walked back and forth across the floor in my sneakers as I waited, glancing now and then at the jerking silver second hand on my wristwatch. *You did a very nice job last night.* Like a guttering flame, her words met the damp tinder of my resentment, sending up not fire but a noxious cloud of contempt. The words sounded foolish. I wanted to feel the pride and pleasure I had hoped for, but all I could think was, *Who cares?* She was stupid for thinking I had done a good job. Stupid. And I didn't do a good job. I had wanted her to like me, but now that she did, I had disdain for her. I wouldn't let her approval in, didn't trust it. She was dangerous. I felt the admonishments and rebukes, the corrections and dismissals stretching out behind me in a span of sour days, and I heard the annoyance that regularly sharpened her words, and my ears burned all over again. Pacing the garage, I reenvisioned bitterly last night and the nice job I had done. It was just one of her many small dinners. William Styron, sitting to Hellman's right, had used the word *verisimilitude*. His clothes looked rumpled. His eyes were puffy. He sawed at the steak I had cooked on the outdoor grill and looked like a cop on his day off, as if he belonged in a powerboat bobbing on the noisome slicks of Buzzards Bay with a beer can in his hand, only it wasn't Styron's day off particularly: he looked that way every time I saw him, no matter the day or occasion—a thin rime of whiskers glittering on his chin, the throat of his shirt open to his sternum, sleeves rolled up, baggy trousers, gray hair a touch too long palmed roughly back on his head. It was hard to make out the bones under the flesh of his face. He looked sleepy and a little annoyed, and his lower lip gathered itself into a small pointed spout. Hellman had directed me to pour her cheapest wine into a decanter—to disguise its provenance from her guests, I was certain. Amused by this little secret, I filled Styron's glass to the brim.

Like a skittish gull plucking scraps of bread from a crowded boardwalk, I had fluttered and swerved and dipped at the table, briskly advancing and retreating, bringing platters and taking them away again, making their dinner pass more smoothly. I felt like a nanny at these dinners, like a tool, and in constant danger of doing something wrong. There was so much to remember I was sick with nerves, while Hellman and the Styrons and another couple whose name I didn't get sat there with ease, eating and drinking and not having to worry about whether the food was arranged right, whether there was enough meat on each plate, whether the pasta was quite hot enough, whether the water glasses had been attended to. Living. That was what they were doing. And having fun. I wanted to sit with them and laugh too. But I pretended not to be listening, pretended not to be looking at them as they lifted forks to their mouths. They talked about Leonard Bernstein. "Lennie," they called him. His sixtieth birthday was coming up at the end of the month, and there was to be a dinner concert at Wolf Trap in his honor. But Lennie wasn't *old* enough for that kind of public celebration, they said. A birthday wasn't an important enough *event* for him to be touting with such fanfare. Mrs. Styron lifted her wineglass and frowned into it, and with a scandalized shake of her head said that, honestly, she was a bit offended by the whole thing. And her husband and Hellman and the others clucked and tched in agreement. It was vain of Lennie. It was self-serving. Frankly rather embarrassing.

Self-serving: the term stuck in my head, while other strange and interesting topics floated in the hot air above the candle flames. Cold drops of sweat trickled down my back as I shuttled between the kitchen and the dining room, between the hot stove and the laughing people. Mrs. Styron kept turning her pretty peach-toned face to me and smiling indulgently, as though I were a famous imbecile miraculously able to perform simple domestic tasks under close watch. When Hellman said from her throne at the head of the table, "I went to Macy's with Claudette Colbert and Bill Blass and we bought the place out!" Mrs. Styron hugged herself with her bare brown arms and exclaimed, "Oh, what *fun* company!" There was information in the way she said it. She knew them personally, *too*. They were *fun*. But what exactly was it about them that was fun? The answer was there in the corners of her white smile: they were fun because they were famous. Famous people were, naturally, fun to know.

Hellman said something dismissive about young people and drugs. Irresponsibility. Experimentation. "Occasionally I smoke marijuana in cigarette form," she said, sounding like a research scientist. "My doctor has offered to prescribe it for my eyes. It eases the symptoms of glaucoma."

I had never seen her smoking it, but I knew where she kept it, hidden in a Marlboro box in her bathroom closet, eight twiggish little cigarettes like twisted lengths of toilet paper. It meant nothing to me. I hated marijuana. Everyone at school smoked it, and I did, too, hoping each time it would work the magic that everyone everywhere said it was supposed to, but instead of making things better, it made them worse. It made me paranoid and afraid and slightly ill. It made the world jiggle unpleasantly. At night my friends and I went out to the cold, slippery soccer fields, where sheets of frost reflected the lights from Memorial Hall, and smoked it. Then we went inside and sat in chairs, and with my arms crossed I watched people talking and thought, *What are they saying? Are they looking at me in a strange way?* Every glance from across the room, every twitch of a person's lip became a menacing riddle, a potential vessel of derision. I couldn't in any way see the appeal of this drug.

Styron cleared his throat significantly and said something declarative. He had a slightly southern accent. When he laughed, his small mouth pursed. Hellman's napkin fell to the floor and she stepped on it, oblivious. Styron talked, and held his glass up to me for more wine. I lifted the carafe and poured. I couldn't stop thinking of John Hersey, who on other occasions had sat at this table. Hersey was so tidy. He was handsome, with straight posture, a diffident manner, and a soft voice. He was attentive, the kind of guy, I thought, who didn't say boastful things and would never be seen with his body in an indign position, bending over with his ass in the air. He was discreet and self-contained. Hellman respected Hersey, I could tell, because she didn't fight with him or with his wife, Barbara, who had a Dutch boy's haircut and the even white teeth and button nose of a ventriloquist's doll. One evening when Hellman and the Herseys were sitting on the couch having drinks and eating hors d'oeuvres, Hersey had tried to spread a bit of smoked bluefish on the stale crackers Hellman had ordered me to pass around, and the damp cracker had collapsed and the whole mess landed at his feet. Hellman didn't see it, and with balletic grace Hersey shoveled it up quietly, wrapped it in his napkin, and placed it discreetly on an empty plate. As I took the plate away he said, "Thank you, Rosemary."

Last night Hellman and her company had talked about Peter Feibleman, Hellman's friend who sometimes called from Los Angeles. His parents had divorced when he was fifteen. "It crushed him," Hellman said. And his mother had tried to commit suicide.

As I gathered up the empty plates and carried them to the kitchen, I wondered why a person would commit suicide. Especially a person who had kids. You'd have to be very unhappy. That kind of self-destruction seemed unnatural to me. In my grade school there was a girl whose mother had killed herself; I remembered the strange feeling I had whenever I saw her, a sweet, pretty, pale-skinned girl with dark hair, dark brows, red lips, and a gap between her two front teeth—she had a heavy cloud over her that she'd have to carry around forever. Why would her mother leave her like that?

When I came back into the room, Styron was putting down his fork and giving his opinion about English men. He smoothed his hair, then dragged a hand with a sandpapery rustle across his chin. Small hands for a guy like him. At rest his mouth was a beak. I took his smiling wife's plate. What was she smiling at?

The mechanic at Ben-David's garage was suddenly in front of me, peering at me out of his sooty face, his watery, pink-traced eyes questioning me with mild blinks, his grin a glistening matrix of decay in a dark frame of dirt and whiskers. "Try smilin', hon'," he said.

I could smell his hair, like axle grease and cigarettes and ink. His breath carried a tincture of garlic and tin. I tried smiling.

"Because," he said, "you look awful glum for a nice young lady like you." He pointed a finger out the door at the car parked at the curb. "Tire's all set."

I had been so distracted I hadn't noticed him working on it. I asked him to charge it to Lillian Hellman.

His eyes stopped blinking, his face went stiff. "Was that *her* fuckin' broomstick I was fixin'?!" As he shook his shaggy head, I saw a segment of startlingly clean white flesh beneath his collar.

The humid wind had picked up speed, and the black sky over the ocean seemed to be hurtling toward me. A canvas awning over a shopfront flapped and beat like a bass drum heralding the storm. As I headed for the car, big viscous raindrops began to fall with the sloppy splat of spit, slapping my cheeks, my hair, the sidewalk. In an instant the warm pavement darkened, sending up the smell of a dirty iron skillet, and before long the gutter began to flow, iridescent as a mackerel's back. Bare-legged figures loped up the street and ducked into doorways. I flicked on the windshield wipers and headed home; the wind flung the hard rain against the car with the crackling bite of rock salt. It knocked trash cans and sent them lumbering and staggering into the streets. Branches came down like twisted shrapnel, metal signs vibrated on their poles.

I went down the back stairs to my room, sat on the bed, and wrote a letter to my mother, the third that week: *Dear Nona: mean, crazy, hate it, should have, why can't I? shouldn't have, will you?* Writing my thoughts down for my mother, I felt secretive and lonesome and slightly sad but somehow safe, like an owl cloistered in a hollow tree. I knew that my mother understood me and would sympathize when she read my words. I folded the letter and put it into an envelope. I organized my two pairs of shoes under my bed, folded my clothes more neatly in their drawers, rearranged the few things I had on hangers, straightened the bedspread, ordered my six paperback books alphabetically, and counted the soft dollar bills in the envelope under my pillow. I checked myself in the mirror, tried to no avail to arrange my face in a way that made it look less round, combed my hair, and sat down on the bed again. I inspected my fingernails, then stood at my gray windows and chewed off what remained of them. The trees billowed and bent, rattling their shining wet leaves. The waves in the harbor were pinkish brown in the storm. Fat clouds slid low across the sky like clumps of dirty wool. The Vineyard felt more like an island when the weather was bad, more like a flat disk of mud floating desperately on the sea. In the wind my screens bucked in and out, in and out, like a body panting.

I put my yellow raincoat on, the same cracked and chipped rubber raincoat I had worn in the sixth grade, clipped its metal buckles, put the letter in my pocket, and went downtown, walking quickly with my collar up and my head bent against the rattling rain. The raincoat was stiff with age and fit me like a clunking cylinder of armor. Its sleeves were too short, revealing my bare wrists, and it pinched me under the arms. Within two minutes my sneakers were heavy with water. Wet leaves flew against my bare legs, and the whipping rain pricked at my face. The planes of Main Street looked immutable in the rain—the tumid sky, the pavement, the clapboard houses staring blankly onto the tree-lined street in a gray light that came from no particular direction. Nothing, not even the wind, could jar this town, and though the air was warm, the day felt seasonless. A few of the houses had dates on their fronts and historic Vineyard names that were echoed on local street signs and showed up occasionally in old books like *Moby Dick:* Mayhew and Vincent, Daggett and Coffin, the first New England interlopers, who, with their prayers and their whaling, had forced the local Wampanoags to welcome them. When I saw these names I saw prim, horse-chinned British people with ruddy skin and dark woolen clothing, thriving on storms and virtue, dried codfish and freedom.

Just above the center of town I passed the tiny pre-revolutionary schoolhouse that had transmuted into a kind of history museum. An enormous wooden flagpole stood in front of the schoolhouse, and as I passed near it my eye was drawn to the copper plaque screwed boldly to the face of the pole. The copper was pretty, weathered to a pale lichen-green, and looked soft as cloth. It bore the raised copper words:

To commemorate the patriotism of three girls of this village
POLLY DAGGETT
PARNEL MANTER
MARIA ALLEN
who destroyed with powder a liberty pole erected
near this spot to prevent its capture by the

British in 1776.
This pole, replacing the other, is erected by the Sea Coast Defense
Chapter DAR
1898.

Rain dripped from my eyebrows. I did some figuring: the pole was exactly eighty years old, had been standing here like this for that long. The girls had done the deed two hundred and two years ago. To prevent the British. I read the three names several times and wondered what the word *girls* actually meant. How old? I was interested in girls who would blow a thing up with gunpowder. Girls were probably allowed to do more in the old days. No, that was ridiculous, of course they weren't. They couldn't, for example, have played ice hockey. Two hundred years later *I* almost couldn't play ice hockey. They had no team for girls at any of the schools I ever went to, no team for girls in my town. In grade school I had to go to the coach and ask if I could play on the boys' team, and it was the same story at St. Paul's. When I was ten I had played street hockey at Milton Academy with my brother Johnny and his friends, but only because my brother knew I wouldn't dare embarrass him by crying or screwing up. If I had, he would have killed me.

We practiced upstairs in the playroom, whipping pucks against the wall, trying slap shots, wrist shots, dribbling, taking splinters from the wide floor boards in the soles of our stockinged feet. Johnny was nearly two years older than I, and in certain moods he would pound me against the refrigerator just for looking at him. He would call me *douche bag* and *moron* and twist my arm behind my back or hurl a ski pole at me with such harpooning force that it punctured first the fabric of my jeans and then the flesh of my thigh, astonishing both of us, and then, half an hour later, forgetting himself, he would tell me I knew how to ride a bike better than Teddy Walsh and that I was the best pitcher he had ever seen. When I asked if I could come and play street hockey with him one Saturday morning, he shrugged and said, "I don't give a shit," which was as close as he ever got to saying yes, then rode off to the game on his bicycle without telling me he was leaving. I glimpsed him from the living room window pedaling down our driveway and ran for my hockey stick, a cracked Koho he had discarded, and raced after him on my bike, slamming in and out of potholes, straining to keep sight of him through the fuzz of new buds on the trees. He was way ahead of me, a small dot furiously pedaling, his bicycle slightly too big for him and his body tilting from side to side as he stretched to keep his toes on the pedals. I thought I saw him turn and look back at me, but he could have been looking at anything.

The boys gathered in the parking lot behind the Milton Academy girls' school, and when he saw me, the biggest one, Fritz Pope, said to Johnny with grinning skepticism, "Mahoney, that's your sister."

The look on Johnny's face said, *No shit,* and into the obedient silence that followed he added definitively, "My sister's playin'."

No one questioned him. He was the best athlete among them. He was small but tough. His eyes were slightly slanted in a way that in the early morning, when he had just got out of bed and pulled on his underwear, made him look Chinese—his straight black hair added to this Oriental illusion. He was pale and thin, and if you had never witnessed the way he threw a baseball, or skated backward, or ran from here to there with liquid agility, or scrambled squirrellike over a chain-link fence, you might have been deceived into thinking he was vulnerable and weak and possibly girlish. His black hair was longish, hovering in sideswept bangs over his brow, and invariably he showed up to play street hockey in brown oxfords with leather soles, the stodgy, downtrodden shoes of a failed salesman. Up and down his bare, skinny shins were scars and gouges and the red welts of flea bites. He could perform excruciating feats of double-jointedness, and, with a lot of fussy plucking and poking, he could deliberately fold his upper eyelids inside out upon themselves, like two gruesome wounds. He could swallow all but the tail of a long string of spaghetti and pull the whole thing out again for his appreciative audience. Invariably he sported a broken arm or black eye or an impressive centipede of black stitches on his chin. I admired Johnny's bravery, his insouciance. He was mysterious and mercurial. His great power lay in not caring. I wanted not to care. I wanted to be like him as much as I wanted to be like my sisters. I wanted to blow something up with gunpowder.

I went into the Bunch of Grapes bookstore and wandered around, glad to be out of the rain, glad that nobody knew me. The store was crowded with damp heads and brightly colored slickers. A bunch of boys were shoving each other around in the kids' book section. They wore brick-red sailing shorts and Lacoste shirts and Top-Siders taped up with duct tape, a kind of rich kid's uniform. They had bracelets of braided rope on their wrists and braces on their teeth that showed how much their parents loved them. Their wary, tanned faces and silky blond heads were like Keep Out signs I wanted to knock down.

A wet leaf had stuck to my bare shin. I rubbed it off and saw a book called *Tropic of Capricorn*. I hated titles like that, but I flipped through it anyway. *With my free hand I unbuttoned my fly and got my pecker out and into position. . . . I could see too that she was enjoying the idea of being fucked half asleep. The idea of . . .* I looked around to see if anyone was noticing me read this book. Every other page had a sex scene. Henry James was a much better writer, but he would never use the word *pecker* or describe sex. It was a completely different kind of writing, and you knew the writer was writing about himself, or some imaginary version of himself. And he didn't even pretend to care about all the women and their cunts and quims and pussies, which I understood was his way of being funny. The women were like zombies, mesmerized by his penis. It was cartoon sex, like the *Mr. Natural* comics that Sheila read. I couldn't tell if it was daring or stupid. I wanted to buy it, but the book was too expensive, and besides, how could I go up to the counter and say to the woman with the scrutinizing eye, "I would like to buy this." I sensed that this woman, with a librarian's pristine omniscience, was aware of every book in the store. I put the Henry Miller back and picked up a skinny little book by Joan Didion called *Play It as It Lays*. The cover said, as a kind of advertisement, THE TRUTH ABOUT WOMEN AS OBJECTS. I opened it. *Maybe she can buy herself a good fuck.* Same general subject as the *Capricorn* book, only this time it was a woman and it was much more serious, with an abortion and a lot of unhappiness going on. I wondered if John Hersey wrote about sex, too, and when I found him on a table devoted to books by Vineyard authors I opened *The Walnut Door*. No sex scenes that I could find. Just a nice book with a nice guy making a pretty door: very nice but a little boring. Lillian Hellman was on the table too, and I eyed her books without touching them. They were a little frightening now that I knew her, and more fascinating. There was a paperback of *Pentimento* with black-and-white pictures from the movie *Julia* on its cover—Jane Fonda and Jason Robards looking serious. Hellman didn't look a thing like Jane Fonda, and it was a joke that they had picked her. Movies were always making reality look better than it was, romanticizing, mythologizing. Well, books could do the same. I had heard Hellman telling somebody on the telephone that she had wanted Barbra Streisand to play her in the movie. That would have been more like it—the big nose and the eyes too close together. The collection of Hellman's memoirs stacked up neatly and brightly and tidily on the table made her seem like something more than she was, something bigger, not even a person anymore but an idea, different from the rest of us. Styron's books were also on the table. I looked at his picture in the back of one. He reminded me of a reveler in one of those Jan Steen paintings we had to look at in art class. Fascinating pictures of Dutch people having fun. But that wasn't quite right, because Styron wasn't happy that way. He was serious. Things didn't seem that funny with him. And he had all his teeth. There was a pile of signed copies of Art Buchwald's book on the table, too. I had talked to Buchwald on the phone. He wrote humorous columns for the *Vineyard Gazette*. I stared at the books and thought to myself that these people had it all worked out.

I wandered toward the back of the store and saw a fat little girl sitting on the stairs in nothing but a yellow bathing suit and sneakers, hiccuping morosely. She stared at me with the devastated look of a jilted lover, lifted a candy necklace from her throat to her mouth, and gnawed on it. I liked candy necklaces, used to buy them at the candy store not far from my mother's house. I wanted to talk to the girl, but she didn't look like the kind of kid who'd be easy to talk to. Her eyes were dark and volatile. My mother would have been able to talk to her, I thought. She knew how to draw people in, particularly children. More than once in my childhood I had approached my mother's car after running in to some store for her, only to find a small pack of young strangers gathered by the open car door, listening to her talk as she sat behind the wheel or watching her pretend to play an invisible flute, her eyes demurely closed, her lips pursed, her fingertips nimbly tapping at the air. Shy in her unpredictable presence, the children would stand at a slight distance and stare with their mouths open, as though at any moment she might float up through the windshield and into the sky. Coming upon this scene, I always experienced a moment of embarrassment, for it seemed that in my brief absence my mother had grown somehow younger than I, delegating reason and responsibility to me. I feared the children would find my mother strange, but my fear always gave way to pride as I saw the deepening interest in their soiled, moonlike faces. They sucked vaguely at their fingers in abstruse absorption and watched as she demonstrated how you could turn the substantial red vinyl bench seat of a 1963 Country Squire into a rocker by releasing the hand lever and sliding the seat rhythmically back and forth to the hilt of its two extremes. One by one they came wordlessly, intimately, forward to lift her hand from the seat lever so they could try it for themselves. On some occasions, moved by their fascination, one or two went so far as to climb into the car with her, her crutches lying between them or across their shins like pieces of driftwood, to experience the rocking. Eventually they would notice her leg brace, whereupon her explanation of how it worked, too, became a game of immense interest and amusement.

I knew what those children felt, for she had worked that spell on me countless times and in myriad ways. Across from the foot of her bed were two windows, and some evenings, as we sprawled on the bed, my mother would lean toward me suddenly and say in a low voice, "Listen, Ra, maybe if we concentrate hard enough, you and I can get this bed to rise up and take off like a sleigh through those windows and over the treetops and take us sailing up over Milton." And she said this in such a mysterious way, with an expression of eager intrigue and her cigarette hand trailing a boa of smoke as it flew up over the covers in imitation of how the bed would go, that I fairly believed it was possible. I braced myself, waiting for it to happen, concentrating, imagining the first rough movements of the bed as it lifted off the floor and how we would sail over the long–idle exercise bike standing sadly in the corner of the room with a motley array of disused handbags dangling from its handlebars, and then over the front lawn, and how it would look to the people below as we proceeded over the Milton Public Library in our nightgowns with the sheets luffing and snapping and the wind fingering our hair. We concentrated and eyed each other with eerie expectation, willing the bed to get up and take flight. It never did. Inevitably our concentration was broken by the sound of the dog stickily licking his chops on his cushion by the radiator. Pretending to be irritated, my mother would eye her beloved dog and say, "How about him, Rose? He never says thank you when I give him his food, and he never shaves his chin."

I left the bookstore, wanting a candy necklace and the Henry Miller book, and drifted up the street, stepping in and out of little shops, the Bowl & Board, Brickman's, Mardell's, David Goulart, Murray's, the Vineyard Dry Goods Store. A handwritten sign in one shop window said JEWERLY. I went into the thrift shop, where all the junk on the Vineyard had landed in a crowded jumble. The place smelled like dust and mothballs and mold and hair, like the ashy bottom of a ragged pocketbook, but I liked it. Its shelves were packed with empty mayonnaise jars and chipped china, plastic picture frames and dented old toasters with cloth-covered electrical cords. I found a blouse for fifteen cents and tried it on behind a brown curtain. As I was changing, I studied my breasts in the full-length mirror; they seemed, unfortunately, to have done all the growing they were going to do. What was wrong with them? They weren't terrible, they just didn't look like the generous, global breasts you saw in magazines. My sister Elizabeth had perfect breasts on a slender body; the simplest rags looked sexy on her. Why her and not me? I bought the blouse anyway, delighted with myself over the fifteen cents, and headed out to the street again.

The rain had abated slightly. Silver puddles rippled and quivered in the wind, and pearls of water glistened on the hard surfaces of the cars parallel-parked along one side of the meterless street. In the wind the taut telephone wires crisscrossing above the street scissored and wagged. A bloated cigarette butt floated in a puddle like a white earthworm. As I was looking at it, a Takemmy Laundry truck came up the street, ripped through the puddle, and splashed my legs with cold water.

On my way to the post office I stopped at the public bathroom, a

small municipal hut at the edge of the A&P parking lot, and was
confronted with a piece of information written on the back of the
stall door: WIGGINS TAKES IT UP THE ASS. I stared in wonder and fear at
the words. I felt a little sorry for poor Wiggins, whoever she was. I
imagined some gormless checkout girl at the A&P and wondered
whether this pronouncement was true, or whether it was just spiteful
slander from somebody who didn't like her. How could the woman
who wrote it know the intimate things that Wiggins did? Whoever
had written it, I decided, was jealous over some guy that Wiggins
liked. Wiggins. What a silly name. Thank God I didn't have a name
like that. Holding the paper bag with my blouse in it on my lap and
looking down at my own muddy footprints on the floor I tried my
name out a few times in the bathroom stall, repeating it softly. *Mahoney*. It was a little bit silly, for some reason. Tough guys in movies
were always called Mahoney.

At the post office there was a letter from my friend Ames Cush-
ing and one from my mother, and when I saw my mother's handwriting my heart was flooded with happiness and sorrow all at once.
It was the most familiar handwriting in the world; each letter, the
way my mother fashioned it, had a bigger meaning for me, as though
the letters were scribbled somewhere within my head or on the
underside of my skull. I saw the handwriting and immediately, with
no effort of recollection, I heard my mother's voice in my ear. I
opened the letter, and a limp five-dollar bill fluttered out from its
pages. This was a habit my mother had gotten into while I was at
school, a five or a ten now and then, and seeing the money now
surprised me and made me sad. I could picture her sitting at her desk
tucking the money into the letter and feeling good about doing it,
even though it wasn't much money. It was less money, in fact, than
she thought it was. The letter was written on the back of my father's
old stationery embossed with his name and address: John P. Maho-

ney, MD, 2100 Dorchester Avenue, Boston, Mass. 02124 Telephone CYpress 6–4000. There were boxes of this stationery stacked up in my mother's office. She couldn't see the point of throwing away good paper.

Dear Ra:

. . . I've been thinking about you and your job. You're a wonderful girl, Ro, everyone can't be wrong. It's not easy to move forward, because risks are involved and it's always more comfortable to stay put. But I know you're ready to take on new challenges, and that's exactly how you grow. The rest of the times we're just on plateaus. You stretch yourself to go beyond your present tolerance, and growth can be endless. I don't think any of us is aware how far we can go. Learn everything you can there. Let Lillian play great lady; she doesn't have much time left to preserve that image. You can cater to her demands and at the same time preserve your integrity. Look on it as a great period for learning how to handle yourself and others. Never be afraid to speak if anything's bothering you, but do it calmly and straightforwardly.

. . . This is a good lesson in self control for you. So often in life we are judged wrongly and there's nothing we can do about it, so you take deep breaths, realize you are right, and go on to the next thing. You would like everyone to know you are right because how we appear in the eyes of others does concern us somewhat, but basically it doesn't really matter if you know it. How to handle disappointments, how to deal with losing, are really excellent preparations for life. . . . In a one-to-one situation, like yours with Lillian, no matter what the other person says you do or don't do doesn't make it true. Their say-so isn't half as important as what you know. You're good, Ra, so you'll do a good job. You ought to relax and just be Rosemary. I certainly think you should speak when it's appropriate. You don't have to be angry.

You'll never have such free time again to read, write letters, and keep
your journal. So do it. Be sure to read some every day. I'll try to write
often, just a few lines here and there.
Rose, I love you a lot.
Mom.

Tears pushed up into my eyes and I pressed them away with the
heel of my hand. I already knew my mother loved me. I knew she
loved me more, in fact, than she loved herself. She didn't have to tell
me. I already knew it, and I knew that what she said was true. But it
was easier to say than do. *Just be you,* she always said. But what was
that? On the back of the letter I had written to my mother I scribbled: *Mom, today was my day off and I also got paid. I don't know what to*
do with the money. She said she made the check out to cash for my sake,
taxwise—or so she says. Is she lying? If I cash it will she get the police on me
and say I stole her money? Love, R.

I mailed the letter and wandered slowly down to the ferry dock
and stared at the boats in the harbor. The masts wagged softly, and
there were so many of them they were like a screen in the air above
the water. From where I stood I could see the roof of the Mill House
tower, its shingles so smooth they looked like thatch. And I could see
the stone jetty hooked around the harbor of sailboats like a protective
arm. Gulls with bowling-pin bellies bobbed and veered like tethered
kites over the dock, their feet tucked back and their yellow beaks
slightly open and touched with a drop of red at the tip, like blood.
The big black *Shenandoah* with its two slanting masts looked unfazed
by the wind. The black woman who was usually sitting in the sand
wasn't there. I missed her; she was only one small person, but whenever I saw her she seemed to fill up the beach. I stood there a long
time, then headed back through the town toward upper Main Street.
I was sick of looking at trinkets in tourist shops, and I had nowhere

else to go. I stopped at the library and looked at books and magazines for a while, then checked out *The Sun Also Rises* and reluctantly returned to the house. The footlights along the path to the front door were on, and in the wetness they threw off a wispy drifting steam like glowing pots of incense. I hated the house from this side; it was plain, and there was so little of it to look at—all you could really see was its flat top, like the roof of an old office building.

When I went down to the kitchen Hellman was making her lunch and drinking a Bloody Mary. "Back already?" she said, glancing over her shoulder at me as I came in.

I put my book on the table and held onto the bag with my blouse in it. My hands were wet and cold. "Yes."

She broke two eggs into a bowl. "Like some lunch?"

I stared at her back, surprised by the offer.

"I'm fixing some for myself," she said, turning her nose to look at me. "If you'd like to join me, you're welcome."

Was she inviting me to have lunch with her? Why was she doing that? It made me nervous. I didn't want to join her. I could say no, but what would I do then? Lie on my bed and stare at the ceiling while she sat out here by herself? That would look rude and even a little weird. I was trapped, like a cat clinging to a log floating down a river. "Okay," I said.

She broke two more eggs into the bowl and stirred. "We'll eat here."

There were ears of corn piled up on the counter, a basket of bread on the table, and beets from the garden boiling in a pot on the stove. As she made scrambled eggs, she sipped occasionally from her glass, its walls furred with soft clumps of red from the tomato juice. Hellman was at her nicest when she'd had a drink. Her face took on a melancholy softness, the slant of her eyes grew more acute, and she moved even more slowly and was more predictable. Carrying a carton of eggs from the refrigerator, she moved with a blind, picking tactility, a crustacean's delicate clumsiness. Her thin neck was draped in soft, loose folds of flesh like pale velvet. The tops of her ears were hidden by her soft hair. I could see she was at ease; her voice had the absent, mumbling tone it sometimes achieved when she relaxed. I felt safer when she was a little drunk, and it wouldn't have mattered to me if she drank an entire bottle of vodka.

I took off my raincoat, threw it on my bed, went back into the kitchen, and offered to help her make the lunch. I didn't want to, but I knew it was polite to offer, especially when I would be eating it.

"Slice a few carrots, if you like," she said.

When I cut my thumb slicing the carrots, she said, "All right?" and though the cut bled steadily and stung with a hard, blaring throb, I said, "I'm fine."

"Not hurt?"

"No," I said, hiding the cut in a paper towel. "It doesn't hurt at all."

I didn't want to tell her the truth. Now that I had my chance, I didn't want to tell Lillian Hellman anything. It was the only bit of control I had over her.

We sat at the table before our two plates and began to eat. "This is a fine, silly lunch," she said. She lifted an ear of corn to her mouth and raked the kernels off with her teeth. She chewed carefully, grinding the corn as if with a pestle. She raised her glass to her lips slowly, carefully, as she always did, and I realized for the first time that she rarely wore earrings. Her naked earlobes were huge. Neither of us spoke for some time. Self-consciousness extracted all the flavor from my food, and lifting the forkfuls of beets to my mouth, chewing and swallowing, I was merely going through the motions. I was acting. She seemed to enjoy every bit of what she ate, not looking up from her plate much, apparently not affected by my presence in any way, as though this were something we had been doing together every day for years. She chewed and swallowed with great concentration, her fork trembled in her hand as it rose from plate to mouth, and when finally she spoke, her voice was wetly altered by some colorful scrap of corn or beet lodged in her throat.

"You're interested in France," she said. Her hand rummaged in the bread basket, like a crayfish picking over muddy rocks.

I looked up at her. What had made her say that?

Before I could respond, she pointed with her buttery knife to the library book on the edge of the table. "The books you're reading. They're about France."

The unexpectedness of this made me sit up straight in my chair. I stared at the book. "France?" I tried to think of the books she had seen me reading. *The American,* Colette's stories, and now this Hemingway book.

Hellman said, "Newman in Paris, Colette in the French countryside, Hemingway's France after the war."

I was startled. I hadn't noticed that connection at all. All I saw was that the books were about people and yet were entirely different from each other; I didn't see them as connected. Which country the stories took place in didn't matter to me. This was a different way of looking at a novel, thinking it was about France. The whole thing had caught me off guard: she had noticed me. She saw what I read and knew that it was about France even before I did. Suddenly I felt stupid and nervous. I felt she was looking through my clothes, and I crossed my arms impulsively. Though I was not especially interested in France, I said, "Oh, yes, I'm very interested in France."

"You've been there, yes?"

I hadn't been there, and I knew that if I said I had she would start asking me what I thought of it. "I've never actually been there," I said.

She looked at me and reached for the salt.

I had hardly been anywhere, and that seemed pathetic and unsophisticated too. "But I've been . . . I went to Ireland. Once."

She lifted a tattered ear of corn to her mouth. "Pretty place," she said into the corn, munching and seeming unimpressed with Ireland.

I moved my fork from one side of my plate to the other. Ireland was better than nothing. "And I'm going again in the fall."

"Vacation?"

I told her I was going there to study. My school was letting me go for my senior year, paying for it with my scholarship money.

"Oh?" She nodded, registering some kind of understanding. "A whole year. I have an Irish friend. Annabel Davis-Goff. She's the wife of Mike Nichols. They'll be coming here. You'll meet her. She's Irish-English actually."

Irish-English. I was pretty sure that meant the woman wasn't really Irish, she was English and just happened to live in Ireland.

"What else do you like to read?"

"Flannery O'Connor," I said blurting out the first name that entered my head.

"Hmph." She frowned and blinked for a minute. "You understand her?"

As soon as she said this, I realized that if there was something you had to understand about Flannery O'Connor, then I definitely didn't understand her.

"I don't know," I said, trying to laugh it off.

"Very taken up with Christianity."

I hadn't really noticed the Christianity part, though I saw the preachers. It didn't matter to me if I didn't get it. I liked Flannery O'Connor. I liked the weird characters in her stories, the wall-eyed goons, the people with handicaps and infirmities saying mean and funny things. I got the jokes, the witty descriptions, the snappy ripostes. "I like Willa Cather," I said, "and John Steinbeck. And I like William Faulkner and Edith Wharton."

Hellman wiped her mouth with her napkin. "You like American writers," she said quickly.

Why didn't I notice these distinctions, these classifications? To me these writers were just people who told stories. It didn't occur to me that they were Americans. I felt as if I had had a blindfold over my eyes, and suddenly I didn't want to talk about books anymore.

"Have you read Melville?" she said.

"Moby Dick."

This was only partly true. I had tried to read it, but only some of the chapters interested me. There were whole dense chapters of that book that when you tried to read them were like chewing on a brick. I knew I couldn't talk about Melville, or really about any of the books I had read. It was like sitting in front of a teacher who had all the answers while you had none. I lifted my napkin from my lap to my mouth; my cut thumb throbbed tightly with hot, metrical taps.

"And you must like Joyce," she said.

"Yes." I did like Joyce; I liked *Dubliners*.

She nodded, sipped.

On the other hand, when I had to read *A Portrait of the Artist as a Young Man* for English class, I couldn't read it. I hated it. I didn't get what everybody at that dinner table was so mad about—priests, God, the government. I got so frustrated with it that in a fit of disgust I swept the book off my bed with a powerful backhand; it skittered across the floor and landed under my bureau, where it stayed for several weeks. I remembered the cover, a drawing of Joyce with his jutting chin and his googly little eyeglasses and his cursory mustache that didn't look right on his small face; it looked like a disguise.

I tried to think of something smart to say. "Joyce isn't . . . he's not American."

Hellman smiled. "No. He is not American."

"He's Irish."

Why did I say that? Everyone in the world knew he was Irish. It was about as useful as saying, "Sixty seconds make a minute."

"What grade are you in now?"

"Going into twelfth," I said.

She nodded. "You have brothers and sisters?"

"Yes."

"How old are they?"

Quickly, perhaps hoping that the numbers would sound different and fewer, I said, "Nineteen, twenty, twenty-one, twenty-two, twenty-three, twenty-four."

There was a silence while she calculated, and then her sparse eyebrows went up and she said, "My God," which was what people always said, and I knew they were thinking, *Hicks.* Barefoot Irish hicks who had no idea where the kids were coming from.

"And you're what? Seventeen?"

"My parents wanted us," I said. "It was all planned out." As soon as I said it I regretted it. I didn't have to defend them.

"What does your father do?"

She was looking at me steadily now, having finished her lunch. I couldn't tell whether she was truly curious, or was just being polite, or was talking to me because she was bored and there was nobody else to talk to. I had already told her my father was dead. She had forgotten. Now she was expecting to hear that he was a cop. I hated these questions.

"He's dead," I said. "He was a hematologist."

"When did he die?" she asked, without offering the usual apologetic pause or expression of sorrow.

"A long time ago."

"Why?" She reached for her cigarettes and plucked a paper match from a flattened Maison Robert matchbook. "Was he sick?"

The question was a surprise. People didn't usually ask that. Was he sick? I had to think about it. I remembered visiting him in a hospital with my mother, long low buildings among some pines in winter, like a Boy Scout camp. There were patches of ice and snow on a thick bed of pine needles on either side of a paved path. I remembered my mother in her blue coat crutching carefully up the slippery hospital steps, her breath bursting white into the clear cold air. We went down a hallway until we found my father's room. He was sitting in a chair and looked pale and strange, wearing pajamas in the middle of the day and his own maroon bathrobe from home. His hair, which he always wore in a crew cut, had grown a little longer. I wasn't used to seeing him like this. Why wasn't he dressed? He said, *Hi, Rose,* and asked me how old I was now, which was an odd thing for him to ask. He was my father. He should have known. He had been there a month, and during that time he had made a little wooden box with tiny brown and white tiles laid into its top in a pretty design. He had never done anything like that before. Nobody ever said anything about his heart or any other ailment. Nobody said anything about sickness at all. A few months later he died. He went to work one morning and didn't come home at night. By the time I went to bed that night he still wasn't home, and later, when I should have been asleep, I stood at the top of the stairs and saw nuns and police coming in our front door. The next morning in the kitchen, my mother told us he was dead; he died of a heart attack at work. I went into the living room and looked out the window; I knew this meant he wouldn't be coming back. After that we hardly ever talked about it. It was a subject to be avoided. I didn't know why I wanted to avoid it, but it seemed to me there was something wrong with it. And it made me strangely uncomfortable to talk about it now, as though a terribly bright light had been turned on me, its heat scalding my face and singeing my hair.

"He had a heart attack," I said.

Hellman lowered her hand from her mouth, and a cottony bulb of smoke tumbled voluptuously from between her parted lips, growing white and round as a golf ball; she snatched it back with a quick inhalation and it disappeared down her throat. With her free hand she lifted the nearly bald ear of corn to her mouth, breathed smoke over it, then chewed. "How old were you then?" she said through her teeth.

"Eight."

There was silence then, and she paused in her chewing with the cigarette in one hand and the corn held an inch before her mouth like a fat harmonica. She was suddenly preoccupied with some complex thought, her unblinking eyes dully searching the air above my head, the big squarish lenses of her glasses reflecting the pale curve of my own forehead. Her fingers twitched as if enumerating. And then she lowered the corn and said with real interest, "How on earth did she manage?"

"Who?" I said, though I knew who.

"Your mother."

I never stopped to think about how my mother managed. Whenever I looked into the well of my childhood I saw first, for a brief moment, myself alone with my mother, sitting on her bed in a silent house, and then, in a burst of sound and color, the surface of the water was broken and the rest of them appeared: twelve other eyes, twelve arms, twelve legs, six other mouths speaking in urgency or demand. Noise came from every corner of the house, hands banging on the piano, scraping at guitar strings, slamming a window shut, a muddy boot kicking a door, cries of delight or violence, a snowball ringing contemptuously against a windowpane, the stereo constantly clamoring with the sound of the Beatles, Bob Dylan, Joni Mitchell, the television spewing out the vaudeville sounds and sights of the *Three Stooges* for seven bodies stretched across my mother's bed like slaughtered soldiers at Antietam, staring dead-eyed. I saw my sisters Sheila and Elizabeth fighting upstairs every morning over some article of clothing. I saw Sheila, with three earrings in one earlobe and a lurid red light bulb screwed into the lamp in her room, dancing atop her desk to the sound of the Kinks. I saw Stephen, Sheila, and Elizabeth crawling out a window onto the roof to smoke pot, Johnny shooting BB holes into a wall, Stephen hurling a metal dustpan at James and accidentally sending it through a plate-glass window. James, with a towel around his narrow waist, banging the bathroom door open and shouting, "Father stinkin' Lyons!" in frustration at some nagging question of my mother's, Ellen and myself jumping around the periphery of the living room without ever touching the floor, couch-to-table-to-radiator-to-love-seat, knocking lamps as we went. I saw Johnny at the Milton Academy skating rink stealing cans of Tahitian Treat from the drink machine by snaking his skinny arm up into its bowels in a Houdiniesque trick of contortion, and Sheila so far ahead of the fashions that she caused a stir at her school by showing up in army boots and a floppy hat and an old lady's dress. I heard James shouting, "Fuck yourself, you bitch," when my mother wouldn't let him buy a motorcycle. I saw the brilliantly lit Christmas tree in our living room tipping over with a crash, the bearded, long-haired boys Sheila once brought home to camp out on the living room floor, one of whom painted a fantastical green-and-red face on a wall upstairs. I saw, for that matter, the entire second floor of our house, which, because the stairs were difficult for her to climb, was just out of my mother's reach and thus had been allowed to flourish and grow wild, like a primeval forest: the floors littered with the play money of board games scattered like autumn leaves, chairs with broken legs, fat worms of compacted dust beneath the baseboards, dirty clothes flung across the floors like cumulus clouds across the sky, twisted apple cores rusting and curdling on the windowsills, Johnny in his new hockey skates, their blades like two gleaming cleavers, traversing the playroom floor in stomping, hacking, strides. I saw that scarred barnboard floor, with its skid marks and stains and copper-colored knots so perfectly round that I was endlessly tricked into thinking they were pennies, and the gaps between the boards wide enough to accommodate pistachio shells, quarters, screws, whole pencils. I saw the notes we left for each other in magic marker on the walls: *Baba sucks* and *Ellen, Marjery Albers caled and she wants you to call her back* and *Hi, Johnny, love me.* I saw the swastika that Johnny, enchanted with the ethos of *Hogan's Heroes,* had scratched into a windowsill when he was ten. I saw the two policemen who, with their bulk and swagger and smell of tobacco, were no less threatening to me than the robbers they had come to sniff out, poking through the upstairs rooms one summer night (we had arrived home from somewhere to discover that our house had been broken into) and confirming to each other with tremulous awe, "The bastards trashed the place." It was plain to all of us that not a single thing upstairs had been touched.

The tiny lines of age radiating from Hellman's lips were like basting stitches in a hem. Slightly slumped, she was looking at me, with her elbows on the table and her hands dangling beneath her chin and her eyes blinking patiently, like a drinker at ease at a bar, waiting for the end of the story. A drop of ash fell from her cigarette onto her empty plate; too late, she made a flicking gesture with her hand, an effort to claim responsibility for it. She wanted to know how my mother managed.

I heard my mother's bright voice ringing out in command: *clean up, put back, don't break, leave alone, eat all of, get off of, get out of, come home from, go down to, don't lie to, don't make a meal of, take your feet off of.* I saw her driving for the thousandth time down to Blanchard's liquor store and sending me, or whichever one of my brothers and sisters was with her, in for a fifth of Seagram's 7 and a pack of Lucky Strikes. I hated doing that; I knew what embarrassment and chaos and blank unavailability it would lead to. From time to time, in a rare and excruciating fit of frankness, I begged my mother not to drink, but she drank anyway. I hated those bottles, saw them as the cause of everything that was wrong with my life, but I went into the liquor store for her because she wanted me to; it was easier for me to hop

out of the car and run in than it was for her. When I refused to do it
and sat stubbornly in my seat, it made her angry, caused her more
trouble, and made me feel guilty and cruel. In the winter if I refused
to do it, she might slip in the snow and get hurt. I didn't want to
make things more difficult for my mother than they already were, but
I despised this job, and as I walked up to the door of the liquor store I
dragged my feet, like a person going to the gallows.

Everything in that store was familiar: the fluorescent lights hanging from the ceiling, the skinny guy behind the counter in the cardi-
gan and faded tie, smoking a cigarette with a yellow pencil behind
one ear and a ballpoint pen behind the other. He wore brown leisure
slacks with a stretch waist and had a stubbly chin and a face gone gray
with smoke and boredom. His hands trembled and his fingers were
shiny-smooth and dirty from handling coins and bills. At nine, ten,
and eleven I was still young enough to be surprised and enchanted by
the store's automatic door, distracted for a moment from my odious
task when the servile door with its gasping, sucking noise opened
wide upon my approach. The place had the toasted, dusty smell of
the cardboard boxes stacked up in rows displaying their bottles. I
didn't have to ask where the Seagram's was, I knew the aisle. The
bottle was brown with a regally crowned red 7 on the front. I would
put it down on the Formica checkout counter, deliberately sliding it
over the lesion of white scuffed into the counter's surface by years of
bottles slid over it in just this way. Slim Jims and Beer Nuts hung in
packages over the counter, and although I hadn't asked permission
from my mother, I pulled down one or the other. I knew she
wouldn't protest; Beer Nuts and Slim Jims were payment for the
service I had rendered: if she got what she wanted, I would get what
I wanted. I asked the man for the cigarettes, and he dropped them on
the counter, saying, "How's mum today?"

I always said, "Fine," and with a flourish that was meant to be
humorous, the man plucked the pen from behind his ear and handed

it to me so I could fill in the amount on the check my mother had given me. I was careful to do it right. I didn't want to disappoint her. On the few occasions when she had forgotten to sign the check, I signed it for her in my juvenile script while the man smiled kindly on this triune of illegal activities. Nona R. Mahoney: it was swervy and swollen and looked nothing like her signature. "Tell mum a big hello for me, will you?" the man would say, and I went out the door with the bottle under my arm, the cigarettes in one hand and the Beer Nuts in the other, tramping hatless across the brittle ice and snow toward my mother's car, a skinny, pale-faced girl with a part fashioned jaggedly down the middle of my scalp and a sky-blue parka decorated with skiing penguins. As soon as we got home, the bottle's pinkish paper seal would be broken.

Looking at Hellman's questioning face, I saw the Thanksgiving turkey falling from a platter in my mother's hands to the kitchen floor with a greasy, mushy thud. I saw five of us standing in the cold outside the closed skating rink, waiting hopelessly for our mother to come and pick us up. I saw Elizabeth and Ellen trying to maintain some modicum of order by cooking the dinner and telling me to set the table. I saw Ellen and myself taking the bottles and putting them upstairs where she couldn't get them, and then, guilty over the unfair advantage we had taken of her handicap, feeling too powerful and cruel, bringing them down again. I saw Ellen, fourteen and unlicensed, pulling up to the trolley station in my mother's car to pick me up when my mother was passed out on her bed; Stephen, fifteen and unlicensed, driving us all home from some New Year's Eve party because she was drunk, and when the police stopped us he told them the truth; they took one look at her, and at the pale frightened faces staring from the back seat of the car, and let us go. I saw Ellen and myself hiding in the woods by our school after the school fair, while people searched for us because our mother was passed out with her head on a table in the school library. I saw myself on long afternoons sitting stiffly in the sunlit kitchen so she couldn't begin drinking, while the shouts of kids playing in the field behind the house drifted through the windows. My watchful, prohibitive eyes, as she potted plants at the sink or did the laundry or prepared a stew, kept her from bringing down the bottle and pouring a drink until the arrival of a respectable hour. She wouldn't pour it in front of me. She had promised she wouldn't drink, but I knew she probably would if I left the room. She always did, filling a tea cup with whiskey and hiding it in a cabinet, and so I sat there doing nothing, pretending that I wanted to be there. She knew, and I knew.

I saw myself in bare feet and a nightgown, waiting endlessly at the dark living room window for my mother to come home from somewhere, endlessly steering her to her bed, undressing her and pulling the blankets up over her shoulders, endlessly lying to people to protect her because I thought unhappiness was shameful. I saw myself hurling a whiskey bottle full force against an outcropping of bedrock beside our house, shattering it into amber slivers on the gray rock.

"She worked pretty hard, I guess." The words dropped like pebbles from my mouth. I knew that they were true, truer than I could explain to anyone who wasn't in my family. Her job was never over. In my discomfort I couldn't bring myself to say anything else.

"I should say so," Hellman said. "I should certainly say so. So many children to bring up alone. Brave woman. She must be very strong."

I placed my hands flat on the table. In their obvious sincerity her words glittered in the air before me like a small gift. Brave and strong. People had uttered the same words about my mother before, but this was different. If Lillian Hellman had spent thirty seconds thinking this about my mother, it was nearly as good as having her think it about me.

"She is," I said, and I knew it was true. She was stronger than anyone I knew.

The wind lurched and a fistful of rain clacked against the kitchen window. "Yes," she nodded, and then, as she crushed out her cigarette, the very atmosphere seemed to tighten around her again, taking on its usual inviolable indifference, and I knew that her eyes had stopped seeing me, turning instead to the next thing in her mind. I knew our lunch was over, that the level platform we had been sitting on was tilting now to tip me back into my place. She got up out of her chair and headed for the sink, and, as though she had forgotten that this was my day off, she asked me to clear the table.

SIX

One August morning she decided to walk downtown by herself to buy a newspaper. From a window in the upstairs hallway I watched her heading off up the steep driveway. With her hat at an accidentally racy tilt, her cane, her cigarette, her pointy-toed flats, and her stylishly flared slacks draping her skinny legs, she looked remarkably like Sammy Davis Jr. going jazzily across a nightclub stage. She had a slow but slightly waggish walk, one arm swinging gently in a rhythmic way, and the rickety precision of her footfalls lent her a roguish air, so that at any moment I expected her to kick up her heels or do a little saltatory dance as she went. Her style was flirtatious, enthralling, her clothes expensive and up to date.

She had asked me to make a batch of cookies from a recipe that Donna had often used, and when she was gone, her bright straw hat disappearing in the haze and the dark trunks of trees at the top of the driveway, I went down to the kitchen and tried to make them. But when all the ingredients had been put together in a bowl and dutifully mixed with a wooden spoon, the dough was so lumpy and dry that it refused to assume anything like the flat disc shape of a conventional cookie. I checked the recipe twice and, unable to see where I had gone wrong, I pinched the dough into little balls and put them into the oven anyway, hoping against hope. I sat at the table and waited, listening to the kitchen faucet drip, thinking, feeling much the way I had upon entering the examination room at school for my math exams. I knew I would fail, knew how cruelly inscrutable the formulas and figures were to me, and yet I sat down at a desk anyway with my chin up and my sharpened pencils in a line, hoping that if I went through the motions, the way everyone else in the room was doing, I would miraculously pass the test.

Hellman had been in another cross mood that day. Earlier she had asked me to bring all of the wine crates stored in the closet under the stairs into the kitchen so she could take stock of what she had. I knelt over the boxes on the kitchen floor, counting bottles and reading labels, while she, sitting in a kitchen chair turned away from the table, checked each label and noted it down on a growing list. The day, though not hot, was thick and fetid; I could smell the low tide, the brackish odor of exposed clamshells and fishy sand and rotting seaweed. Hellman looked tired and pale and very grave as she scribbled meticulously on her pad with a felt-tipped pen. Her seriousness about these tiny household matters both bored and impressed me. "Mouton-Cadet," I read. As she leaned over to see the label on the bottle in my hands, double-checking what I had said in a way that annoyed me, her cheek struck the top of a kitchen chair beside her, unsettling her glasses and knocking the entire chair slightly sideways with a scraping rattle. Her hand flew to her cheek and she sat back abruptly, eyes closed, mouth gathered into a tight knot of pain, and after a moment she said with dry objectivity, "Well, that was stupid." Hearing her say this about herself made me feel, for a moment, exultant. I put the wine bottle down, stood up, and asked her if she was all right.

"I think I'll need some ice," she said.

"I hope it wasn't your eye," I said, trying to sound concerned.

"Thank God, no. My cheek, my cheek."

"I'm sorry," I said, and, bundling some ice into a tea towel, I sat down next to her. She took the ice and pressed it to her cheek, making tiny tching noises of pain and fear. "Is it bleeding?" she asked, removing the ice for a moment so I could check it. I leaned closer to see: a red welt had already risen on her delicate flesh. I could smell the perfume on her clothes, the nicotine on her fingers and lips. I could see into her big shiny ear, the map of tiny wrinkles on her forearm like the lines on a crumpled piece of paper smoothed flat again. This close to her, I could feel her vulnerability and confusion.

"There's no blood," I said, "just a red bump."

"Silly fool," she said, and for a shocking moment I thought she was addressing me, but it was herself she was talking to, and though she was being droll, I could see she was shaken. "I didn't see that chair at all. It was right in front of me. You can't know what it's like not to be able to see properly. Does this ice smell funny? Are my cigarettes anywhere?"

The ice did smell funny—it smelled like onion—but I didn't answer her, fearing she'd blame me. The cigarettes were behind her on the table. I handed them to her. With shaking fingers she pinched one out of the pack, poked it between her lips, and asked me to light it for her. As I held the quavering match flame to her cigarette, I felt a little sorry for her, sensed the frustration she felt at the way her body was failing her. The word *creature* came to me as I looked at her, so distracted by her pain. She was like a freshly hatched crow in a nest of twigs, weak-necked and pink, with a beak too comically large for the small body, vivid in its palpating animalism. She was old. Several days before, I had taken her to Martha's Vineyard Hospital for a blood test, and on the way there she had looked pale and nervous in her seat, smoking one cigarette after the next and saying, "You know, I hate needles." Coming out of the hospital that day she was visibly diminished, radiating exhaustion, fear, violation, and uncharacteristic resignation. She looked helpless, her skin a little green, a Band-Aid in the crook of her arm. On the way home in the car she kept pressing and checking it, like a child. I sensed that no disaster was as upsetting to her as physical disaster.

Despite her accident she insisted on finishing the wine inventory. As I was putting the crates away in the closet and she was preparing for her walk, the doorbell rang, and she said, "Go up and get that." I ran up the stairs and opened the front door. It was a man grinning and sweating and clutching glossy brochures to his chest. He tipped his hat and said eagerly, "Mrs. Hallman?"

I said, "Just a minute, please," and ran down the stairs, and as soon as I reached the kitchen doorway I knew I should have asked him his name.

"Who is it?" she said, touching her wounded cheek.

"A man."

Her face radiated mistrust, as if an unexpected man at her door was a trick being pulled on her, a plot she needed to untangle before it ensnared her. "Did you ask him his name?"

"No."

"You must always get a name. Go up and say I'm not home. Then get his name." As I turned to go, she said, "No, no. Wait a minute. I'll see what it is."

On her way out of the kitchen, her cigarette grazed the doorjamb and knocked ashes onto the hallway carpet. She struggled up the stairs to meet this man, her hand on the banister, her lumpy face curdling with impatience. I watched her climb. She had no rear end; her legs seemed to hang directly from her tiny waist. It took her many long minutes to reach the upstairs landing, and I hoped that by the time she got to the front door the man would have left. I sensed this wasn't going to go well, and I felt responsible. I had a feeling she was going up to see him just so she could stick it to him. I stood at the bottom of the stairs and listened to her making her way down the hallway, and I rubbed her cigarette ashes deep into the carpet with the toe of my sneaker so she wouldn't tell me I hadn't done the vacuuming. Her cigarette was like an eleventh finger, carried about with the same confident neglect as the other ten. She used it absentmindedly, never looking at it, oblivious to its burning tip, the ashes growing and bending under their own weight, spilling down her shirt front or onto the furniture. When she waved her hands the lit end grazed draperies, tables, other people's sleeves, sending sparks fluttering. There were ashes in one spot or another in every room of the house.

I heard voices from upstairs, soft vibrations at first. There was persuasion and a touch of unctuous zeal in the man's voice, but I couldn't make out the words, and then came a louder rumbling, and finally Hellman roared with alarming clarity, "I don't need a new vacuum cleaner! And if you don't get the hell off my property, I'll call your company and tell them their machines stink!"

The front door slammed shut so forcefully that the banister trembled under my hand. When I heard her croaking, "Rosemary!" I ran up to see what she wanted. She was standing in the hallway putting on her hat.

"Carly Simon and James Taylor will be coming over for tea this afternoon," she said brusquely. "I'd like to serve them those cookies, so you must start them while I'm gone." And then she went out, caning her way up the concrete steps to the driveway.

Several minutes passed before her words registered. Carly Simon and James Taylor are coming for tea. Was she joking? I didn't think so. Lillian Hellman had a sense of humor, but not with me. I couldn't believe my ears and was torn between terror and delight. To me, James Taylor was far more famous and thrilling than Lillian Hellman. I loved his songs. And he was handsome. I couldn't imagine myself shaking his hand and saying, "How do you do?" It was too strange.

I sat at the kitchen table, waiting for the cookies, getting up now and then to peer through the oven window, sitting back down to stare at my hands and fret. The cookies looked like eyeballs. They had swelled and cracked with the heat in an unpromising way, and every time I peered into the oven it felt like looking in on a suffering creature in a brightly lit incubator. Why did people think of cooking as an art? It was much more like science. There was a right and a wrong answer, and in the end you didn't really have much control over how it turned out. Down at Cronig's market there were rows of perfectly good cookies in boxes and bags, all ready to be eaten, with no trouble involved. But no, Hellman had to have me go back to the beginning and mix the raw ingredients, like a peasant in a mud hut, because it was supposedly better this way. I was certain I had never tasted a homemade cookie as good as an Oreo.

I sat and thought about the mistakes I had made since arriving here, and about the ones I hadn't made that Hellman had accused me of making. I felt I would never quite get a grip on this job, never feel assured. A few days before, she had insisted that although she had explicitly told me to turn it off, I had left the sprinkler running on her patch of corn at the top of the hill. I had no idea what she was talking about. She had never asked me to turn the water off. When I told her that I didn't recall her asking me to turn it off, she snapped, "Oh, yes, I did!" The cookies, if they didn't work out, would be another mark against me. These tasks I seemed to keep failing at felt like an endless line of hurdles that were impossible to clear, so I had no choice but to bash through them, leaving my shins scuffed and scratched and bloodied. I wasn't used to failing with this kind of regularity, wasn't used to feeling stupid. Failing and being wrong and being somehow pathetic were what I feared most, and I did everything I could to avoid any situation that might make me appear that way. In school I had exhausted myself in the struggle not to fail, and the task of staying on top had become so distressing that finally I had found an honorable way to leave it behind, by choosing to spend my senior year in Ireland on what the school called an "Independent Study Project." People at school said it was brave of me to want to go off to Europe on my own. I knew it wasn't bravery but a kind of hardihood inspired by fear, recklessness inspired by a desperate desire not to be tested anymore. I was a good runner; on the track team I had broken the school record for the girls' mile run. If I went away, I wouldn't have to do that again. I wouldn't have to get good grades. I wouldn't have to try to be funny. I wouldn't have to run five miles every day and be a pioneer girl in the hockey rink. I wouldn't have to be the captain of the soccer team again. I wanted to get out. In general, that was what I wanted: to vanish.

And now the cookies were a sensational failure. As I was sitting at the table, staring at them and wondering whether it would be worse to throw them away, start over, and possibly mess them up again, or to show them to Hellman and risk the consequences, a woman appeared at the back door, tapping at the screen and saying softly, "Hello? Hello?"

I got up and opened the door. The woman had a long, startled-looking face. She was middle-aged, with kinky hair that hung to her narrow shoulders. She pointed at me with one thin index finger and said, "Oh. Good morning. Is this . . . Is this Lillian Hellman's house?"

I said it was.

She sighed with great feeling, pressed her pale hand flat against her chest as if to still her fluttering heart, and stepped back momentarily to take in the full view of the house. Her softly protruding front teeth, which rested perforce on her lower lip as she squinted up toward the balcony of the second floor, made her appear slightly wounded. She wore a T-shirt that looked slept in and jeans that clung tight to her wide thighs. A pink sweater was knotted around her waist. Adjusting the leather bag hanging from her shoulder, she came toward me again, smiling expectantly, and with a quick duck of her head, as if to rein in her brimming excitement, she said softly, "Is Lillian . . . Is she . . . here?"

I said she wasn't.

Her frizzy bangs hung to her eyebrows like raveled wool. She fingered them and peered intently at me, as though desperately trying to come up with a way to rephrase the question and this time elicit from me a different, better answer.

"I'm sorry," I said. "You just missed her. Was she expecting you?"

"Expecting me?" She looked distracted and disappointed. "Oh, no, she wasn't. She wasn't really expecting me. A guy at the ferry told me how to find the house. See, I'm a writer who lives in Arizona. Lillian doesn't know me yet, but I feel like I know her. I've read all of her work and it speaks to me so powerfully. And I've always wanted to meet her, always *knew* I would meet her and . . . could I just come in for a minute?"

With a darting hop that was at once abashed and aggressive, devious and forthright, like the skulkingly self-conscious movement of someone cutting into a waiting line, the woman stepped over the threshold and into the kitchen in her sandals.

". . . and I came East this week to visit my sister in Hyannis and so I said to myself, hey. And ha! Here I am." She grinned nervously at me, wide-eyed, startled at her own boldness and good fortune. Her face was flushed pink with excitement and damp with perspiration and humidity. She glanced about with her hands uplifted, as if to greet the room. "Wow!" she said breathlessly, looking around. "I can't believe I'm standing in Lillian Hellman's kitchen! This is a real step for me, coming here. I can feel her karma. Beautiful. I just love her work."

This was the second time this had happened since my arrival here: a female fan had sniffed out Hellman's house and simply showed up on the doorstep to tell her story. The last woman had been a writer, too, from Boston.

When her eyes fell on me again, the woman said eagerly, "And who would you be?"

"I work for her," I said.

"Like her secretary or something?"

"Well, I help her out with lots of things."

"Wow. What a trip! That must be really! You must have the greatest conversations and see the most wonderful stuff!"

"Yeah," I said.

"And so how do you get a job like that?"

"I asked for it."

With sudden and very visible comprehension she nodded vigorously and slapped her broad thigh. "Hey, that is a step! You asked for it! Imagine. God, I wish I had come up with that one. You must be a fan of hers, like me."

"Yes."

"Yes. And so here you and me are standing right here in her very kitchen! It just goes to show that when you really really want something, you'll find a way to get it, right?!"

She grinned at me, waiting for an answer. "Right," I said, though this summary comparison, this presumptuous pairing of her interest and mine, irked me. She shifted her weight monumentally from one foot to the other, as if to encourage her soft body to take in fully the significance of this moment, and then she went to the table, moving as in a dream, her inner thighs rubbing together with a fricative whisper. She stared sweetly at the deformed cookies. "Baked things. Gosh, she made them?"

"I made them," I confessed.

"Still. It's her stove and her oven, right?"

"Right."

"Wow. You can't beat it." She turned her face to the window and looked out. "And so is that her garden right there and everything?"

"Yes, it is," I said.

"Because I know how important her garden is to her." She

smoothed her bangs with her fingers and looked at me. "And so, do you think I could have a glass of water or something?"

Her excitement, the avid momentum of her speech, made me wary. I felt strongly that I shouldn't give this woman anything, that in fact she really shouldn't be in the house, that it was probably part of my job to discourage a visitor like this, but I wasn't sure how to do that, so instead of saying anything I went reluctantly to the sink and filled a tall glass from the tap and handed it to her. She sipped timidly, as though unsure of its temperature, stared at the glass, and said, "Lillian Hellman's glass." She giggled and sipped again, getting used to the idea. The wonderment and naive belief in her darting eyes embarrassed me.

"Well," I said, "she's not home right now, so maybe you could . . ."

She seemed not to hear me. She went to the door and stepped out onto the back lawn with the glass in her hand, like a woman at a party. Anxiously I followed her out.

"I just *have* to take a look at this garden," she said, wandering around the edge of the flower bed. She walked unsteadily in the grass, like a hobbled donkey, her thick thighs slightly hindering her progress and giving her stride the suggestion of teetering, high-heeled imbalance. "I always wanted to come here. Gosh, that's some view of the water!"

In fact, through the haze that day it was a very poor view of the water. The air was so thick and slack that looking across the beach grass to the sea was like looking through the cloying gauze of a nylon stocking. Horseflies and sandflies and mosquitoes luxuriated in the brightly buoyant murk. Orange monarch butterflies throbbed as if drugged in the flowers.

"I always imagined it would be just like this. You know I have this real feeling of belonging here. She's so . . . how can I put it?

Noble! And that romantic man Dashiell Hammett." She shuddered with pleasure. "If I didn't love her so much, I'd be positively jealous!" She tore a large, ripe tomato from a vine and sank her teeth into it with a wolfish lunge. She chewed and looked around with narrowed eyes, drawn into herself momentarily, fueling her thoughts with what she saw. She looked like a woman standing alone on a city street, staring covetously, longingly into a shop window. Suddenly she stopped chewing, held the tomato up with a bashful smile, and said, "Hope it's OK."

"It's OK," I said, though I was sure that it was not OK. If Lillian Hellman saw this taking place, she would hit the roof.

The visitor stood perfectly still for a moment, staring intently at the torn red flesh of the tomato, while the damp air and the dense sunlight filled the crevasses of her complex hair, and then, as if furthering the salient point of a great debate, she said, "Dash told her the truth. He helped her, steered her the right way through thick and thin. Not to say they didn't fight. Sure, there were fights, plenty of them."

I nodded. I wasn't the slightest bit interested in Dashiell Hammett. I hated detective stories, and to me he wasn't what stood out most in Lillian Hellman's work. I didn't care about their relationship, didn't think she needed the guy, and I could never understand why middle-aged women always focused on him when they talked about her books.

The visitor polished off the tomato in two bites and dragged the back of her hand across her shiny chin. "You see, what I want is a man to tell me the truth. Lillian is such a life force for me. So affirming of the power of women. She said fuck you to men all her life. A large portion of me would like to do the same."

As the minutes passed, the woman seemed, distressingly, to loosen up. She plucked an orange zinnia from its stalk and tucked it behind her ear. With surprising self-assurance she stepped onto the sun deck and, like Goldilocks, sat down in one of the chairs and made herself comfortable at the table under the umbrella. My heart sank. I knew now that I should be getting rid of her. In the sunlight I could see that the frizzy hair was threaded with gray. "God, if my friends could see," she said, putting her feet up on the chair opposite, throwing her sweater onto the table and sitting back meditatively with her arms stretched out on the arms of the chair like a woman relaxing in a sauna. "I just loved it when she smashed that fountain!" She made a little smashing gesture with her fist.

I stood nervously at the edge of the deck.

"You seem like a nice girl," she said. "You seem like you can listen. What's your name?"

"Rosemary."

"Woo. Rosemary Woods. Remember? And Nixon. Yuck, don't mention his name to me. That House Un-American asshole. Thank God for Carter." She narrowed her eyes in scornful delight. "And what about Martha Mitchell?" She did something pantomimic with her fingers, a web over her eyes indicating absurd eyeglasses, and said contemptuously, "God, she reminded me of my mother. My mother is one of my issues. My name is Elaine, by the way. Well, it's really Ruth, but call me Elaine."

She took another sip from her glass of water, blew a fallen eyelash from her wrist, and said, "So, does she have any lovers?"

"Who?" I said.

"Lillian, of course."

"No. I mean, I don't know. I don't think so."

I hadn't thought about that part of Hellman's life. She was old, she was irritable and feeble, she looked terrible; lovers, I assumed, were a thing of the past. In the time I'd been with her she had had no romantic episodes that I could detect. She talked on the phone to a lot of men, a lot of women, too. She talked to Feibleman and it was clear that she cared about him, but I didn't think that was romantic. The guy was about half her age. In cleaning her desk one day I had seen a pile of old letters, a lot of them from somebody who signed his name with a small j. They were dated 1953, when Dashiell Hammett was still alive, and were full of statements like *You know I love you.* I had noticed that in her books she often talked about men and how interested they were in her—Cowan, Hammett, Hemingway—but I hadn't seen anything like that here.

The woman narrowed her eyes and fiddled with the zinnia blooming above her ear. "Because, you know, the truth is it's the women who want sex after forty. Men don't want it. Guess how old I am."

"Fifty-five?"

She shut her eyes and shook her head and gave me an obliterating smile that meant *I'll pretend you didn't say it!* "No! I'm forty-five. I know I don't look it. I exercise. I haven't done menopause yet. In fact, I could be pregnant right this very minute. Jesus, I could have killed the guy. I told him to be careful, but you know how men are, Rosalee."

I did not know how men were. I didn't know the slightest thing about them.

"They don't listen and they're very selfish. Right?"

"Right."

She smiled at me. "They are *so* selfish."

She seemed thrilled by how selfish they were.

She took a sip of water, put the glass down on the table, looked around her, sighed, and raised her shoulders with the pleasure of her accomplishment. She smiled at me some more. She didn't seem to mind that I had nothing to say. She lifted her eyes toward the upstairs windows of the house. "Can I see the rest of the house?"

"I don't think that's such a good idea," I said.

"Aw, how come?"

"She might come home. She won't be gone long."

"Hey, even better! I'd get to meet her!"

"I don't think that would be a good idea."

"It's a great idea! I'd love to see where she works, where she rests her head at night."

The woman was probably harmless, but like an oil spill, she was spreading and growing more difficult to contain. I felt afflicted by her garrulous persistence. If enough time went by she'd be in the living room lighting a fire in the fireplace, or sitting at Hellman's desk, or lying in her bed. I knew Lillian Hellman would hate her. I wanted to say, *Because if she sees you here she'll rip your face off and mine too!* I knew I could swiftly deflate her fantasy of Hellman if I wanted to, but why bother? She had read the books and, like me, she believed in an image she herself had created, fertilized by the words of a person she didn't know. She wouldn't have wanted to hear what Lillian Hellman was like. She had come all this way because she wanted what she thought she recognized in Hellman's work, because, spurred by vanity and insecurity, she hoped to make her person known to Lillian Hellman and receive a self-assuring echo. She wanted a view of herself.

I wanted very much to get her to leave. I said, "See, she's usually kind of tired around this time of day. She needs to rest. She's getting old. And sometimes she gets into kind of a bad mood."

The woman closed her eyes and raised a hand to assure me. "No, no. You don't understand. It would be totally different with me. I'm not a pushy type of a person. I'm a giver, I'm not a taker. I have a high sensitivity to other people's boundaries."

And she rambled on about boundaries, and Timothy Leary, and men again, and where she was from, until, with a kind of screeching halt she looked up and said, "How old are you, Rosalee?"

"Rosemary."

"Huh?"

"My name is Rosemary."

"Right. Of course. And I'm Elaine. So how old?"

"Seventeen."

"Oh, to be young again." She leaned back, put her feet up on the deck chair opposite, shut her eyes, and tilted her face to the sky, as if to take in the sun's sickly rays.

"Well," I said, "maybe you ought to come back another time. Maybe when she's home."

She blinked amiably at me and touched her bangs. "Oh, sure. That's fine. I'll come back another time. Maybe I can give her a call. What's her number?"

Dropping her feet to the deck, she hoisted her big handbag off the table, plopped it down on her lap, and scrabbled in it, muttering, with her knees together and her hair falling in her eyes. She produced a pencil stub and a torn envelope and looked up at me, waiting for the number.

Although I was skillful enough at lying, I wasn't quick enough to come up with a phony number, and in my confusion I said, "Six nine three one two six three." A hot wave of horror engulfed me as soon as I realized what a serious mistake this was. If Lillian Hellman found out that I had given her telephone number to a total stranger, she would roast me on a spit. "Listen," I said, "maybe if you walk back into town right now you'll be lucky enough to run into her on the way. She should be on her way back here. I'm sure you could find her. That way you wouldn't have to call her."

"You think?"

"Sure."

"Ok. Here. Here's my card." She produced, with great pride, a bent business card that said ELAINE. "Give her this, and if I don't find her, she can call me."

She gathered her things and stood up. "Will I know her if I see her?"

"You can't miss her," I said. "She's tiny. She has a cane."

"A cane?"

"And a hat."

Not more than sixty seconds after the visitor went off up the outside stairs, Hellman returned to the house through the front door. It would have been utterly impossible for the woman to have made it out to Main Street without running into her on the driveway. But if they had met, they couldn't have had much of a conversation in such a short time. Hellman didn't mention it, so while she was preparing her lunch, I asked if she had met anyone on the driveway. She said she hadn't.

"You didn't?"

"No. Why?"

"Oh, I was just curious. I thought I saw someone up there just before you came in."

"No," Hellman said. "I don't think so. I didn't meet anyone."

Unless the woman had clawed her way back up to Main Street through the brambles and trees in the untended berm of Hellman's land, this was impossible. The two must have met, but I didn't persist, for in my heart I felt that it was better not to know what had transpired.

When Hellman saw the cookies, she adjusted her glasses and said simply, "I don't recognize these as the same cookies Donna made." She seemed more baffled than angry. I explained that the batter was dry, and she suggested I call the Herseys' cook, Mary Bruce, for advice. I had met Mary Bruce several times on my messengering trips to the Herseys' house. She always opened their kitchen door and said, "Good afternoon," and I said, "This is from Miss Hellman," and handed her a head of lettuce or a basket of tomatoes or a book or a pound of smoked fish wrapped in foil or a bunch of pink roses, and that was the extent of our conversation. I would wait while Mary Bruce wrapped up something for me to bring to Hellman in return. Mary Bruce was a genuine cook, a professional. The Herseys' large kitchen was more her room than theirs, a laboratory that she commanded with stately calm. She could crack an egg on the edge of a bowl one-handed. She never had to measure raw ingredients or look at recipes. A frying pan was like an extension of her own powerful arm. Her seeming perfection answered that of the Herseys: they had got the housekeeper they deserved. Mary Bruce was a solid woman. She was always called Mary Bruce; I never heard anybody call her just Mary, and it was unclear whether Bruce was her last name or her middle name, or whether her first name was actually Marybruce. When I telephoned her about the cookies, she seemed not to understand my question, in the way a genius sometimes finds it difficult to understand the obtuse incomprehension of the layman. The notion of having done something wrong to a trifling batch of cookies was so far beyond her purview that she said, "Tell me again . . ." Mary Bruce's eventual solution was to add orange juice to the cookie batter; miraculously, it worked.

As she finished eating her lunch, Hellman said to me in an offhand way, "You didn't grow up in the country, did you?" and I stiffened at the implied criticism. Something in the tone of her question carried scornful pity for people who didn't grow up in the country. I knew Hellman prided herself on the farm she had owned, was pleased at having worked it herself. Being able to identify flowers and animals was a kind of virtue in her world; being able to kill animals was, too. Our house had been the carriage house at the edge of what was once a farm. We had woods and fields and rocky ridges, pheasants and screech owls, bobwhites and whip-poor-wills, mushrooms and loosestrife, milkweed and bittersweet, red-tailed hawks and rummaging raccoons and once in a while a red fox slinking along a stone wall with his head held low and the extravagant plume of his tail trailing behind him.

I asked her what had made her think I didn't grow up in the country.

"You don't seem to recognize vegetables."

This ridiculous postulation infuriated me more than anything she had said all summer; I couldn't let it pass. "What haven't I recognized?"

"Mint, for one."

I peered at her, my mind furiously scrambling for a defense. "I grew up in the country," I said. "Mint isn't a vegetable."

There was silence then as she crumpled her napkin and crushed out her cigarette, smiling in that tightly forced way, her lips drawn together in a downward grin over her teeth. In her eyes was a studied expression of amused boredom. "Well, Rosemary," she said with a sigh, "it looks like you are winning this argument, so we won't carry it any further."

I couldn't tell whether she was joking or annoyed, and then I thought it was all the same thing with her. She was annoyed all the time, angry, eager to provoke with her sudden routing gibes. Bringing the conversation to an abrupt end was a way of winning, of controlling things. She was the boss. She was never hesitant, she always had an answer. She was also very smart. Calling it an argument, she had made my defensiveness look foolish. I wanted to fight her. Suddenly I wanted very much to fight her.

———

Carly Simon and James Taylor arrived at four o'clock with their two children, Ben and Sally, and a babysitter not much older than I, who had a long straw-blond braid and a pair of square-toed leather boots and looked eerily like a younger Carly. They pulled up to the house in a boxy white Marathon, an old Checker cab with the softly rounded curves of an antique toaster. I was struck by his bespectacled eyes and her horselike teeth, her long arms and his long legs, his incipient balding and her leonine hair, and by the height and slimness and loose-jointedness of both of them. She wore what I thought was a wampum bracelet; he wore boating sneakers. There was a brief meeting between Hellman and her guests in the hallway, a lot of friendly small talk, and then a descent to the kitchen, where, in an unconvincing attempt at grandmotherliness, Hellman passed out cookies to the kids, offering them a few emollient words laden with the sort of fulsome insincerity the witch had used on Hansel and Gretel. And then the adults disappeared into the living room, the children and the babysitter went outside, and I sat alone in my chair in the kitchen, waiting.

The babysitter irritated me. She sang loudly to the kids in a way that seemed to suggest to the world that, like her employers, she was an accomplished singer. She tickled the children mercilessly, flung the boy up into the air, poked him in the stomach, saying, "Silly boyska." She was obnoxiously happy with her job. And she looked good, better than I did. Though her clothes were casual—jeans, a blouse, the fashionable boots—they managed to give off a sense of sophistication, of self-possession, of planning. She had a figure and a tan and dangling earrings. In the room with her I was painfully aware of not being this kind of girl. She seemed to know something I didn't know. She allowed her personality to spill freely across the kitchen and over the two kids with no inward hesitation or reserve, no apparent sense that she would be judged or checked by anyone present, no thought that her noises and her gestures, her loud expressions of self-satisfaction, would be rebuked. She played with the kids on the lawn, swinging them around by the hands, her long, thick braid whipping stiffly through the air as she spun, like a racquet handle. The little boy tottered toward the roses, dazzled by their nursery color, their soft, secretive folds, and when the plump spider of his hand reached up to grab one of these creamy trumpets, the babysitter snatched at his wrist and restrained him. I saw her mouth moving at him, but I couldn't hear the words. She held a rose stem between her fingers, showing him its hidden dangers, the razor-edged corners of the thorns, and then pretended to prick her finger on one, stagily wincing in mock pain and bringing the finger to her lips, while he stood with his eyes lifted up at her, absorbing the performance. I watched them through the window and then, in a haze of disgruntled disgust, I got up and went to stand in the shadowy hallway between the kitchen and the living room. Leaning against the hallway wall, where Hellman and her guests couldn't see me, I eavesdropped on their conversation. James Taylor's voice was a rounder version of his singing voice, deep and rich and softly southern, and familiar in the way my brother's voices were familiar, calling up a string of events and images from my past for which his wounded, unadorned voice had provided a kind of mirroring accompaniment. Carly Simon's voice, too, was so like her singing voice I was mesmerized. And every time Hellman's voice entered with its grating grit, I was startled to realize that hers was the unfamiliar sound.

They were talking about drugs. The subject seemed to arise in this house with great regularity. He said something muffled about antidepressants, but it was unclear who exactly was depressed. Hellman said, "My doctor has said he would prescribe marijuana for my eyes if I want it. For the glaucoma."

Why did she keep telling people that? It wasn't that interesting, and I had never seen her smoking pot. Was she hoping to impress them because they were young and marijuana was a young person's drug? I felt my mouth jerk sideways in a conformation of contempt, and then suddenly Hellman called out my name. I knew I couldn't just jump down the two steps to the doorway of the living room because it would be obvious I'd been lurking there. I tiptoed back into the kitchen, turned around and came out again, going tremulously into the hallway, down the carpeted steps, and into the airy living room as if into a furnace. I stood stiffly before her, not daring to look at the two blurred icons sitting with magnetic force on the periphery of my sight. I tried to listen to the waterfall of words that tumbled from Hellman's vividly moving lips. In my muddied vision her thin lips clapped together like a cartoon clam's or a dog snapping his jaws around a luckless fly. Her words were overwhelmed by the humming vibration of my own awe, my own buzzing struggle not to turn my head and drink in the fantastic sight of Carly Simon and James Taylor. I feared that if I met the eyes of either of these unbelievable guests they would detect my silly, intemperate awe. Hellman said, "Coffee," and I was desperate to stay cool. When her lips stopped moving, I said, "Yes, Miss Hellman," turned, and proceeded toward the door, conscious of every inch of space my person occupied, one foot stretching out in front of the other in what seemed less like walking than like uncontrolled skidding on a wide, thick swath of bacon grease. I felt their eyes behind me, scanning my back, searing the flimsy fibers of my clothing. I was dressed in a skirt—a green cotton wraparound—and the flowered blouse I had bought at the thrift shop. On my feet was a pair of black cloth Chinese slippers with plastic soles the color of bricks. I was aware how bluntly shoddy and haphazard the slippers were; they seemed now like flapping rubber flippers spanking across the oak floor. As I passed through the door and out of the room I felt I was narrowly escaping a fiery explosion.

They wanted coffee. That much I had gleaned. I put the kettle on, got out the cups and saucers, sugar and milk, spoons, freshly ironed napkins, a plate for the cookies. As I waited, I rehearsed the way I would reenter the living room, the order in which I would present each cup, the words I would use to offer each item. If you planned ahead, you couldn't get it wrong. I rubbed the spoons on my shirtsleeve to make sure they were clean and piled eight of the repaired cookies on a pretty porcelain plate. Through the window, I could see that the babysitter and the children had moved down to the water's edge: they moved with the happy jerkiness of puppets through the late afternoon light slowly draining away to the west.

With everything prepared, I carried a tray into the living room, set it down on the sideboard, picked up two cups of coffee, and walked toward the talking people. The moment I began to move I knew I was in trouble. My wrists seemed to jiggle at the ends of my arms, and the pretty cups, painted with brightly colored butterflies rendered in Audubon-like precision, chattered in their saucers. Deranged with nerves, my hands were shaking. Undeniably they were shaking. I watched the cups tremble as I walked, watched the softly leaping ripples of coffee skip over the rims of the cups. In a blur of momentum I handed Hellman her skittering cup. She took it, and before I could turn to the two smiling guests, she said with chilling softness, "This won't do, Rosemary."

Holding a single cup with both hands now, I paused in fear to read her face. She plucked her glasses from her nose and laid them on the table. My heart lurched, its beating momentarily irregular, shockingly out of sync with a lifetime of orderly beating, a clutch of palpating thumps too fast for my veins. I could feel the color rising in my neck and cheeks.

"This saucer is sloppy. It's spilled. Please take it back and get a clean one."

I looked at her hands and then at mine. It was true: each coffee cup sat in its saucer, ringed by a steaming brown moat of spillage. I put my free hand forward, took her cup from her, and out of habit was able to say, "Yes, Miss Hellman," and headed for the door.

Mortification does not begin to describe the heartache and embarrassment I felt following this correction. The ignominy of the moment was so great that I remember next to nothing about the minutes in which I returned to the kitchen, filled fresh cups, and rectified the badly botched service. I know that I went back into the living room with clean cups in clean saucers, so numbed now by my bufoonish mistake that I wasn't able to see much but the feet and then the mouths, still stiffly smiling, of James Taylor and Carly Simon. I heard Taylor say, "Thank you," when I handed him his cup. My shame and failure and sorrow were so great, that my overburdened brain began, mercifully, to zone out the circumstantial details, and I heard nothing else.

After dropping Hellman at the Herseys' house for dinner that evening, I took her car to Edgartown just for the sake of driving. I was still numb with disappointment and embarrassment over the afternoon's mishap and took the longer route to comfort myself. Beach Road beyond Hart Haven was, to me, one of the prettiest and most exhilarating stretches of road on the Vineyard. The strip of South Road beyond Abel's Hill toward Allen Farm was another, and the road by the airport out in Katama that came to an abrupt end at the silky white sand and tossing green waves of South Beach was a third. These slender roads had a rich openness, an abundance of light and warmth, soft color, and huge vistas in the absence of trees. The shoulderless gray pavement just beyond Oak Bluffs, surrounded by so much unmanipulated nature, itself looked natural: a sun-baked, stone-gray slab that managed in its uninterrupted smoothness not to offend its surroundings. It was soothing to drive along this slim bridge of sandy land, literally at sea level, with the rolling Atlantic on one side, jagged and multihedral as a pile of discarded roofing slates, and the mirror of Sengekontacket Pond, flat and salty, on the other. There was little to distract the eye but broad sky and palmy, bowing sea grass. You could see nearly all the way to Edgartown on this road, for the tallest things here were the rosa rugosa that dotted the short dunes, with goldfinches dipping suddenly over them. To me, such an open place offered lightness and safety. Nothing could sneak up on you here. State Beach was public, and therefore considered tawdry, but I thought it was pretty. The sky in the west was orange and purple and tainted with a swirl of stringy yellow clouds that seemed to have spun, whiplike, off the edge of the earth.

I couldn't see a sunset like this without thinking of my mother. When I was seven my mother took me to Provincetown, and as we drove down Route 3 the sun was setting brilliantly above the scrubby pines that streaked past the car window. My mother pointed to the lurid sky and said, "See the pastels, Rose?"

I didn't know what pastels were.

"Soft colors," she said and named them. "Salmon, cantaloupe, orange, shrimp, peach, raspberry, lime."

I watched my mother's mouth, lit by the slanting sun, and listened. "Food," I said.

My mother hadn't noticed that she had rendered the colors edible and was pleased I had noticed, and I was pleased that she was pleased.

I thought about my mother all the time. Unexpected things reminded me of her. In truth, nearly everything reminded me of her. As I drove along this road, the many smooth knuckles on the grip side of the steering wheel were effortlessly translated to the identically knuckled handgrips on my mother's crutches. The crutches were Canadian: aluminum, with a metal cuff around the forearm. They made a lightweight metallic clinking noise when their tips touched the floor, the delicate sound of a penny being sucked through the pipe of a vacuum cleaner. My mother could use the tips of her crutches to delicate ends; she could inspect a tomato plant in her garden with the tip of one, turning its leaves this way and that, or flip a light switch with the crutch raised like a long-barreled rifle, or prod a footstool across the floor, or flush a toilet, or straighten a picture on the wall. She could pick up a wad of paper or a Styrofoam cup between the pinch of her two crutch tips, working them like the forelimbs of a mantis, delicately lifting the object up and into a trash can. She could wake the sleeping dog—yawning and stretching—and poke him out of her path with a tinkling of tags. With the tip of a crutch my mother could fling off the front porch and into the snowy bushes the bloody rabbit carcasses that our scarred tomcat regularly pulled in for our approval; she could knock icicles off the gutters of the house and stop a five-dollar bill from blowing away. She could block a hasty child's way with one crutch, lifting it across his belted waist like a tollgate until the child answered her question. And if the answer was insufficient or untruthful or impertinent, she could ad-monish him with the crutch, bringing it across the backs of the legs in a manner more surprising than painful. Once, when she had fallen down on the walkway to the house and was unable to get up for several minutes, she killed a hovering bee with the narrow rubber edge of her crutch tip, fearing that when he lit on a brick near her nose he was gearing up to sting her.

As a child I found it pleasant to upend a crutch and punch its rubber tip solidly against the ceiling of whatever room I was in. My brothers and sisters and I conducted sword fights with the crutches, took them outside and tried to balance them tip-down on the palms of our hands, like Chinese jugglers balancing spinning dinner plates at the top of a stick, and when the crutches fell and flew askew into the bushes, we found that incredibly funny. We careered through the house on them, knocking pictures off the walls, upending lamps, and fantasizing about being lame. We did the same with my mother's brace when she wasn't using it, strapping it on and clomping giddily up and down the hallway, pretending to be her, calling out our own names, sharply and with urgent authority, the way she did when she was looking for us. My mother's brace was to her as I imagine a gun would be to a soldier: a hard, angular machine with movable metal parts, heavy, grim in its purpose, but necessary to survival and therefore to be treasured in all its ugliness. At night, when my mother was in bed, her brace lay empty on the floor nearby, bent at the knee, straps loosened and cuffs splayed, like a gape-mouthed drunk asleep in a doorway. The knee pad of the brace was brown and hard and curved like the shell of a horseshoe crab; it cupped her knee perfectly. When I was younger, I loved the brace. My mother needed it and so, therefore, did I. The brace, like her crutches, were part of her, and I liked being near it. These orthopedic tools were like trusted friends, and also a bit scary when my mother was out of the room, in the same way an absent person's eyeglasses or winter coat can so vividly call up that person's essence. Some part of my mother had been invested in these props, incorporated into them—they seemed animate, wed to her as they were. I could frighten myself at will by imagining what it would be like to see them after my mother had died, and then, properly frightened, I had to quickly shake the image out of my head and replace it with another, easier picture.

I thought about my mother as I drove. *Just be who you are,* she always said to me, but a stubbornly faithless part of me believed that it was what other people thought of me that counted, believed that other people were forever on the brink of thinking I was unworthy. When I was at school so many thoughts and uncertainties flapped and fluttered in my head that I began to find peace only when I was

alone. Alone, there was no wearying struggle to fit in, no need to
hold in check all the uncertainties that plagued me with their grinding, jostling angles and planes. Solitude was comforting. At school I
was most at ease when I sat on the bed in my dorm room listening to
my Billie Holiday record and staring out the window at the winter
sun setting over the school garage, hurling its pink light onto the
steep snowbanks and turning the icicles that dangled from the gutters
into dripping golden spears. *Smooth road, clear day, but why am I the
only one traveling this way?* Billie sang it in a roguishly sad and careless
way. There was a hint of the wise guy in her voice that I liked. I
didn't notice that it was a song about love; I thought it was a song
about life, mine in particular. My loneliness was acute, and my feeling of falseness further isolated me and compounded my fears. Self-
doubt sucked up my energy in greedy gulps.

As I neared Edgartown, the traffic began to thicken, and I passed
a school of helmeted people mooching along on rented mopeds,
their sunburned knees akimbo and their tiny motors straining under
the strain of their weight. At the top of Main Street I drove slowly
past the court house. COUNTY OF DUKES COUNTY COURT HOUSE was
printed importantly over the door. Redundant, I thought, and had to
read it twice, craning my neck and slowing down to make sure it
really said that. I knew it couldn't be a mistake; Edgartown was too
correct for that. They would have some archaically proper reason for
calling it this. Still, it looked silly.

I turned left on North Water Street and saw Audrey Baird, a
friend of mine from my school, heading down toward the yacht club
with her gymnast's walk and her raven-black ponytail swinging, but I
was in too sour a mood to go after her and say hello. I didn't want to
talk to anybody. I drove on up the street, looking at the picture-
perfect houses, tidy and white and well defended by their eminent
age, advertent sameness, wealth, and tight proximity—they were like
bright and blocky rare books tucked neatly on a shelf. Not a single

one of these houses showed peeling paint or uncut grass or dusty windows. Some had widow's walks that looked across Edgartown Harbor to Chappaquiddick, others had American flags dangling limp above their porches like damp shirts on hooks in the stillness of the evening. I followed the street along to Starbuck Neck, gaped enviously, resentfully at the hulking gray shingled mansions there. Edgartown was an impossible dream, a movie set of Colonial New England, and in its egregious prettiness it made my gloomy mood somehow worse. I steered the car up Fuller Street, then headed back toward Vineyard Haven along Pease Point Way.

The house was dark when I returned. Hellman was still at the Herseys'. I went in, switched on some lights, turned Hellman's bed down, put a jug of fresh water on her night table, put her eye medicine on ice, closed the shades against the purplish residue of the day's light, emptied the ashtray into the wastebasket by her desk. Among the cigarette packs and Bic lighters on her desk, the paperclips and felt-tipped pens, the matchbooks and scribbled-on bits of paper, a copy of a letter caught my eye, a letter she had written to some acquaintance about a book being written about him by someone called LeVey. I skimmed the page. Hellman seemed displeased with some of what LeVey had written and wanted to make some changes in the book, which, oddly, would cost a lot of money. The changes cast the person she was writing to in a more favorable light than the one LeVey had cast him in. One change that stuck in my mind was to call his wife Irish-English instead of Irish, which seemed strangely insignificant. Hellman had called Mike Nichols's wife Irish-English. Maybe this book was about Nichols. But why did she care what his wife was or what she was called? And what was the matter with Irish? One line in the letter referred to *the boys who would do the job for one*

hundred fifty thousand and the cheaper boys who are just plain fuck-ups.
The language spooked me—it was like something out of a mobster
movie. I didn't know what it was about, but I was afraid to read more
of the letter. It felt sneaky and risky. There was an invitation lying on
a pile of papers that read, "Mrs. Jouett Shouse cordially invites you to
Plantation House (adjacent to Wolf Trap Farm Park for the Performing Arts) on Friday August 25 for a Toast to Lenny after the Gala,"
and I thought of Hellman and her dinner guests saying *Lenny's not old
enough for that kind of celebration.*

From the brick hearth of the fireplace in the corner of her room I
gathered up the pile of old newspapers she had asked me to get rid of
and went down the stairs thinking about the ethnic slurs she tossed
out willy-nilly. She was always saying *Chink* and *Jap* and *nigger,* which
in *Pentimento* she claimed she would never say. I put the papers on
the kitchen table, went into my room to get my journal, rummaged
in the refrigerator for some food—a bowl of leftover spaghetti and a
hardened bun—and sat down to eat. Through the open window I
could see the greenish lights of fireflies signaling above the lawn.
Scores of tiny bugs danced and popped and circled in a kind of
airborne fountain around the floodlight above the back door. The
night air was warm and smelled of roses and the ocean. In my journal
I wrote down what had happened that day. Going over the day in
words was like licking my wounds, saying all the things I hadn't been
able to say during the minutes I was actually living the experience. *I
think she is a humbug and a hypocrite,* I wrote. *Often I find myself
comparing her to other old women I know. . . . She must think it's a
fashionable trait always to criticize and be verging on rudeness. . . . I think
she is like an immature child.* It made me feel better to write it down; it
strengthened my nerves and solidified my place in the world. My
thoughts were the one thing I knew were mine, which was why I
liked reading: the writer may have chosen the words, but I was the

one making pictures out of them in my head; the book was the author's, but the pictures were mine.

Finished with the journal, I flipped through the old newspapers, mostly the *Vineyard Gazette* and the *New York Times*. I liked looking at the photographs in the *Gazette,* pretty black-and-white pictures by Peter Simon and Alison Shaw that made the Vineyard look even more rustic and pretty than it already was—somebody driving a tractor at Pimpneymouse Farm, boats moored in a harbor, sand dunes striped with the shadows of a picketed wind fence. There were articles about what was going on in the various towns ("Mrs. Robbins Talks to the Garden Club") and letters to the editor about provincial things that life on the island rendered monumental: *I live at Katama, out near the town boat ramp. I raise chickens for my family . . .* or *I have a blooming plant in my garden that I would very much like to have identified . . .* or *we truly appreciate your kindness in accepting the affection of our 2¹/₂ year old beagle . . .* I rustled aimlessly through the rumpled wide-format pages in a pleasant trance, looking at the ads (Tashtego, Dutton's) and the editorials ("Marking the Summer Off," "On Washing Away"), moving from week to week until my eye fell on a tiny but shocking editorial headlined THOSE "STOP" SIGNS:

"Stop" signs at intersections in Massachusetts now mean just that, with additional emphasis. All vehicles are required to stop at such signs, and yield to oncoming traffic. The old law allowed the driver of a second or third vehicle in line to proceed after stopping just once, but not the new law. Each succeeding car must stop upon reaching the "Stop" sign. . . . It may be noted also that a "rolling stop," the invention of some ingenious drivers, in contravention of dictionary meanings and Newton's Laws of Motion, is not acceptable. Every stop must be a dead stop. No rolling.

I couldn't believe my eyes. It seemed like a joke. What new law? I wondered if Hellman had seen it, but then I was certain she hadn't; if she had, I would have heard all about it by now. The paper was several weeks old. The very sight of this notice stunned and infuriated me. Even though I knew Hellman didn't know one way or the other what the law was, or that it had changed, I went outside and rammed the newspapers deep into a trash can and said, *Fuck her,* then went into my room to sulk.

At ten-thirty, while I was lying on my bed reading Hemingway and listening to the crickets chisel the thick night air and hoping to kill a mosquito that had been strafing my ears, I heard a rustling outside my window, followed by the sound of fingernails scratching at the screen. I jumped up, startled, dropping Hemingway to the floor. It was my sister Ellen and her friend Nina, their tanned faces pressed goofily against the screen and their white teeth nearly phosphorescent. "Rosie," Ellen whispered. "It's us!"

I opened the outside door to my bedroom and they clamored in, tripping on the doorsill.

"Jesus, you scared the shit out of me!" I said. I was delighted to see them.

Ellen threw her arm across my shoulders and whispered furtively out of the side of her mouth, "The Witch home?"

"No, thank God. What the hell are you wearing?"

They were dressed in strange clothes. Nina wore a fedora, baggy white pants, an argyle necktie, heavy boots, and a woolen vest. Ellen wore a bomber jacket, a turquoise wool scarf, and a woolen driver's cap; they looked like fancy boys.

"We're going to a costume party at the Styrons'," Nina said. "It's Tommy's birthday. Come with us."

I knew about this party: the day before I had driven to the

Styrons' house to deliver a fifty-dollar check from Hellman for some charitable cause Rose Styron was involved in, and I had seen the dance floor they were building on the lawn. "You're going to the party as boys?" I said.

"No. The guys from *The Great Gatsby,*" Nina said, grinning and patting her argyle necktie with comic pride. "I'm Gatsby."

"And I'm Buchanan," Ellen said.

"And Emily is Nick," Nina said. Emily was Nina's older sister. "She's meeting us there."

"Nick who?" I said.

"Isn't there somebody named Nick in that book?"

"Maybe the narrator," I said. "What's his last name?"

Nina shrugged and showed her brilliant teeth. "We don't really know."

"Or care!"

They laughed; that they didn't know seemed to make them even happier than they already were. As a pair, these two achieved a brash power that was larger than the considerable power each of them had alone. They inspired each other to greater ebullience.

"Just don't tell Emily there's no Nick," Nina said, examining her fedora in the mirror and giving its brim an adjusting tug. She pulled a pack of sugarless bubblegum out of her vest pocket and held it out to me. "Piece of gum?"

I took a stick. Ellen pointed to the dark doorway that led into the pantry and the rooms beyond. "If Lillan's not home, can we snoop?"

"No, you cannot. She might come home any minute. She's going away for a couple of days next week, for her eyes. Snoop then."

"Does she have anything good to eat?" Ellen said.

"Tripe and tongue and brains."

"Come off it."

"It's true. She eats that shit."

"Gross."

"What's the matter with her eyes?" Nina asked.

"Going blind," I said.

"So this," Nina said, looking around, "is your room?"

"More like a cell," Ellen said, opening the closet door in the corner, peering in, sniffing, and closing it again. "Puny."

I had been getting used to the room. In fact, I had come to think it was a little nicer than my room at home, but now, with three of us crowded into it, casting big shadows against the wall in the orange light of my one lamp, it seemed tiny again. "At least I have my own door so I can get out if I want," I said. "And I can see the ocean."

The two of them nodded politely, but it was obvious they thought it wasn't much. They both wore lip gloss and unusual bracelets and smelled of shampoo. "This job sucks, huh?" Ellen said.

"*Sucks!*" I said. "I'm so bored. I can't wait till she goes away."

Ellen flopped down on my bed, plumped the pillow under her head, and crossed her booted ankles. Her wrists were brown and her eyelashes were nearly blond with sun. The three gold hoops traveling up her right earlobe glittered in the lamplight. She swung her turquoise scarf in the air above herself like a lariat, let it drop to her chest, then gathered it up and sniffed it. "Moth," she said softly, frowning.

"Mothball," Nina corrected.

Ellen and Nina were always high-spirited, adventurous, and mischievous, but tonight, I could see, they were truly electrified. For several years Nina had worked with my two sisters at Helios, a little Greek café. Ellen was living with Nina's family for the summer. They called each other Miss in imitation of what their customers called them and were always pulling pranks. When Helios was still an outdoor café in Edgartown, they went upstairs at the restaurant and, leaning out the window, rolled raw chickpeas down the sloping awning onto the customers seated at the sidewalk tables below. After work, late at night, they rode their bicycles up North Water Street and snuck into the empty pool at the Harborview Hotel to swim. One time, when they were ready to leave, they threw the hotel's lawn chairs into the pool, and another time they let Nina's dog, Minnie, jump into the pool with them. Now and then they carried a little pair of scissors and late at night clipped a rose or two from the bushes that reached over the picket fences on Water Street. They knew all the words to the songs from *Grease* and sang them as they dove into the waves at No Key Beach. (The beach, really called Black Point, was private, and members had to have a key to open the padlocked gate across the dirt road that led to the shore, but Ellen and Nina had discovered that the lock was always open, and, pushing through the gate, they'd say, *We don't need no key!*) I loved them. They were capricious. They were always overflowing with wry humor. They were three years older than I was and in college and both very pretty, and I thought they were clever and fun and brave. They had sailed a Sunfish all the way from Edgartown to the Cape Pogue Lighthouse. They had won ribbons at the Agricultural Fair for things they had knitted and baked. Now here they were in my room, asking me to come with them. I was thrilled.

Ellen jabbed my arm affectionately.

"Did I get invited to Styrons'?" I said.

"Yeah," they both said at once.

"I did not."

"No," Nina said. "Really, you didn't, but it doesn't matter."

"I can't go anyway," I said.

"How come?"

"Lillian."

"That bitch." Ellen scowled. "Don't you get any time off? It's nighttime. You can do what you want. Just come for an hour. We'll sneak."

"But what if Lillian's there?"

"Why would *Lillian* be there?"

"She's a big fat friend of Styron's," I said. "She goes everywhere, has to be in on everything. If there's a party with famous people at it, she's there. The Herseys probably took her there."

"If she's blind," Nina said with brimming optimism, "she won't be able to see you!"

"But what if Styron sees me?"

"What if?"

"He knows I work for Lillian."

Ellen looked at me as though I was insane. "So *what?* What's the matter with you? Just because you work for Lillian doesn't mean you can't have a life."

She was right. But for some reason I had thought it did mean that. I realized I was afraid to do anything or go anywhere. I didn't want to make Hellman mad. I never wanted anyone to come over and see me here, because I thought the very sight of my friends would annoy her. Whenever my sisters or friends called on the phone and Hellman was at home, I whispered into the receiver that I'd call them back from a pay phone in town when I had a chance, and hung up. I had warned even my mother not to call too often. And when Ellen or Elizabeth stopped by, we always whispered in my room for a while and then I shunted them off up the back stairs. But the truth was, Hellman had never told me I couldn't go anywhere in my free time or have a friend over. I just sensed she wouldn't like it.

"It'll be a big party. Nobody will notice. They're all in costumes anyway."

"I don't have a costume."

With a flourish Nina lifted the dirty apron hanging off my chair and threw it toward me. "Wear that."

My sister picked up a wool hat. "And this."

Nina got the mop leaning in the pantry doorway and put it in my hand. "And that."

"There," Ellen said in triumph. "A costume. Styron won't know you."

"Yes he will," I said. I pulled off the hat. "This is how I *always* look."

Ellen pulled a pair of sunglasses out of her jacket pocket and put them smartly on my face. "Now Styron won't know you."

"It's nighttime. I'm not wearing any sunglasses."

"Rose, it's a *cos*tume," Ellen said. "Come on. You have to come."

"But what am I supposed to be?"

Nina said, "It doesn't matter. As long as it looks weird enough, nobody cares."

I looked at myself in the mirror. It was pathetic: I was going to a costume party as my own subordinate self. I turned to look at my visitors. Moths hugged my screen door, and a few tiny-winged bugs that had gotten inside clung to my warm lampshade. I was torn, afraid to go. I knew I'd feel out of place. I didn't want to crash a party, particularly Styron's, and I wouldn't know anyone there but Ellen and Nina. They were cool. I wasn't. They knew the whole island and everybody on it. I didn't. And I was worried that Hellman would come home, need me to do something, and be angry that I wasn't there. I felt strangely exposed and confused. I felt if I didn't go, I would look fearful. I wanted to be like them: brash and fun and daring. Finally I agreed to go, and we headed out and up the outdoor stairs.

I could see the ghostly outlines of trees through the dark. Not far away a screech owl warbled like a loon. As we neared the top of the hill I saw the headlights of a car turning into the driveway from Main Street and, fearing that it was the Herseys bringing Hellman home, I made Ellen and Nina duck into the bushes with me until the car passed. The beams wheeled and grazed the tangle of branches above us. The darkness looked darker when the lights were finally gone. My mop snagged in a bush, and as we headed off again, a tiny yapping dog from a neighboring house began to chase us. We ran. I could hear the dog behind us, choking on his own rasping breath and tearing at the pavement with his tiny paws, stirring up pebbles, tripping on his nails, trying desperately to bark as he ran.

The Styrons' long driveway was lined with parked cars. We could hear the party before we saw it: loud music and shouts of laughter. As we neared the house, I took the dark glasses out of my apron pocket and put them on, low on my nose so that I could see over the tops of them. The Styrons' house was pretty and white and graced with a smooth lawn that went all the way to the water. In the middle of the lawn was a little guesthouse. Styron was rich; that was what his property showed. And yet there was an air of recklessness here; nobody really seemed to be in charge. I thought I saw Styron himself standing in a doorway, looking grumpy and tired, his arms folded on his chest. The party was big, with people trampling the lawn, silhouetting against the lamplit windows of the house, dropping beer bottles into the flower beds, milling on the dock, dancing barefoot on the temporary dance floor. Tommy Styron came to greet us and give us all a hug. He had white teeth and wavy black hair and was handsome and slim. Nina's sister joined us. She had a mustache drawn onto her upper lip and wore a man's shorts and boots and kneesocks and a necktie like Nina's. Wandering through the party I had a powerful hollow feeling; I was a carved wooden decoy, tilting and stiff-eyed, among a clutch of busily paddling and preening real ducks. It was only by accident that I was here; though I looked as properly odd as all the other disguised people, I knew I wasn't really a part of this. The uneasiness I felt was old; there was some makeshift, ill-fitted, unacceptable thing about me that I felt would have to remain hidden if I was to pass through the world. In grade school once, riding out of Dover in a carpool, I told the friendly mother driving the station wagon (she'd been softly complaining about a vacuum cleaner badly in need of repair) that of all the housecleaning jobs there were I hated vacuuming the most. In truth, I didn't mind cleaning the house at all. I actually liked washing windows and sinks—anything that involved water—but I hated vacuuming because it was a nuisance to pull the vacuum cleaner out of the closet and fit all the hoses and metal pipes together and drag it around after you like a fat metal dog on a chain. At eleven I had already developed a preference for Comet over Ajax and for a terrycloth rag over a sponge. Sleepily off guard, I went on about this to the carpool mother until she turned her head and looked at me with the squinting stillness and open mouth that denote surprise. She gave her hairband a pat and asked how a girl my age knew so much about housecleaning. Her interest immediately made me uneasy. I had revealed too much. And I sensed that in what I revealed there was something unusual, something unsuitable about me, about my home. I knew that when I was inspired to clean the house it went beyond regular chores. It was a desire to battle disorder; I *wanted* to do it. In the reflection of this woman's comment I felt embarrassed and stayed silent across the six miles to Dedham. For several days I worried about what I had said. The woman's reaction seemed to confirm what I had already suspected: my family was different from everyone else's; by extension my very presence in this carpool was a hoax.

As we moved toward the edge of Styron's lawn I turned my head and saw Carly Simon among a group of laughing people. "Is that Carly Simon?" I said.

"Yeah," Nina said. "It's her birthday too. Want to meet her?"

"Oh, no," I said. "Really, that's okay."

"Come on," Nina said.

As we approached the group I felt like a solitary figure sitting in an audience, peering out of the darkness, with only the faint reflection of the footlights playing on my featureless face.

SEVEN

The morning of her trip to New York, Hellman stood in the kitchen drawing up a list of things for me to do while she was gone. As I was putting pots and dishes away in the cabinets, she began reading the list aloud. I listened, stacking dishes, putting some silverware in its slotted drawer, drying the cast-iron frying pan with a dishtowel. Suddenly Hellman snapped, "If you pay attention, Rosemary, you won't forget what I'm saying."

I put the frying pan down and turned to look at her. "I'm paying attention."

The buzzing of the oven clock seemed to parody the irritation in my voice. She lowered her eyes to the list and read on. With her head tilted down at this angle, the lenses of her glasses made her look weirdly Japanese. She wore a creamy silk slip and a lightweight bathrobe, a kind of cotton kimono. With her sloping shoulders, her boxer's nose, her knobby knees, and the folds of her robe hanging loose around her like great idle wings, she looked like a downy marabou picking through a swamp. Her eyes were swollen and she looked unwell; for several days she had complained of having slept poorly. The end of her nose was the color of liverwurst. She had smoked nearly half a package of cigarettes since breakfast, and the afterdamp of her breath was blunt. She had read this list once already and asked me if I understood it. There were two cases of wine to exchange, mousetraps to check, plants to water, shopping to do, blouses to iron, windows to wash, and the guest rooms to prepare for the visitors who would be coming soon after her return from New

York. Feibleman would be arriving first, and Mike Nichols and his wife a day or two after that. I didn't mind the work, as long as she wasn't going to be around to harass me about it. I was delighted that she was going; I'd have two full days to myself, a welcome rest. The hour that remained before I was to drive her to the airport seemed like an eternity. I listened as she read. She coughed with her fist to her mouth, shoulders shaking, and read some more. When she was finished, I said—to show that I had been listening—"A man from Jim's package store is coming this afternoon to pick up the wine boxes we marked yesterday, is that right?"

She patted her uncombed hair and raised a concurring finger at me. "Yes. Two cases of white. The two boxes at the front of the closet. Jim's package store will pick them up this afternoon and deliver two cases of red. Is that clear?"

"Yes," I said.

The day before, Jim's had delivered the wrong wine, and she had called them up and berated the delivery boy at the top of her lungs and demanded a discount for her pains. I had heard the whole thing. Now the boy was coming to fix the mistake.

"The two cases of white at the front of the closet," she said firmly. "He'll take those away and deliver two cases of red. You must be sure and point out the correct boxes to him. Are you certain you know which boxes?"

"The two cases of white at the front of the closet."

"We marked them yesterday."

"Yes," I said.

She peered at her list, paused to think, then peered at me. "They have RETURN written on them."

"Right."

Suddenly her face seemed to curdle, her head tilted back, her mouth opened wide in a horrible grimace, her eyelids fluttered, and with a violent nod *yes* of her head, she let out a roaring sneeze, jarring her spectacles loose on her face and freckling the front of her slip with damp grayish spots. She blinked dully, and her mouth hung open while the teeming body of the sneeze swelled and settled in the sunlit air between us. She straightened her glasses and tamped at her nose with the back of her wrist.

"Bless you," I said.

"Thank you. Two cases of white," she said, sniffling. "That's clear, right?"

"Very clear."

I was beginning to wish I had never asked. I knew those two boxes too well. We had looked at them twice that morning, and I was the one who had, at her command, written RETURN in black marker on each box.

She fished a cigarette out of her pocket, touched it with the flame from her lighter, and pushed smoke through her nostrils, as if to clear away the sneeze. "At the front of the closet, yes?"

"Yes, Miss Hellman."

Shoving the list into the pocket of her robe and pitching her hands forward to set herself in motion, she said, "We'd better go and have a look at them to make sure you know which ones."

I knew which ones. Only a moron could get this wrong. I was supposed to give the Jim's guy this wine and he was supposed to give me some red wine. I knew that. Why was she doing this? It was as though she saw me as brain-damaged. Or as though she herself was brain-damaged. This was the most inane conversation I had ever had. I didn't want to go and stare at those two boxes a third time, but I knew it was inevitable now, so, rigid with frustration, I decided to feed the fire and see how big it would grow. "Miss Hellman," I said, "it's the two boxes of white in front, isn't it?"

"Exactly," she said with no sign of irony or annoyance or even surprise. "That's correct. At the front of the closet."

"Yes," I said dumbly, "I think I know the boxes now."

She was shuffling out of the kitchen, trailing smoke and tea-rose perfume. Her hand was on the doorjamb. "I'll show you again."

I stared at the back of her straw-colored head, at the gown billowing around her, the axe handles of her ankles, the soft flimsy slippers, her fingers groping at the shadowy air of the hallway. I wanted one of us to disappear. I could go or she could go, it didn't matter to me which. "Good," I said. "And they'll replace them with red?"

"Two cases of red in exchange for the white."

Spurred by my own boredom, I shut my eyes, threw back my head, grimaced with my tongue hanging out, and followed her that way for a second, my feet splayed out crazily like an ape's, and then, straightening up and listening to the sound of my own voice as if it belonged to some beetle-browed cretin, I said, "He brought the wrong boxes."

"He certainly did." She actually pronounced it *soitany,* like Curly on *The Three Stooges.*

"Awful mistake," I said.

"Oh, believe me, they're very capable of getting it wrong." Her throat seemed to fill with satisfaction as she said this, as though she thrived on the mistakes this liquor store had made, and on other people's mistakes in general.

We stood before the closet. *That box and that box,* she said, pointing with her pen, and I touched each box and said, *This one and this one?* For the tenth time she asked me if I had everything right now, and, goaded into recklessness over this moronic rehearsal, I said a little too vehemently, *"Yes,* Miss Hellman."

"Don't answer like that," she said, and turned away to go up the stairs. "I need to pack my bag now. Please come up and help me."

I followed her glumly up the stairs to help her pack and listened to her sighing as she pulled herself upward along the banister with the grasping fingers of one hand, one foot plucking after the other with meticulous concern. It was like climbing the Matterhorn, a little like going up a flight of stairs with my mother. It took her so long to reach the top that I had time to study the pictures hanging on the stairwell walls—a pastel costume design for *Candide,* five bell-skirted dresses in yellows, reds, and blues; a black-and-white photograph of a man; a landscape in oil—and to stare out the landing window at the harbor. Another bright day filled with lucky people steering sleek sailboats out to the sound through the winking white-caps.

In her bedroom Hellman shuffled about from closet to drawer to bathroom, draped in cigarette smoke and breathing through her nose, gathering her effects and handing them to me. In the bathroom she rummaged in the medicine cabinet, taking bottles down and asking me to read what each one was. As I read the labels for her, she flicked the stub of her cigarette into the toilet bowl with stunning quickness and accuracy, and with a spitting sting to the water the cigarette went dead. I folded blouses and tucked them into her suitcase, found the two pairs of shoes she wanted in the hallway closet, collected her medicines and makeup and put them in a small bag. We hardly spoke. But as our work was nearing completion and she was preparing to dress, she turned to me suddenly, her face long, hands hanging by her sides, and said solemnly, "You are perfectly right to ask questions, Rosemary, but when I give you an answer, don't get upset."

My mouth opened but no sound came out. All this time she had been thinking about how I'd answered her, and her words seemed less like a criticism than an appeal or a plea. I was astonished. "I wasn't getting upset," I said. "I only wanted you to know I understood you. That's all."

But I was getting upset, and her commenting on it in this somber, earnest way was new, was different. She had been oddly subdued that morning, not her usual combative self, and with a pang of remorse I wondered if I had gone too far, frightened her, pushed too hard. The truth was I didn't really want this job anymore. I wanted to go home. In my anger and disappointment I had perhaps begun to dare her.

While Hellman was in New York I rode my bicycle all over the island. My happiness was immense. I rode to Edgartown to see my sister, pedaling furiously, the wind just brisk enough to rattle my cheeks and whip tears out of my eyes and fling a fly to its death against the hurtling wall of my forehead. Ellen and I took our bikes to Chappaquiddick on the little ferry—a floating platform, really, like a steel-plated version of Huck Finn's raft—and rode along winding Chappaquiddick Road, shadowed by the leaves of tall oaks and sassafras to Dyke Bridge, pinching acorns beneath our tires and sending them shooting like bullets onto the shoulder of the road. We rode across the bridge (marveling at how such a tiny, pointless, splintered little slab of wood could have become, overnight, so famous) to East Beach. Our tires plowed wavering serpents into the soft sand. We locked our bikes to a weathered post and spent the afternoon on the beach, bodysurfing and talking and watching seals just offshore. Sometimes they looked like chocolate Labs as they surfaced, and other times, when they paused to float and observe us, like whiskered nuns looking on in disapproval, their oily foreheads glinting. Sitting on the beach I felt that the world had never been more vivid. Though erratic footprints cratered the sand, not another person was visible on this soft-duned stretch of shore. We lay in solitude and listened to the waves crumble and slip flat again and watched the speeding sky. A lone laughing gull wandered overhead, muttering to himself in a retching, choking way, and higher up a silver plane smaller than a lapel pin inched toward Europe. Anxious sanderlings wheeled up and back on the slope of the beach in mimicry—or mockery—of the lace-edged waves' push and pull.

When I licked my lips I tasted greasy seawater with its bloom of metal, gasoline, and blood. I watched Ellen beside me, what she did with her hands, how she curled her hair behind her ear, how she talked and brushed dried sand from her thigh, how her mouth moved. Her wrists were bony and brown; mine were padded in pink bracelets of baby fat. Her legs were waxed; I raked a razor across mine when I remembered to. She wasn't religious, but she wore around her neck a tiny gold Saint Christopher medal my mother had given her. I had no chains, no rings, only two silver bracelets and one pair of hoop earrings that I never took off. I wanted to be more like my sisters. They knew the best beaches on the island, the sandy short-cuts, the restaurants. Elizabeth was always trying to help me fix my hair in a more sophisticated style, saying, "See, Rose? Like this. It's easy." I looked at Ellen's hair on the towel beside mine. We had come from the same place, and though Ellen struck me as infinitely more glamorous and graceful than I, we were alike, and both like our mother. We were all, my sisters—and brothers too—like Nona in one way or another. I knew that my family offered the one world I truly belonged to, a private constellation that I shone rightfully within, regardless of what anyone else thought. They were the people I really knew, the people who knew me. They were the only foundation I had, and it was truer than I realized then that they were the measure against which I judged everyone and everything else.

Ellen and I hiked over the hot dunes through the brittle grass to the salt pond and skimmed clam shells over the still water. The banks of the pond were splattered with soft goose droppings, like spills of coal tar. Waterlogged cormorants floated and slithered serpentlike under the surface for their dinner. In the dunes I found a pearly bird's egg the color of an old bed sheet, perfect but for a tiny indentation knocked into one end. This was the summer I had wanted.

———

The night before Hellman returned from New York I dreamt she was standing in the upstairs hallway in a black dress and a wig, with her bags packed to go to New York. She was waiting for someone to come and pick her up, and she looked robust and round and solid, nothing like her true self. A car came down the driveway, a long silver Cadillac with three shady-looking men in it. Hellman went out to greet them while I carried her bag. When a little girl climbed out of the car, Hellman picked her up and handed her to me, saying, "Take care of her while we are gone," and suddenly I knew she wasn't going to New York at all, that she had lied to me, that something else was going on. I held the little girl's hand, frustrated because I had been hoping to have freedom and fun while Hellman was gone, and now I was saddled with a child to mind. When Hellman and the men drove off, I went looking for my mother and found her in the parking lot of a shopping mall, sitting in a car with two of my brothers. As I was explaining to my mother what Hellman had done, the silver Cadillac pulled in to the lot and parked two cars away from us. My mother got out of her car to go over and tell Hellman that I wasn't going to be working for her anymore, but the driver saw her and pulled out again, trying to get away from her. In his hurry he rammed the tail of the Cadillac into someone else's car, and the dream ended in a confusion of sirens and angry shouting.

The next day Hellman came through the door of the little Dukes County Airport, stabbing her cane at the ground and squinting toothily up at the broad-shouldered stranger who was carrying her bag and guiding her by the elbow. I had been sitting on the warm hood of the car, listening to its cooling ticks, waiting for her and watching the flimsy little planes career out of the early evening sky, wavering and tilting and whining, buffeted by gusts, like pigeons floating their unstable way to the sidewalk. I jumped up to meet her.

In the short time she had been gone she seemed to have aged considerably. Her dress was wrinkled at the waistline, a sliver of her slip showed just below her hem, and she tottered across the lot in a fearful way. When, in her conspicuously sexy fashion, she smiled and blinked her eyes and cooed her thanks for his help, the stranger tipped his baseball cap at her and said, "Pleasure."

I guided her the rest of the way to the car, while she muttered and mumbled about her feet, her back, a crick in her neck and, worst of all, the operation her doctor had said she might need for her eyes. The medical examination hadn't gone well. "My eyes are getting worse," she said gloomily to the windshield as we turned onto Airport Road. It frightened and worried her. "God knows, I don't want an operation," she said several times. She seemed so frail and upset that I found myself driving very slowly back to Vineyard Haven, as if to keep from jarring her body. She wanted kale and sausage for dinner, and asked me to stop at Woodlands Market for the kale. When I came out of the market and returned to the car, she was asleep, her head tipped slightly forward and her hands loosely open, palms up on her thighs, as if in resignation. In the fading light her hands were like two wilting white tulips. For a moment I feared she was dead, but when I slid behind the wheel she muttered and lifted her head and asked, "We there?"

"Not yet," I said, thinking how like a child she could be. "But almost."

In the kitchen, as she prepared her dinner, her mood retrogressed from sorrowful to sour. She asked me to get the jar of pickles out of the refrigerator, and although I seemed to remember putting the empty pickle jar into the dishwasher, I looked anyway. When I told her there were no pickles, she snapped, "Don't always be so sure of everything!"

My scalp and the soles of my feet tingled in a way that had

become too familiar now, and I thought to myself, *She is crazy*. It was a big jar of pickles that she had made herself from her own garden cucumbers, but I knew we had used them up for company. I stood in front of the refrigerator, at a loss for what to do. "I'm pretty sure we used them," I said, and she stumped and scraped her way toward me and brandished her hand and said, "Look some more. I can't see them, but I won't believe they aren't there. We couldn't have used them all."

The pickles weren't there, and I knew it. I hunkered down and looked some more to humor her, and when I lifted my face to her again, hopeless and empty-handed, she grew fierce. "I'm sure they're there! Don't you remember we put them in that Mason jar?"

I didn't remember. I had never pickled any cucumbers with her. I said, "I think that was Donna."

"Why do you always argue?!" she yelped. "What does it matter who it was?!"

She was in a rage. Anything I said now would be wrong, I knew that. "It doesn't matter who it was," I said. "But I don't remember. There aren't any pickles."

"Don't question me! Of course there are! Just find them. And move faster."

Like a dog, I put my head down and obeyed, looking over the same bowls and cartons and moist plastic bags and jars with colorful labels. I reached in with both hands and shifted things around, but as much as I wanted to I could not make the jar of pickles appear. I stood up, shut the refrigerator door, and looked at her. What could I say? I had asked for this job. I had come to her. I had needed her as much as she needed me. I crossed my arms on my chest to give myself strength. "I'm not questioning you, Miss Hellman," I said. "The pickles just aren't here. I'll look as many times as you like. But there aren't any pickles."

She lifted one foot in what looked like an attempt to stamp it, but she was tipped slightly off balance and had to clap her hand onto the countertop to steady herself. "Well, where the hell did they go?"

When I told her that people had eaten them, she opened her mouth and bayed, *"What* people?"

Something about her big teeth was very frightening. They were yellowish and solid and slightly jutting. They were unnaturally even. They were like the cattle catcher on the front of a freight train. "Your people," I said, because I couldn't think of anything else to say, and turned away from her. I couldn't look at her anymore.

She snorted through her nose and went back to the stove. Her kale was roiling in its pot, seasoned with the fatty bits of ham she had thrown in. The kitchen felt tight and damp and smelled like vinegar. *Your people* rang in my ears; I knew there was something odd and sad in my saying it. I felt a vast chasm between her people and mine. When the kale was done, she asked me to strain it and put it in a serving bowl, then give her a plateful. As I was filling her plate from the bowl, she came over and pointed at my hand and snapped, "No, no! I said put it on this plate."

I stared at her. "I was putting it on the plate."

"You weren't," she insisted. "You were taking it off the plate. I asked you to put it on my plate. Please do that now."

I couldn't argue with her. She seemed a little insane to me, though I was sure she wasn't. It may have been her eyesight. But if it was, how could she go on bulldozing through the world with the same confidence she had always had? She had to be right about everything, though her blindness made that nearly impossible.

She ate her dinner alone in the living room, drinking wine and staring at nothing. As soon as she dismissed me, I went into my room without saying goodnight and tried to write in my journal. I was unable to get much beyond *I don't want her to be a friend of mine, because I don't respect her.*

————

Two days later, at the end of a beautifully clear August day, Peter Feibleman arrived at the house. Hellman had been increasingly excited about his visit, delighted, visibly nervous. She wanted this to go well, I knew. That morning she had wandered distractedly from one room to another, adjusting flowers in vases, rearranging photographs and ashtrays on tables, checking light bulbs. She went into the guest room he'd be staying in, the one at the end of the hall, and checked and rechecked the way I had made the bed and washed the windows and cleaned out the bureau drawers. I had moved a table into the room for him to use as a desk: he was, she said, working on a novel. At nine o'clock she went out with Jack Koontz, her fishing partner, to look at a boat. When she returned at ten-thirty I was ironing a pile of linen napkins and several of her blouses. She came to stand by the ironing board, gently pinching her lips between thumb and forefinger, like the handle of a teacup, and stared absently at what I was doing, obviously organizing something in her mind. It made me nervous; I was ready to have her criticize the ironing. I was ready to have her criticize just about anything. But she was too distracted to think about me today. Annabel Nichols would be arriving tomorrow, and we needed to be ready for her as well. Hellman asked me to call Gilbert at Café du Port on Main Street to make a lunch reservation for her and Albert Hackett and his wife, Frances Goodrich—the two Anne Frank people. "And then call Mr. Hackett to confirm the date." As soon as I had done so, she told me to call Gilbert back and change the time of the reservation. Then she sat down in her armchair in the living room, perfectly still, with her chin raised. She appeared to be thinking, her eyes looking no farther than the lenses of her glasses. She sat that way for five minutes, got up again, went upstairs for one minute, came back downstairs, straightened a picture on the hallway wall, went out the door to stare at her garden for three minutes, came back in, banged her knee on a chair, searched for a fresh pack of cigarettes, sat in her armchair again, and made some telephone calls. She called somebody and complained about the BBC's request to film an interview with her at the house in September. "A fellow named Peter Adam," I heard her say. ". . . television . . . they want two or three sessions to be sure they get it right . . . waste my time . . . bunch of fucking amateurs . . . I want the right to edit . . . sure they'll screw up." She called someone else to talk about a writer named Johnson, who, from what I overheard as I dusted the baseboards in the living room, would be writing a biography of Dashiell Hammet. She seemed conflicted about Johnson, liked her but then didn't, trusted her but then didn't. She mentioned Styron's name once or twice, crankily. Her grumbling was general that morning. With her face cradled into the telephone receiver she talked about a guy who had recently called her up to inform her that some woman, obviously an acquaintance of Hellman's, had died. Hellman put on a heavy southern accent in imitation of the caller and hollered at the person she was talking to, " 'Scout's honor, Lillyun, her almost *dyin'* words were *How I looove Lillyun Hellmun!* Her almost *dyin'* words! *Oh, how I* looove *that Lillyun Hellmun.* ' "

Gathering the empty bottles from the bar and putting down new ones, I listened to her cackle for several minutes over this. She coughed and laughed and added in her own deep voice, "And then he shouted to his wife, 'Oh, say, Daybruh?! Say, Daybruh?! Come hyeah and say hello to Lillyun Hellmun.' " She roared and coughed and slapped her thigh and tilted her face up at the ceiling and crowed, " 'Her almost dyin' words were *How I loove Lillyun Hellman! Dear Lillyun Hellman!*' "

She found the whole thing so hilariously funny that I thought she would choke. And the way she told the story, it was indeed funny. It was the "almost dying words" that killed her. She did a brilliant job of making the man, whoever he was, sound foolish and fawning, and

I caught myself smirking into the ice bucket over it. She used the word *jackass* to describe him. Her laugh, with all its liquid volume, was infectious. She was funny, though she had never once been funny with me and wasn't the sort of woman you could slap on the back and guffaw with unless you were invited to, not the sort of woman who shrugged things off. I was happy when I could watch her from under the cloak of my work, sometimes glad that she paid me no attention. It was as though I didn't exist, and therefore she said and did things in front of me that she might not have done in front of others.

Soon after Hellman returned from her lunch date, William Styron stopped by the house. His nose was sunburned and shiny. Hellman and he were gruff with each other, teasing and bickering in a good-natured way as they fixed themselves drinks. She was planning a dinner in honor of her guests for Wednesday night, and the Styrons had offered to bring the main course: twenty quail, which Styron himself would cook on her stove. They talked about this, about cooking, about Styron's wife, his daughters, about their work. As I had suspected, Hellman was writing notes to her memoirs, and it sounded as though Styron was writing a novel about the Holocaust. Their faces were bright as they raised their glasses to their lips.

When Styron left, Hellman changed her clothes, smoked eight cigarettes, turned on all the lights downstairs, flipped through the *New York Times* with a magnifying glass pressed to her face, checked her watch, had another drink, and went upstairs twice to make sure the outdoor lights were on for Peter Feibleman. Finally he appeared. He had taken a taxi from the airport, and he walked in the front door with a suitcase, dressed in a loose-fitting shirt and soft trousers. He was even younger than I had expected him to be, and he greeted her with the familiarity of a son. I could see that Hellman was truly happy to see him and, more than that, relieved, as though some horrible burden had been lifted. She introduced him to me. He was friendly, cordial, and soft-spoken and had a gentle manner. He shook my hand. He had hairy wrists. He seemed nervous, a little uneasy. His dark, wavy hair was touched with gray at the temples, and I noticed that his upper lip was very like Hellman's. He wasn't tall, but he was broad-chested and strong-looking, with dark eyebrows and long sideburns.

Hellman and he sat in the living room and had drinks, and she grumbled about her eyes and a lot of other things. She opened up with him, was not on guard, was not defensive. In his presence she looked brighter. It seemed as if this man was her one real friend.

As I was going out the door to meet Annabel Nichols at the airport, Hellman said, "She is tall, blond, and very very pretty. You'll know who she is right away. Just wait at the door. She'll be alone. Her husband is coming tomorrow."

At the airport several tall, blond, and very pretty women came out the door. In fact, it seemed that all of the women getting off planes on Martha's Vineyard were tall, blond, and very pretty. I asked each one, "Are you Mrs. Nichols?" Finally, one of them was. Annabel Nichols was long-faced, with white skin and big eyes that had a slightly sad slant, which made them prettier. She looked game for anything but also delicate, as if she might bruise easily and get badly burned by the sun. She had flown in from New York. In the car, heading back to the house, she had the look of a person just coming to life after a long sleep, a slightly bewildered air of freedom, as though she were getting used to her own body, felt a little stunned by the green leaves and winding roads and antique houses, by the closeness of the sky, all the space, after the narrow plastic-and-metal enclosure of the airplane. When I mentioned that Hellman had said she was Irish, she smiled and fiddled with an earring and said, "Well,

I was born in Ireland." She was from Waterford, she said. When I told her I was going to Ireland soon to study Irish, she laughed and said that her parents had paid for her to go to a private school so she wouldn't *have* to learn Irish. I smiled and nodded knowingly, but the statement annoyed and insulted me, and as she talked in her fancy way I thought to myself, *Planter.* She was friendly, but the clean elegance of her clothing and her accent unnerved me. Her shoulder-length hair was thick, and her skin had a ringing clarity. I was dressed for housework on a wooded island; she was dressed for a day at the races. She didn't sound the least bit Irish. She had long lashes and well-tended brows, thick hair to her shoulders and an exceptionally full lower lip. I felt dark and oily and backward beside her. I felt like the chauffeur that I was.

The next morning, while her guests were still sleeping and I was making a pot of coffee in the bright kitchen, Hellman came in, opened the freezer door to search for something, stood there for a minute with cold mist winding about her head, and suddenly said, "I have never seen so much frost on any freezer in my life! Between you and Donna, this freezer should have been taken care of long ago!" She shut the door, shuffled to the sink, tore at the hot water faucet until a milky pole of water twitched from the spigot, and began filling a pot with hot water. "If it happens again I'll *shoot* both of you," she said, and I knew that through her vexation she was being facetious. "Defrost it now."

She stood by me as I began the job, which made the task unpleasant. To my way of looking at it, there really wasn't much frost. It seemed strange for her to be angry about it, a strange job for us to be focusing on when there was so much else to do, with all these visitors here. As I worked, removing the rocklike packages from the freezer and packing its shelves with steaming pots of hot water, I saw a tiny mouse slide across the kitchen floor toward the oven and said, "Oh, a mouse," more in interest than alarm.

Hellman went stiff. Her head turned slowly, as if not to draw attention to herself. "Mouse?!"

"Yes, by the oven."

"I can't see him. Are you certain?"

"Yeah," I said, "it's a mouse. I think I might be able to catch him. He's just sitting there."

"Just *sitting?*" She was incredulous.

"He's not really running away from us."

"Not running? That's impossible. God, I don't want to see him."

"He's just looking at us."

Hellman moaned with disgust and put her hand to her throat. "What does he want?"

The mouse sat still in a patch of sunlight on the linoleum. He was tiny and dusty, all haunch and rump, with a hairy little nub for a head and his tail stretched behind him like a length of gray shoelace. He seemed to be trembling. As I searched for an empty coffee can, Hellman muttered, "Jesus Christ," several times to herself, and with amazing alacrity hoisted herself onto a kitchen chair in the kneeling position. She fitted an unlit cigarette between her trembling lips, took it out again immediately as if to say something, was mute, put the cigarette back again, clutched the back of the chair with both hands, and muttered around the bobbing cigarette, "Don't let him over here, will you?"

The sunlight streaming through the kitchen windows lit up her brilliant hair and formed a kind of halo around her head. She was breathless with fear, which fascinated me. It was like a parody of squeamishness. I went over to the mouse and fitted the coffee can gently over him. "I caught him," I said.

"You *caught* him? Jesus. Where?"

"Right here."

"Oh, good for you. Wonderful. Can you . . . can you get rid of him? Can you kill him?"

I didn't want to kill him. Besides, he looked unwell, probably poisoned by the D-Con she had asked her handyman to put down. I got a piece of newspaper, slid it under the can, and picked the mouse up. I could feel the negligible weight of his body on the palm of my hand, his little feet scratching and poking and hopping on the paper. "I have him here," I said, lifting the can for her to see.

"Oh, God, don't show him to me. Just kill him. Flush . . . flush him down the toilet."

I knew I couldn't kill him. "I could just put him outside," I offered.

"No, no, he'll come back. Flush him. Hit him with the broom."

Now that the mouse was actually in our possession, her fear and anxiety seemed to have increased. I pretended to go into the bathroom but went into my room instead, opened the door and put the mouse down on the lawn. He didn't run. He was sick. His eyes were big and black. I knew he'd never make it back. When I returned to the kitchen, she was getting off the chair. She saw me and said, "Done?"

"Yes."

"He's gone?"

"Yes, he is."

"Wonderful. That's wonderful. Good for you. Brave. You . . . what did you do? You put the can over him? Magnificent. I couldn't have done it. And you flushed him down the toilet."

"Yes, I did."

"All the way down?"

"Yes."

She tried to light the cigarette, realized she had broken it, put it in her pocket and found a fresh one. In the slanting sunlight her thin eyebrows were like the caramel-colored hairs on a coconut. "Thank God. I'm going to go to work now," she said shakily. "Thank you. You can finish the freezer yourself."

Catching the mouse was probably my biggest success of the summer, and for that one moment every other blunder was redeemed.

That afternoon, when Donna arrived to help prepare lunch for the guests, I mentioned Hellman's cranky reaction to the freezer, hoping for solace and commiseration, but my plea backfired, and Donna chided me. She was uncharacteristically short with me that day, and as she dragged a sponge across the back of the kitchen sink she said sternly, "Rosemary, this place needs to be kept cleaner."

I stewed and tried to make things better by telling her about the mouse, but she didn't seem to be listening. I did whatever she and Hellman told me to do, and when the lunch was ready, I was allowed a few hours off until dinnertime.

I walked down Main Street, sweating and fretting. In the pocket of my shorts I found the paycheck Hellman had given me and went into the bank to cash it.

The Martha's Vineyard National Bank was a pretty building made entirely of stone—smooth round cobblestones mortared together—and the roof was red pantiles. It looked to me like the carriage house of a Tyrolean castle. Inside, I handed my check to a young teller. She inspected it, flicked at it with a red fingernail, glanced at my face, and shook her head. "I don't think, Miss," she said.

"Think what?"

"We can cash this."

"How come?"

"Is it your check?"

"Yes."

The woman raised her brows at me in a look that said *Tell me another one.* "Are you Lillian Hellman?" she said smartly.

"No."

She pursed her lips. "Because for one, you don't appear to look like Lillian Hellman. And for two, this check says Lillian Hellman." She held the check up for me to see and gave me a knowing look. "What would you agree?"

"Well, yeah," I said, "it's her check, but it's my check actually. It's my paycheck. She gave it to me."

The woman leaned back on the stool she was sitting on, crossed her arms. "Why wouldn't it be made out in your name then?"

"I don't really know. She did it that way for some reason. But it's OK, you can cash it."

"Miss." She paused for emphasis. "It is most certainly not OK."

"I promise you it is OK."

"Not to us it isn't." She sounded personally offended. "It has to be made out in your name for you to cash it, which this check is not made out in your name." She pushed the check back across the counter to me, but before I could take it she snatched it up again. "On second thought, I think we'll be keeping this here."

"But it really is mine," I said.

The woman stared in a wincing, pinch-mouthed trance of disbelief.

"You can call her up. She'll tell you."

"Mary," she said, turning to her coworker at the next window, "can we call Lillian Hellman?"

Mary looked up from a fan of stiff twenties she was snapping up with her fingers. She stared grimly at my teller, then at me. "Yeah, Betty," she said, "we can call Lillian Hellman, as long as it's you not me who's calling. I'm not being responsible for Lillian today."

My teller got off her stool. "What's your name?" she said with a sigh. I told her, and she disappeared into a back room. I waited. The bank was cool inside, and tidy and pretty, with polished brass and creamy marble everywhere. Through the glass front door the sunlit street was blindingly bright; cars and people passed by, sharp and quick, like photographic slides shuffling through a projector. The teller came back, put herself back onto the stool, folded her hands on the counter, and said sullenly, "We called her. She's not home."

"That can't be right," I said. "I just left there. She was sitting down to lunch."

The girl shrugged at me. "Sorry, miss. She is not home."

The palms of my hands were sweating. I pressed them to the counter to cool them and looked at Mary, twisting a rubber band with an expert's vicious flair around her clutch of money. She looked back at me. They thought I was a crazy con artist. The teller held the check out to me pinched between the tips of her fingers, as though it were soiled. I took it and went out to the street. I feared I might begin to cry. Either the bank had called the wrong number, or Hellman had made Donna pull the not-home trick. In the dark shadow of the bank's little stone porch I felt betrayed and enraged. Across the street Thomas Palmer was coming cheerfully out of Cronig's in his green apron, pushing a shopping cart. He saw me and waved. I waved and tried to smile, but I knew the smile looked indignant and the wave was stunted by my feelings of betrayal into an awkward convulsion of entreaty.

I walked down to the ferry landing and sat on the beach, my sneakers filling with sand. I was too upset to bother taking them off. I always found comfort in the sight of boats, a reminder that there was a way to leave. I sat there on the beach in the sun in my long-sleeved shirt and listened to the vessels of my own thoughts popping in my head. I didn't really care about the money. It was her trickery and her scheming that made me burn. What was she thinking of? *My taxes.* I knew it was bullshit. It had to have been in her interest somehow to try to pay me this way.

I thought of a scene in *An Unfinished Woman* in which Hellman and her black housemaid, Helen, got into an argument. Helen had accused Hellman of making her into a slave and Hellman had called her a liar and Helen had ripped up a check Hellman had given her and said, "You think money and presents can buy me. You're wrong." And then Hellman had dramatically suggested that Helen move out. And then they had both had some kind of revelation and it was patched up. Sitting there I didn't think life was that easy. And the person I had imagined and admired in Lillian Hellman, the writer I had envisioned sitting at a desk as I read her books, seemed very far away now. It was difficult for me to remember what it was about her that I had loved.

A fat gull cried like a baby overhead, and the white bulk of the ferry began to slip away from the dock. People came and went in the shimmering parking lot behind me, but I hardly noticed them. I was too busy conversing in my head, only vaguely aware that my eyes were narrowed to slits and my lips were moving dryly and small sounds of irritation were escaping from my mouth. Eventually I looked up and saw that the strange black woman who was usually sitting here had appeared out of nowhere and was standing a few yards away, watching me with skeptical interest as I muttered and rocked and tsked and shook my head and stabbed at the sand with my fingers. When I caught her eye she looked quickly away and moved grandly off down the beach. Like me, she was wearing long sleeves on this hot day. Her strong feet stirred up big plumes of sand peppered with black twists of dried seaweed. She was like a person waiting for something that was certain to arrive, confidently biding her time. The waiting made her strong. She was free, and in her freedom she was powerful. Nobody told her to leave the beach or to do anything at all. That afternoon I envied her.

I went to the public phones outside the Steamship Authority ticket office and called my mother. Her voice was beautiful. She had no accent that I could hear except the long Boston *a*—she made *half* and *bath* and *calf* and *laugh* rhyme with the *a* in *Ma*. She only faintly dropped her *r*'s. Her voice was like a dancing figure. "How's everything, Rose?" she said brightly.

"Awful," I said. "I want to come home."

There was a cautious silence from my mother. A man coming out of the ticket office shouted, "Hey, Ginger!" and the same crying gull that had been slipping through the sky over my head seemed to answer with a perseverative barking call.

"You want to come home?"

"Yes."

"Today?"

"Yes. Now."

"Why?"

"I hate it here."

Another silence, and I knew from the timbre of it that my mother was torn between my unhappy feelings and what was best.

"She's awful, Nona. She's a jerk. And an asshole. And I wish she would die."

With a familiar theatrical sadness in her voice that appealed to my higher sympathies with just the right touch, my mother said, *"Die* is a harsh thing to say about anybody, Ra. I know she's tough, but quitting won't solve it. You can come home anytime you like, you know that. But I know you. You'll feel better if you stick with it. You'll see. You made her a promise. She needs your help, even if she's not nice to you. It's a good experience. Later on you'll laugh about it. Remember how many times you called me from school and said the same thing? You got through that."

That was true. That spring I had called my mother many nights from the phone booth out among the pine trees by the school garage and said, *I want to come home,* crushing underfoot the orange tassels of pine needles littering the quilted metal floor of the booth, my tears tapping the front of my bulky down jacket. I always felt vulnerable in that booth; when I pulled the accordion door shut behind me, it switched on a fluorescent overhead light, exposing me, advertising my presence for whatever bear or nut case might come along through the dark stand of trees.

I couldn't imagine laughing about any of this. This was the worst summer I had ever passed.

"You thought it over when you were cool and calm," my mother said gently. "Now the heat is on. Don't crumple. Have faith."

My mother always said, *have faith,* and though I knew she was right, the slow, abstracted nature of faith itched on my skin and made me want to lash out at everything. It reminded me of the dry, tortuous books we had read in religion class at school: Paul Tillich and Alan Watts and their obscure and nonsensical dronings about existential disappointment and the *leap of faith.* Their numbing treatments of how to handle all the things we couldn't know zigzagged in a crazy cat's cradle over my head, just out of reach. I knew there was something in their philosophy, yet not understanding it, knowing I'd have to bluster my way through some pointless test, made me hate it all the more. The notion that there was one "right" way to anything scared and perplexed me, and I felt too distracted by my daily life to think clearly about these ideas. I debased those books by doodling stars and boxes all over their covers and writing *fuck this* and *idiot* and *oh, thanks, Paul, this really helps* in their margins.

I said to my mother, "Why should I?" which was what I always said.

"Because," my mother said, "that's all we have. And it's a lot. Stay. Something will be there for you. You'll see."

———

Toward dinnertime I walked back to the house, and as I turned into the driveway I met Rose Styron coming out in her car, driving a little too fast. Through the windshield I could see that she was conversing intently with herself. She was red-faced, looked angry, the corkscrews of her soft blond hair hanging around her face. Her tires fairly squealed as she gunned the car out onto Main Street. In her preoccupation she hadn't noticed me on the road, and I felt the rushing heat of her car door rip by inches from my knuckles.

When I went down to the kitchen, Donna told me that Rose Styron and Hellman had had a heated argument during Rose's Scrabble visit. Rose had stormed out of the house, swearing that she and her husband would not, after all, be bringing the twenty quail for the dinner party Hellman had planned for the next night. In fact, they would not be coming to the party at all.

I knew it must have been bad. Hellman and the Styrons were old friends, but when they fought, it was bitter, with loud voices and brilliant stinging insults and shredded egos.

I tried to lie low. Donna and I served dinner for Hellman, Feibleman, and Annabel Nichols: bluefish that Hellman had caught herself. Hellman had made a tangy mustard sauce to put over it. While Donna and I sat at the kitchen table eating our fish, she told me she was leaving the island soon, the twenty-fourth of August, and how much she would miss Hellman when she was gone.

"I like her so much," Donna said. "She's so nice."

I looked up to see if she was kidding. She was not kidding, and this was so baffling that I stared at my plate and kept eating. Donna rarely screwed up the way I did, so Hellman had less cause to be irritated by her. Donna was a good cook, and Hellman respected that. Hellman never yelled at her. But *nice?* Who could say that? "Yeah, she's nice," I said pathetically. I chewed a piece of bread, thinking and worrying. Through the window, the ferry was just leaving Vineyard Haven, its many windows glowing with a lemony light like a string of lanterns over the water. I could hear Annabel Nichols's high sweet laugh running through its dressage in the other room. The fine hairs on Donna's arms were golden in the light as she raised a forkful of steaming white fish.

Donna told me that when she had first taken this job, the summer before, she was very quiet and reserved and fearful of Hellman, that she felt she couldn't be open or relaxed in her presence. "You're much more relaxed here than I ever was my whole first year," she said.

"I am?"

"Yeah, much more."

Impossible. I had become mouselike and uncertain here. I felt Hellman was after me all the time. She was like a lion lurking behind a clump of bushes. I felt awful, and though I tried to hide my fears, I wasn't relaxed. "Donna," I said, "did the bank call here at lunchtime today?"

Donna sipped from a glass of water. "Bank? No. I don't think so."

"They said they called."

"They must not have. The phone never rang. What were they calling about?"

I stood up to begin clearing the table. "Oh, nothing really."

When we had finished cleaning up the kitchen, Donna and I went upstairs to turn down the beds. Donna reprimanded me again, this time for doing Feibleman's bed wrong. *"Rosemary,"* she said. "This has to be neat!"

I hurried to neaten the bed, patting and smoothing the spread briskly, giving the sheet a resentful yank, but it was difficult for me to understand why it mattered so terribly, and why Donna, who was a smart person, cared. I didn't care; turning down another person's bed seemed to me the most pointless and precious activity anyone had ever thought up.

The next day Mike Nichols arrived with fourteen ounces of Beluga caviar. His face was smooth and round, his eyes hooded, his nose finely winged, his hair a sleek sloping mass, like a Frenchman's beret. He wore stylish tan trousers and a white shirt. He put the can of caviar down on the kitchen table and hugged Hellman and his wife. He had big thumbs. They all stood around in the kitchen talking and sipping iced tea. I didn't know what to do or where to stand, so I retreated to my bedroom and sat on the bed until, a few minutes later, Hellman called me out to rinse the teapot. I rinsed the teapot and then I was left standing by the sink again, doing nothing while they talked. Annabel Nichols had made a salad, and Feibleman and Nichols had shucked some corn. There was nothing for me to do.

For lunch, at the kitchen table, Hellman gave her guests corn and salad and Nichols's caviar. They drank Beck's dark beer in tall glasses and tore at the loaf of bread lying in a basket. Nichols drummed on the table with the tines of his fork and leaned back on two legs of his chair like a young boy. He crossed his arms and uncrossed them. He was restless. When he stuck his finger in the little pitcher of salad dressing and raised his finger to his mouth to lick it, his wife said, "Mike, your manners," and he hunched down in his chair and pretended to look chastised. I could see that Hellman was proud to have him here. I knew he was famous, but I had no idea what for. I liked him. He was tall and loose and funny.

With other people in the room I had a chance to stand idle for a moment and watch Hellman talking. She lifted her hands into the air as she spoke and waved them slowly like small paper fans, then folded them together in the way of the Pope greeting the throngs from his balcony. She touched a fist gently to her knee to emphasize whatever point she was making. I could hear her beer gurgling loosely in her throat as she swallowed. Her gold watchband clacked and scraped on the table as she reached for the salt, and when she was finished eating she sat back with one hand on her hip and looked at her guests, like a foreman surveying his dock workers. Listening, she had a habit of touching her thumb lightly to each fingertip, as if in counting, and occasionally her jaw slid off center and she tapped her teeth together softly. She had big nostrils, and sitting at the table with her friends, she seemed to be repeatedly battling a fugitive smile, relaxing and letting it rise, then straightening it flat over her teeth until it crept slowly, slyly up again. She looked better without her glasses, and her eyes were nearly pretty when she laughed. She used the phrases *It's my belief* and *I've long felt* and the words *shabby* and *fine*. To me she was as fascinating to watch as a small nocturnal animal. Just before lunch, in the living room, she had asked me if the water on the bar was clean, and when I said "I'll check," she had raised her barnacled hand suddenly and stopped me with that brown look of dissatisfaction, the hushed voice of irritation, and sternly informed me that I had been here long enough to know when to check the water on the bar and that it was annoying for her to always have to tell me these things. Her quiet mode of admonishment was more frightening than her noisy yelling. It felt downright sinister; her cheeks fairly trembled and her top lip actually curled. Her eyes, angry, took on an expressive, nearly pleading look. She had never had to say anything to me before about fresh water on the bar, but it didn't matter. I bothered her. There was no question about this.

Naked, bellies up, their little legs kicked into the air and their pinkish yellow skin pimpled with tiny bumps that made them look checkered and chilly, twenty quail lay on two platters on the kitchen table. The argument had been resolved. The Styrons had relented. The day, which had been nearly perfect in its beauty, was slowly shutting down. Crouched in the shadow of the hill, the house and garden were still and cool, and the sun was visible only as it murmured in flecks of gold and orange to the very tops of the dark green trees behind the house. Birdsong came more softly and less frequently out of the trees, the watery whistle of a house finch, a jay's rusty wheedling. The eastern sky over the water was cobalt blue and glittered every so often with the silver flashes of a far-off gull's wings catching the sun.

The kitchen was crowded. Styron stood at the stove, preparing to cook his quail, I was at the cutting board making colorful mounds of minced garlic, diced red peppers, onion, and ginger, and Donna was setting up frying pans on the four burners. The dinner was for ten people, not counting Donna and me. There was spaghetti with the pesto that Hellman and I had made that afternoon, ham and quail from the Styrons, and two chocolate rolls that Donna had made. Donna dropped hunks of butter into the frying pans while Styron turned up the heat, bending his knees to peer at the knobs on the stove. Without a word he took the cutting board and knife out from under me, flicked garlic and onion into the four pans, and handed the cutting board back. The frying pans hissed and sizzled and sent up humid clouds of smoke into the yellow light under the hood of the stove. Donna turned on the stove fan, which began to breathe loudly, and without looking at her Styron snapped it off again. The kitchen grew hot. Styron squinted into the pans, sipped at a clear drink tinkling with ice cubes, and flicked perspiration from his brow with the tips of his fingers. His graying hair looked damp. The way his puffy lids slanted made him look dissatisfied. He didn't smile. He talked loudly. He scared me. I thanked God Donna was here; she had greater authority in the kitchen than I did and thus greater responsibility. I was delighted to be relegated to chopping, unwrapping, stacking, and washing; I could hide behind these simple tasks, odious as they were to me. Donna and I worked quietly, trying not to invoke anyone's wrath. Now and then Feibleman ducked into the kitchen on the balls of his feet, slicing a lime, observing for a second with a hand on his hip, and disappearing again. Something about the set of his mouth always made him look as if he were about to nibble at his upper lip.

At one point I looked up from my chopping to see Donna gesturing at me from the shelter of the dark, cluttered pantry. I made my way slowly and strategically toward her, wiping the counters and moving plates in a phony show of necessity as I progressed to that side of the room.

"We don't have enough butter for the quail," Donna whispered out of the darkness. "He'll kill us. Ride your bike down to Cronig's, will you, and get some more?"

I snuck out my bedroom door and sped the wrong way down one-way Main Street. Drivers had begun to switch on their headlights in the bluish dusk, and the cars curled by me like big dark hippos in a river, or a parade of mattresses. My apron formed a tilting white bowl between my knees, light filling it as a car approached, then leaching away as it passed. Ripping wind grabbed at my ears. I had a hard time seeing the road. Still hot from the day's sun, the pavement sent up waves of warm air that touched my bare ankles and shins and pushed against the cool breeze coming out of the trees. A young couple was locked in a kiss at the top of Owen Park. I wanted to ride all the way to Gay Head on this pleasant evening. At Cronig's I grabbed a block of stick butter, paid for it with $1.59 of my own money, and when the freckled checkout girl tossed out her usual jaunty, "How's old Lilly baby?" I said, "Shitty," and ran out the door.

Rose Styron arrived shortly after I got back to the house. She smiled widely, yet she looked tense and jumpy as she introduced the people she'd brought with her, a bony-faced writer named Peter Matthiessen who, somebody said, had written a great book about the Himalayas, and an English woman whose name I didn't hear. Hellman smiled and shook their hands and said how pleased she was, but I sensed that the fight with the Styrons was just barely patched up, the anger temporarily tucked behind their faces.

I worked fast. I had already made one mistake, had heard Hellman in the other room telling Styron I had put out the wrong plates "again," heard her use the words *little* and *Irish* to describe me. She had a thing about Irish people. In fact, she had a thing about ethnicity in general, Jews included. We were all figures of ridicule and predictability—she alone was somehow exempt; she had the superior Jewishness of Jesus, which was like no Jewishness at all. "Take these back and get the right plates," she had told me. She fussed over which wines to serve, made me check the ice on the bar twice, asked me to get candles and matches, salt and pepper shakers, and set them out on the dinner table.

Coming out of the hairdresser's that morning Hellman had slipped off the curb and nearly fallen, and had had to grab at my arm to steady herself. Her efforts had been worth it. With her freshly vested hair and expensive silk gown, her long gold chain dangling ropelike to her waist, she looked striking. Her eyebrows, shaped and thickened with pencil, were like strokes from a calligraphy brush arching high above her powdered blue lids. On her feet she wore a pair of slippers, thin soles bound to her tiny feet with a few fine leather straps crisscrossing the tops. She was nervous, sipping at her drink, smoking, padding in her hipless way from one side of the kitchen to the other, a lighter clutched in one hand. Now and then she stopped to stand and stare at nothing, thinking, tasting her teeth, the painted corners of her mouth sagging. She released tiny puffs of smoke into her own face and brushed ashes from her bosom and offered oblique comments on what Styron was doing. Her perfume and cigarette smoke battled with his simmering garlic and ginger. She couldn't leave him alone. His cooking techniques put her on edge. Was he sure the heat was high enough, were the quail clean, was he burning the butter, how would the cooked birds be kept warm until everything else was ready? She spoke to the oval of sweat darkening the back of his shirt. He directed his gruff answers at the frying pans. She kept pausing to hover over the plates of food laid out on the kitchen table, commenting on whatever dish caught her eye. Bending over, her cigarette held out behind her, straight-armed and away from the table, as though she were handing it off to a relay runner, she poked at the vernix on a small wheel of Brie. She peered at the ham Styron had brought, and then at the plates of quail, and tsked and hemmed and muttered what sounded like *salmonella*. It was hard to tell whether she was joking. She wasn't smiling. She was like a horsefly, nagging him, nipping at his flesh, then chiding him for being short with her, until he accidentally backed into her on one of her pacing passes through the room, nearly crushing her brittle feet. "Lillian!" he roared. "Will you get the hell out of here?! You're getting in my way."

"I'm only trying to be helpful, Bill," she croaked, cocking her head like a robin, trying to see him better, then slunk out of the room, sulking and wounded, the heels of her sandals dragging and clacking beneath her.

While the Herseys and the Nicholses and the rest of the guests sat in the living room drinking, Donna instructed me to gather up the dinner plates and begin warming them with hot water. Warming the dinner plates, like turning down the beds, seemed to me the height of superfluity—no one had ever needed to do those things for me.

More than any others, these two exercises made me feel machinelike and invisible. Donna and I held the platters of quail for Styron as he dropped them one by one into the frying pans. The whole thing seemed like a tremendous amount of bother; with the energy that was going into this meal we could have painted the kitchen or laid down a new tile floor or planted a field of roses. Cooking did not strike me as a useful activity, but these people were mad for it.

Styron's gray hair brushed the collar of his shirt as he moved. Why did he seem untidy to me? I knew he was smart from the way he talked, and people liked his writing, and his wife was nice. There must have been something good about him. As I watched him rummage through the utensil drawer, I saw, on the periphery of my vision, several slender shoestrings of black smoke snaking up from the lip of one of the pans. The sight was paralyzing. Styron saw it too, and for a strange second he stood, like me, perfectly still. Then his mouth opened, his hands jerked out of the drawer, his body pitched massively forward. Grabbing the handle of the pan, he gave the birds so brutal a shake that his cheeks jumped. Dark smoke furled upward into the muffled orange stove light. He cursed and banged the pan down on the stove and immediately turned his sweating face on Donna and upbraided her for not paying attention. "That was *your* job, dammit!" he said.

I slipped to the sink and began washing the tangle of greasy crockery and tin that lay discarded there, my face turned safely to the wall. The kitchen went deathly quiet as Styron began forking the cooked quail onto clean platters. I felt my back and shoulders bracing for whatever blow, verbal or otherwise, might come at me from behind. Styron sighed and grumbled. The meal was ready. He went out of the room to sit with the guests.

I turned from the sink to look at Donna. Her cheeks were scarlet. She wiped her palms on the front of her stained apron. We stared at each other. She shook her head, shut her eyes, and blew a stream of air into her eyebrows. Her forehead was shiny with sweat. I wondered if my face was as red as hers. "It wasn't my fault," she said, dragging her forearm across her forehead.

I knew she was right.

With two powerful punches Donna crushed her long sleeves up over her elbows. She was fuming, beset, her lower lip held a faintly perceptible tremble, as if Styron's stinging words had frightened it. "Come on. We have to get it ready."

We looked at the quail: cooked, they looked more like live creatures, their crooked wings on the verge of flapping. They looked toadlike to me. Four of them bore coal-black smudges on their backs. As she arranged the quail on the platters with flourishes of parsley and lemon, Donna said, "Just wait. As soon as we bring this out, he'll tell everyone it was *our* fault. *Donna and Rosemary burned the quail.* I bet he will."

She seemed to have been through this before with him. And, as she had predicted, when we walked into the living room with the two platters, Styron made a scraping sound in his throat and said, "My apologies for the few that are singed. The girls lost control of a burner."

Donna's face remained expressionless as she carried her platter first to Hellman at the head of the table. I carried mine to Mrs. Hersey, lowering it to her left. She smiled politely at me, lifted the serving forks, and scooped up one of the leggy brown packages. Around the table the expectant faces and hands of the guests glowed in the apricot candlelight. They were delighted to be here. Hellman blinked and grinned and held her wineglass beneath her chin in both hands, like a priest performing the consecration at the altar, yet she looked small and dazed, as if she had somehow lost command of the evening, surrendered control, as if she too had become a guest. Matthiessen's face was a mask of crags and hollows. The English woman giggled at something he said, covering her mouth with a pale hand.

Donna nudged me and shifted her eyes to the bottles of wine on the sideboard, a sign that I should pour. When I filled Hellman's glass she blinked and shifted her lips into a sad smile and said, "Ank you," with a pleasantness that suggested she had no recollection of who I was. But her laxity wasn't comforting. Hellman rarely looked uncertain. It was built in with her: be in control. Never falter. Always have an answer.

Donna and I worked without pause. Back and forth from kitchen to living room, shuffling plates, tending dishes yet to be served, replenishing others, checking faces in anticipation of small needs, while at the end of the table Hellman seemed to be moving in slow motion. The conversation was leaving her behind. Every so often she lifted her chin and reached for one of its shimmering threads, but before long it slipped away again. The bowl of soup on the plate in front of her was untouched. Quietly Feibleman urged her to eat. She lifted her spoon, lowered it again, groped at her cigarettes and wineglass instead.

Nichols talked to Styron. Annabel talked to Hersey. Matthiessen talked to Rose Styron. Barbara Hersey and Feibleman and the English woman talked to each other. Hellman nodded her head, smiling at all of them. I had no time to listen to what anyone was saying. I noticed only the faces lifting up at me to see what I was offering. Rose Styron gently touched the shadowed gulley above her collarbone with the fingertips of one hand and gave me a smile. Nichols pinned the serving spoons with his big thumbs. Styron dragged his teeth across a quail's scapula. Before long, Hellman was utterly mute, slumping like a straw effigy, her eyes narrowed to slits, her mouth set with the lower lip protruding slightly, like a barracuda's. I knew she couldn't see anything. She was overwhelmed with fatigue and wine and nerves. Her guests talked on, occasionally addressing her, but she was useless, and finally her head tipped forward and she was asleep.

In the kitchen Donna looked concerned and said, "I wonder what's the matter with Miss Hellman."

With a large spoon I flung pesto onto a pile of noodles and thought, *She's drunk.*

Presently Feibleman got up, went to Hellman's side, suggested that she might want to go to bed. She agreed and held his hand, clinging to it. "It's my eye medicine. It affects me so," and her guests nodded in sympathetic agreement. It was clear to me she had had too much to drink. She apologized for having to say goodnight, and several people stood up as Feibleman helped her out of her chair and across the room to the door. She walked in tiny steps, her feet lifting cautiously, too high off the floor. She seemed to be trying to escape her own dainty shoes, as though the soles had been smeared with hot glue.

There was a strange silence at the table once Hellman was gone, a tender, tentative puzzlement, then reverent murmurs, and then, as the surprise of her exit began to wear off, the volume of the voices increased, eventually striking a level above its previous setting. There was tolling laughter now, and immoderate exclaiming, and cigarettes rakishly lit from the flames of brandished candles, and more gushing wine as Donna brought out the chocolate rolls she had made, and before long, having finished the dinner, they pushed back their chairs and moved farther into the living room, leaving the ruined table littered with linen napkins like wilted cabbage leaves.

Donna and I cleaned up, filling trays with dirty plates, pushing in the chairs, washing dishes, scraping spaghetti and quail bones into the garbage, sweeping the floor, scrubbing the stove. My feet hurt. Donna's eyes were growing tired. I shuttled back and forth, back and forth, glancing at the guests as I worked. The English woman, the Styrons' guest, was curled up like a cat in the corner of the white couch, her bare feet tucked under her, cradling her wineglass, and sucking on a joint. Voices clashed and collided, bottles clinked on the bar. Someone cried, *So! As you were saying!* There were noisy exclamations and barks and screeches of laughter and glasses that left wet moons on the tables. It was as if the party, liberated from the constraints of Hellman's elderly gaze, had sprung noisily to life, opening suddenly with ominous strength, like a night-blooming cactus. The Herseys left early, and eventually Styron left too, but the others stayed on. It was growing late.

Once we had cleared away most of the mess, Donna took off her apron and said goodnight. Alone in the kitchen, I began scrubbing charred quail fat from the last frying pan with a hank of steel wool. Feibleman had put on some music that seeped through the house now, and every so often a stunned-looking guest came into the kitchen searching for something. I took my hands out of the rancid brown dishwater, wiped them on my apron, fetched lemons, limes, clean ashtrays, a bottle opener for whatever person stood in the middle of the room staring at me with elbows crooked and hands dangling. Rose Styron wanted another piece of chocolate roll. Feibleman wanted ice and a bottle opener. One or two people came into the kitchen to make telephone calls, summoning other people to the house.

I went back to the sink with a hollow feeling. No one was in charge. Who would tell them to leave? The hilarity, the pot smoke, the corks popping. I was in the house but not at the party. I would have to go to bed in my small room with all this going on around me. It was like so many nights at my mother's house, when she was passed out on her bed, like the night of the huge snowstorm when I was eleven and my mother was drunk and Sheila had two seventeen-year-old boys from California at the house. They made pot brownies and sipped at Nona's bottle of gin and went sledding at midnight, then brought the dripping sleds into the living room, where they built a huge fire in the fireplace, forgot to open the flue, and filled the house with black smoke. They put *Abbey Road* on the record player and let the boys' two scar-faced dogs curl up on the couch. I wandered through the house worrying, going in to look at my sleeping mother, then back to look at Sheila. The kitchen was a shambles. They had left the back door wide open, and someone had accidentally kicked the dog's water dish and spilled a silver slick of water across the floor and into the raw skid mark in the linoleum in front of the sink, worn down over the years by my mother's one dragging shoe. Every light in the house was ablaze, which I knew my mother would have hated. In each room the black windowpanes threw my scraggly-haired reflection back at me. I kept putting the lights off and Sheila kept turning them on again. When I gathered the enraged courage to tell her she shouldn't smoke pot in the house, she said, not unkindly, "Listen, Rosie, Nona has her drug, we have ours. We have a right. It'll all be fine. Go to bed." She laid sleeping bags in the living room and put lit candles about. With their long, stringy hair and torn blue jeans and red-traced eyes they were all going to camp out there. I couldn't go to bed. I had to be here, bailing the punctured rowboat with my watchful eyes, keeping a balance, ensuring that the water didn't rise too high. My vigilance was corrosive; it wore my nerves thin.

I knew Sheila didn't care if the house burned down. She was a person who upset my mother and took LSD and ran naked through the sprinkler on the front lawn, her seventeen-year-old breasts bouncing. She had political impulses and was always abstractedly complaining about the rights of Huey and Bobby and Angela and the U.S. government and the military in Vietnam. *Two! Four! Chicago Eight! Free the People, Smash the State!* was a slogan she often blurted out, in case the world was confused about the nature of her sympathies. She had taken to standing in Harvard Square with a tin can in her hand, helping to raise funds for George McGovern's presidential campaign, and then, forgetting her good intentions, spending the funds on cigarettes and bras. Her teachers sometimes sent her home from school, saying, "Mrs. Mahoney, we cannot control her." Although she was good at math and science and helped me with my multiplication and division homework while tears of frustration ran down my cheeks, I thought Sheila was crazy. That past summer on the beach she had stood at the edge of the water and poked her painted toenails into the soft wet sand and said to Ellen and me, "So, what do you guys think about Daddy?" We said, "What about him?" And she said, "Well, you know, that he killed himself." We looked at her as though she were a dragon rearing up out of the sea. What stupid, scary things she said. What utter nonsense. When we ran to our mother and reported what Sheila had said, Nona shook her head and held our wrists and said, *Don't believe what Sheila says.* We knew that must be right, for Sheila was often the cause of upheaval and strife in our house. She twisted the head of every person she met—with a talent only a bright and furious teenager could possess—in the direction of exactly what they didn't want to see. Though Sheila's sudden words had knocked hard against a fragile pod of mystery that hung perpetually at the back of my heart, jarring loose a picture of him looking foggy in a hospital room, I was sure I knew how my father had died. My mother had told me many times. He had had a heart attack. He had gone to work in the morning, though he wasn't feeling well and his nose was cold, and had had a heart attack there and died. He was forty-six. I had even read it in the newspaper. *The funeral will be Saturday . . . with a solemn requiem high Mass in St. Pius X Church.* It was foolish to believe anything Sheila said. And my mother would never, of course, lie to me.

I gathered up the dirty tablecloth and took it outside to shake crumbs from it, moving to the edge of the garden, out of reach of the backdoor floodlights. I didn't want any of the guests to see me. The house was aglow, like the festive ferry in the harbor, every window but mine lit up. From where I stood in the cool darkness and glittering wet grass, the yellow-walled living room looked hot and airless. Someone stood at the bar in the corner of the room, lifting a bottle to eye level to see how much it contained, another person leaned with an elbow on the mantel, then turned and with a long arm plucked a book from the shelf behind him. A foggy nimbus of cigarette smoke glowed purple around each lamp. Heads nodded, elucidating white hands with sketching fingers lifted swiftly into the air and fell out of sight again. It was hard to see facial features from this distance, just dark spots where mouths were, widening and shrinking in speech. Heads were yanked backward with laughter that sounded pained, reaching me in waves borne along on the breeze. In the windows above the living room, I saw that Hellman's bedroom light was still on, the curtains wide open. She had been too out of it to care tonight.

When I returned to the kitchen, Rose Styron was opening the refrigerator door. She smiled at me. I went upstairs to turn down the beds. At the top of the stairs I saw that Hellman's bedroom door was open, and before I began to move down the hallway to the guest rooms, I realized with a stunning jolt that she was lying stretched out on her bed stark naked, her arms and legs flung wide and her breasts spilling from her chest into the rumpled sheets. I stood in her doorway, shocked. The yellow glow from the bedside lamp fell on her brownish yellow skin. Her nipples were the size of Oreos. Her twisted toes poked up out of the ruffle of the sheets. She breathed softly, dead to the world, rib cage rising and falling, while her fancy guests laughed and chattered downstairs, smoking and enjoying her wine. She was the oldest person in the house by nearly ten years. She was like a wayward granny. Her body was so skinny and old it was like a scientific event looking at it this way, like finding a large fragile fossil embedded in stone, or the mummified remains of a three-thousand-year-old man preserved in a bog, his prunish face flattened and smeared and warped, like a face pressed against a windowpane. I had once seen one of these men stretched out in a museum, and looking at him in his glass box, every joint visible beneath his dusty film of skin, I half expected him to sit up, with the floppy, corky creak of folding leather, and say, *Yes. Here I am. Again.*

Anyone leaving by the formal second-floor entry that night would have to pass her door and see their famous hostess dumb and naked, snoring and muttering on her bed. I stood there staring, floating in a wave of scorn and pity. I could punish her, leave the door open, and let people catch the terrifying sight. Or I could close it and protect her. I argued with myself. She had been so hard and unwelcoming. She hadn't allowed me in and had forced me to block her out. Everything here seemed bitter and sour to me. It wasn't what I had expected, wasn't what I had wanted. And I felt embarrassed and angry for not having been wiser, for not having anticipated how complex it would be, how marginal my person was in this place. I hated surprises. I hated not knowing things.

I stared at her nose, at her lips hanging loose in her oblivion. The thin lips fluttered with her breath, rattling softly through pockets of phlegm lodged in her lungs. Though she was unconscious, her body went on in its organized way under its own direction. What made it do that? What kept it going? Beneath her skin the blood rushed, the heart beat, the hair and nails grew, the breath advanced and retreated, advanced and retreated, steadily, wetly, uninterrupted, like the waves on East Beach, with no visible cause. The sounds of her guests below, the shrieks of laughter and hoots and murmuring babble, were jarring in contrast to her deathly quiet. All the preparations, the worrying, the effort and expense, it mattered not at all to her now. The eyebrows she had so carefully prepared stuck up in spikes and spears, thin and pale. Her hair was a glossy jumble on the pillow.

I threw a sheet over her. I went to the end of the room and closed the curtains. I turned off her light, took the doorknob, and gently pulled her door shut.

EIGHT

Feibleman and Hellman sat in the living room drinking coffee and talking. Feibleman wore shorts and no shoes. His legs were brown and muscular and his wiry hair had been carefully combed. He smiled at me and nodded as I gave him his coffee. A sheet of white sunlight fell across the round wooden table between the two arm-chairs, and the *Vineyard Gazette* lay rumpled and skewed on the footstool in front of Hellman. August was coming to an end, and I could see that the summer's light was already changing, diminishing. With nearly a month still to go at this job, I had begun counting the days on my fingers.

On the table, by Hellman's arm, was a hardcover book, a recent novel by Annabel Davis-Goff Nichols, who had left the island alone early that morning. She was a writer too, I had discovered. And so, for that matter, was Rose Styron. A thin book of Rose's poetry lay on a bedside table in the middle room upstairs. I had seen it when I was vacuuming the rooms and, curious, had opened it while the vacuum cleaner roared at my feet, its head knocked upside down and its mouth sucking furiously at the sunlight. Now I tried to remember one of the lines: something something over the dunes, someone is whistling a birthday tune. I liked it. I hadn't known she was a writer. They were all writers. Maybe Mike Nichols was a writer. If he wasn't, what was he? I had never heard of him before this summer, and it remained a mystery to me what he was important for.

I stood in the hallway and listened to the voices drifting out of the living room. Hellman was talking again about the movie they had made of "Julia," still grumbling about how she had wanted Barbra Streisand to play her, not Jane Fonda. She was speaking sharply, her voice rising emphatically, then falling to a pinched whisper, about somebody, a woman, who had used her name in an interview.

"How dare she?" Hellman said. "How *dare* she?"

Her voice ran creeklike through the room, gurgling and twisting softly, then roaring over a particularly rocky place in the sandy bed. I thought she was talking about Jane Fonda, but hovering outside the living room door, out of sight in the hallway around the corner of the liquor closet, I couldn't be sure. I held my breath and turned one ear toward the door, but still the voices were a jumble—shards and shreds and exasperated cries. The refrigerator, with its furry electrical buzz, had switched on in the kitchen, making it more difficult to hear. I wanted for once to just walk into the living room and say, "What are you talking about?" I wanted to know what had offended her so, but I was sure that once I knew, it would seem silly, a mountain she was making out of a molehill. She was like that, could turn another person's careless comment into a catastrophe. I listened, staring out through the little slit of windows next to the hallway door. From where I stood, one high white cloud hung precariously in the whitish blue sky. A pole of sunlight slanted through the window onto the hallway floor, and in the time I'd stood eavesdropping, the pole had inched slightly leftward, crawling onto my foot, heating my toes inside my sneaker. In the morning, this side of the house was slapped with sun, like a wall of hot whitewash slung from a bucket. Every room in the house held bald patches of bright light; walking through them was like dipping in and out of warm bathwater.

I was too familiar with this narrow neutral spot in the house. I had spent a lot of time here listening in on conversations because there was nothing else to do, and because in all her fierceness Hellman had become as compelling to me as a scab that wanted picking. Though I was close to hating her, my interest in her had not diminished—in fact, it had grown intense. I had heard a lot standing here, but a surprising amount of what I heard meant nothing to me. I couldn't understand some of what Hellman talked about. There were names I didn't know, literary journals, reviews and organizations I had never heard of. William Phillips, the *Partisan Review,* Jerome Wiesner, George Will. I didn't read the newspaper much and was usually bored or disgusted by the television news: Israelis fighting Palestinians, Aldo Moro's bullet-ridden body, Pope Paul VI dying, the Panama Canal being given away. It wasn't important to me to be "up" on any of that. Just before Feibleman's arrival I had seen in the wastebasket by her desk an invitation for something called the Committee for Public Justice. *Lillian Hellman and Orville H. Schell cordially invite you to attend an important discussion: Whose Country Is This?* I never thought about whose country it was. Whose country should it be? It was nobody's country. I certainly didn't think of it as mine. I was aware of the great gaps in my knowledge, that when it came to current events I often gave in to my own whims, to whatever caught my eye. Usually what caught my eye referred back to me somehow, reminded me of my own life. Vietnam had caught my eye only inasmuch as Sheila seemed to blame my mother for it, and then, toward the end of the war, when I saw on my mother's television the open-sided helicopters struggling up out of Saigon, fleeing that muddied, ruined place at the last minute, and the black-haired people so desperate to climb on, to be saved from certain doom, hanging onto the feet of a helicopter with their legs swinging and, as it lifted away, slipping off and down like heavy droplets of water, the image caught my eye and reflected my mood with chilling accuracy. I thought I knew that sensation of slipping, of being left behind, and as I watched I was glad for the safety of my mother's bed beneath me.

I sensed that Hellman was bothered by something in her life, that something was wrong, and her health was failing. The night before,

Katherine Graham and a guy named Gil Harrison had come to the house for a cold chicken dinner, and as Mrs. Graham was leaving the house I heard her say to Feibleman that she had never seen Hellman "like this," and Feibleman murmured his agreement that it was, indeed, worrisome.

I knew there were people she had had literary and political quarrels with, enemies and detractors, that she wasn't always happy, but none of it was clear to me. Her politics were not what had drawn me to her; it was the stories I had liked, the people, the way they talked, the crazy things they did, and the way she had handled herself with daring and certitude. When she talked about Dashiell Hammett I usually stopped listening. What I cared most about was my place in her house, what she thought of me, whether I was doing well or not, how I would get through to the end of my obligation here. I knew critics had argued about her book *Scoundrel Time* because I had heard her talking about it. I had read the book, but not with the same interest as I had read the other memoirs—there was too much political confusion in it, too much history that seemed remote to me, too much that was vague and cryptic. It was like a letter written in agitation to her peers, with references to things I'd never heard of. I knew about Joseph McCarthy and his hatred of Communists, but her wrangle with his committee, the legal ramifications, struck me as tedious. I skipped pages because at times it was unclear to me what she was talking about. When she wrote in a parenthetic aside, "Obviously nobody could have anything to do with the governments of Coolidge and Hoover," I thought it would be a lifetime before I figured out why that was obvious. I had no idea who Whittaker Chambers was and didn't want to have to know (although the fact that he had hid documents in a pumpkin stuck in my childish head and made him interesting). I was waiting for *Scoundrel Time* to tell me something about myself, to involve me in the vivid way her other stories had, but nothing in it was familiar to me except the image of a movie mogul smacking his assistant's hand as it reached, uninvited, for a sandwich. But my ignorance of political matters didn't bother me enough to cause me to rectify it. I had simply assumed that Hellman's political intentions were good and right, but now, when she sat evenings in her living room and complained about somebody named Kazin and another named Kazan with the same mystifying loftiness and bossy tone of that book, it bored and rankled me.

That morning a lot of people called on the telephone. Robert Brustein, Hackett, Art Buchwald, Richard Poirier, Palevsky again, and someone named Nadia. Hellman kept making me answer the phone. "Get the name," she said, "and repeat it so that I can hear it. If I want to talk, I'll take the phone. If I don't, just tell them you can't find me at the moment and take a message."

Those were her solemn instructions, like a checklist for an air raid alert, and with each call we danced our clumsy way through the charade. Every time the phone rang in its too-bright corner of the kitchen, beside a vase of yellow snapdragons, I dreaded the task anew. It seemed so obvious and flimsy and awful, and she was too old to be ducking the telephone this way. After pacing through the act four times, I stumbled on my own confidence and said to the fifth caller, "Sorry, she's busy right now." It was a horrible mistake, I knew it as soon as I said it. Hellman flapped her hands at me and bit at her lower lip and struck the air with the butt of her fist, as though stamping a document. "No, no, no! Not like that," she whined when I had hung up. "If you say, *She's busy,* then they think I don't want to talk to them!"

I wanted to say, *Well wouldn't that just be the truth? You* don't *want to talk to them,* but all I could say was, "Sorry. Sorry."

Everything was annoying her lately. Now she was complaining to Feibleman about Rose Styron. Feibleman listened patiently, moderating her mood. His voice was steady and sleek. Rose Styron had called that morning, and when I answered the telephone in the kitchen, she had asked to speak with Mike Nichols. I had told her that Mr. Nichols was in the bathroom.

"Please tell him," Mrs. Styron had said, "that Ted Kennedy will be here tonight, and I'd like him and Lilly to join us for cocktails."

"OK," I said, "I'll tell him. And do you want to speak to Miss Hellman?"

She didn't necessarily want to speak to Miss Hellman. "Just give Mr. Nichols the message." And then she thanked me and hung up.

Hellman had appeared at my elbow, her cigarette held between thumb and forefinger, pointed at me like a skewer. I turned my head and there she was, the big eyeglasses glinting up at me. "Who was that?" she said in a voice soft with suspicion.

"Mrs. Styron."

"She didn't want to speak to me?"

"No, Miss Hellman."

She stood there for a second, breathing onto her cigarette. I could see the blond hairs in her nostrils. "Who'd she want to speak to?"

"Mr. Nichols."

"Mr. Nichols?"

"Yes."

"She asked for him?"

"Right."

"I see. And what does she want?"

"She wants me to tell him that Ted Kennedy will be at her house tonight and she would like to have him and you over for cocktails."

Hellman stared over the top of my head at the bright windows, her mouth frozen open until this small coin of news fell into its proper slot and snapped her jaw shut. "I'll be damned," she said finally, and with a shake of her head that dislodged a dirty rag of smoke from her mouth she turned and went clumsily back to the living room.

Now she was complaining to Feibleman: Rose Styron just *had* to get Mike Nichols to her house to impress Ted Kennedy. It could have been predicted. And where *was* Mike anyway?

Still in the bathroom. I could hear water surging in the pipes behind the walls. The coffee I had prepared for him was heating on the stove, filling the house with a dry dark smell, rich as loam.

"He's in the bathroom, Lilly," Feibleman's voice said.

"He's been in there for ages," she barked. "Why does it always take him so *long* in the morning? What the hell does he do in there all that time?"

There was silence from the living room then. The refrigerator had muttered to a halt. I sniffed at my fingers; the smell of garlic from the night before was so strong on my hands it was like a yellow balloon in front of my face, pushing into my eyes. The water in the pipes abruptly stopped gushing. Through the kitchen door I could see silver drops of water slipping from the low faucet into the sink. The silence in the living room persisted, which annoyed me. I had grown used to the burbling company of their conversation. Curious, I peered around the corner of the closet and saw Hellman's face appear with breathtaking suddenness in the living room doorway three feet from me, looking downward, overseeing the movements of her own shuffling feet. Opening her mouth she blatted, "Rosemary?!"

This close, her voice was like the searing flame of a blowtorch. She had no idea I was here. I put my back against the wall and slid quickly along it until I could duck up the stairs over her head and out of sight.

"Rosemary!" she shouted as she climbed the little fall of stairs from the foyer to the kitchen.

I took the upper stairs two at a time, reached the safety of the middle landing, smoothed my hair, counted to five, and bounded down again, hoping for a look of preoccupied innocence. "Yes, Miss Hellman?"

"Please prepare a breakfast tray for Mr. Nichols. He'll take it in the living room."

I went into the kitchen and she followed me, hovering, waiting impatiently for Nichols to appear. She wanted him out of the bathroom; she wanted to report on Rose Styron. She stood squinting and pale in the blazing kitchen sunlight, uselessly adjusting the snapdragons on the table, then moved to the window and looked out at the garden.

Finally Nichols came in. He said good morning, stretching his body, then settled himself into a chair at the kitchen table. There was something soft about him. And sandy-faced. His nose was long and slender and fine, and his nostrils were large but narrow. He reminded me of a rooster. In the sunlight his few freckles were the color of ginger.

"Mike?" Hellman said.

Nichols smiled pleasantly at her, showing his long nostrils, his teeth. "Yes, Lilly?"

"Rose Styron wants you."

He blinked at her. Between frowning tastes of her teeth Hellman explained about Ted Kennedy and the Styrons' party. Nichols seemed to like the idea, wanted to go.

"Well, I don't want to go, Mike," Hellman said, turning her back and shuffling to the stove. "I don't want to go. So you'll have to go without me."

The statement bristled, stood erect in the middle of the room like a surveyor's pike, like the stiff flag the astronauts had poked into the moon. If Nichols was going to be loyal to Hellman, he would have to say no to Rose Styron and Ted Kennedy. But he wanted to go. He laid his freckled hands flat on the table. "Lilly," he said sweetly, as if to suggest she should try being a little bit reasonable.

Hellman watched as I poured the muddy coffee into a cup, carried it to the table, and set it on the tray. Nichols reached for it.

"You're going to drink it in here?" Hellman said.

He shrugged. "Is that all right?"

"Fine," Hellman said coolly. "Fine." She pulled at a chair across the table from him and sat down uncertainly on the edge of it. "What will you eat?" she said.

"Toast."

She waited, scratching at her scalp, with a blank look on her face, as if this scratching was all there was and all there would ever be.

"Just toast." Nichols drummed his fingers on the table.

"Not an egg?" Hellman said.

"Just toast for now."

Hellman looked at me and translated, "He'll have toast."

I went to get the bread. The phone rang. I looked at Hellman. She waved her hand. I answered it. I could feel the beam of her impatient gaze, like the hairy touch of a spider's feet, brushing my face as she waited. It was Mrs. Styron again, looking for Nichols.

"Mr. Nichols," I said, "it's for you."

Nichols reached for the phone. Hellman pulled her two hands off the table, as if to spare them from the plummeting blade of a guillotine. While Nichols chatted with Rose Styron, Hellman's mouth worked itself into a smile, a closed-mouth grin so false and sickly it amounted to a grimace.

Nichols hung up the phone. With a dry laugh, Hellman said, "Oh, she *wants* you, Mike. She really wants you."

I went to the stove and needlessly wiped its surface with a wet sponge. I felt embarrassed for Hellman. Rose Styron was Hellman's friend; I had often watched them as they played Scrabble together.

They sat at the table with their iced tea and their friendly utterances of competition and encouragement, and the wooden grid in front of them burgeoning into a map of clever verbal conjunctions, and they talked the way close friends talk, leaning toward each other, without the polite need for eye contact, about personal matters. They seemed to enjoy each other's company, but there were aggravated disagreements, and though Hellman was pleasant in Rose's presence, she found subtle, cheerful ways to criticize her to others. I was, of course, aware that people talked behind each other's backs, was often guilty of it myself, and that I had believed Hellman would be any different seemed silly to me now. I had hoped, naively, that she would provide evidence of a better way of being, had admired her for her honesty and strength, but watching her stick it to Rose Styron now, that person I had wanted so much, the strong and noble figure, was gone. I had a strong sense that Hellman couldn't help disliking pretty women, that she was threatened by them and Rose Styron was beautiful. Hellman was easily made jealous, preferred men to women, and didn't like it when the men she knew were interested in the women she knew. I had begun to think she actually disliked women, had seen this streak glinting now and then through the weave of her personality. At times she seemed to think that women were downright stupid, and I saw that as a flaw in her, an indication of something awry in her self-perception.

Behind me, Nichols repeated his desire that they join the Styrons that night, and Hellman insisted that she, for one, would not be going.

Hellman and her two guests went out after breakfast. I cleaned the oven, gagging on the metallic clouds of Easy-Off that crept up my nose and down my throat as I worked. I did the laundry, ironed a shirt for Nichols, two for Feibleman, washed the kitchen floor, dusted the living room. When Hellman returned, I asked if I was free to leave. She said, "Yes, but be back at five."

I took off my apron, walked down through the grass to the beach, and headed toward the ferry landing, plodding glumly over the slipper shells, my sneakers twisting and bumping on the uneven terrain. I was supposed to have that evening off, but Hellman had forgotten again, and I no longer had the energy or the desire to protest; I knew she would realize her mistake when Donna showed up to prepare dinner. It wasn't worth getting into it with her. Hellman was like a dark sky coming closer and closer to the ground, pressing me down. The less she seemed to see me, the more she pressed me. I walked with my head down. She always had the final word. On one of these crowded days with her house full of guests, they had all gone down to Menemsha and returned with thick paper bags full of lobsters. They ate them with corn from Hellman's garden, and during dinner they debated at length about the proper way to eat the corn. Each smiling face piped out its way of doing it. I hovered in the kitchen doorway and listened to the sounds from the dining room. *Rub the butter on with the knife, like this. Put it right onto the stick of butter and spin, like this. Melt the butter and pour it on. No, no, just put a pat of butter on your plate, and roll it there. Salt and pepper is all I use.* Until finally Hellman's grumbling voice said jokily, *Oh, eat it any fuckin' way you want!* sealing the subject in silence.

There was a small boathouse near Owen Park, and beside it was beached a pretty little sailboat that I liked. It was green, freshly painted, big enough for one person, with the rounded lines of a kayak. It looked homemade, had a handle on its stern so you could drag it up and down the beach. Its name was *Luna*. I sat down beside it, studying it, and imagined myself sailing around East Chop to Edgartown in this little box. I wished it were mine, though I didn't know how to sail. The idea of being alone and free on the sea, under your own command, was the only good idea I could think of. I stared at the sea. Before too long I'd be traveling to Ireland. Though I was apprehensive about how I would manage alone in Dublin, I was relieved not to be going back to school, and my relief was like a soft bed I could lie down in. When I had come up with the idea of spending a year in Ireland, my mother had encouraged me to pursue it, had helped me with my proposal for independent study, had helped me organize my thoughts. And when I faltered and said, "Oh, forget it, it's a stupid idea. The school will never let me do this," my mother had said, "It's not a stupid idea. It's a good idea. You want to do it. Just tell them and see what they say. What can you lose?" My mother had faith in me, had more faith in me than I had in myself, and knowing that she did made me try to find faith. She believed in trying things. She always said, "If you don't try you'll always be wondering what would have happened if you had tried. That's not a good feeling, Ra."

Farther down the beach I could see the black woman sitting in the sand by the ferry landing, a tiny, straight-backed figure, staring, like me, out at the sea, her dark head perfectly round and still. She seemed to like it here. I lay back in the sand in my clothes and looked at the sky. When I had time off, it wasn't as if I could leave my workplace, go home, and relax. Hellman's house was supposedly my home, but the only place I could go to rest was my own little bedroom. I couldn't just kick off my shoes and prop my bare feet up on her coffee table in the living room, with a book I'd yanked down from her shelves, and that truth made me feel homeless. This was the only place I could sit and be comfortable, staring at the water, watching the scoters that wandered in and out of the moored sailboats, the sandpipers with their white collars. The tide was going out, leaving its flatus behind it. Fine green seaweed covered the few exposed rocks like steamed spinach. Dragonflies and white butterflies traced the air. I turned my head and let one cheek touch the soft sand. There was a slow breeze, and the air was filled with the shuffling, tinkling sounds of cutlery and china in a busy hotel dining room—the clinking of halyards on metal masts, the ruffling of unfurling sails, distant children's voices. An outboard motor muttered. A dog's bark bounced and echoed across the flat water. The early moon was a holy host in the sky, nearly transparent, like tissue paper, its bottom end dissolved, its dark spots the same pale blue of the liquid sky it floated in. Clouds had begun seeping in from the south.

When I came back to the house at five, Nichols and Feibleman were getting ready to go to the cocktail party at the Styrons'. Hellman sat silently in her chair in the living room, reading Annabel Nichols's book, the handle of the magnifying glass gripped in her fist, looking up now and then to see who was coming into the room. She looked skeptical and nervous, distracted, waxen and weak and small, struggling to see the words on the page. I could see she was worried about being left behind. As I approached her, I saw one of her eyes rendered enormous through the magnifying glass, a great watery marble swimming in milk. I sensed her helplessness, and rather than waiting for her to ask me to do something, I said, "Is there anything you need, Miss Hellman?"

She lowered the magnifying glass, shifted the book on her lap, picked the glass up, put it down again. She ran through the usual list, the standard daily things—the ice bucket, the fresh water, the medicine on ice, the ironing. Everything had been done. She stared at the table, thinking. She seemed uncertain. How could a person who could be so frightening sometimes appear so weak? She looked at her hands. Presently she put the magnifying glass and book on the table with a certain prim resoluteness and said, "If . . . if you wouldn't mind, I'll need some help dressing. We're going to the Styrons' tonight for cocktails. You can come up and help me."

I felt relieved. It was a little sad to think of her sitting there alone with her magnifying glass while her friends went out. I put out my arm to help her up from her chair and followed her up the stairs. Her hand was cool. She stood in the entrance to her bathroom, thinking about what to wear, then decided on a particular dress. I found the dress for her and laid it on her bed. I brought her the shoes and the necklace she wanted, and when she went into the bathroom I heard her muttering something to herself about Ted Kennedy.

When she was dressed and ready to go, she poked a cigarette between her lips and lit it. Why weren't her lips blistered with all those thousands of cigarette filters raking across them all day long? Before I went out of the room, she handed me another paycheck, again made out to cash. I finally managed to tell her there had been a problem with the last check she had given me.

She held the cigarette in front of her chest, like a Popsicle stick, lit end down. A fiddlehead of smoke curled out of her fingers. "Problem?"

"The bank wouldn't take it."

"Why not?"

"They said it has to be made out to me."

She looked confused. "But I've done it this way many times." She paused, thinking, and her eyes narrowed with interest as she said, "What did they say when you gave it to them?"

"They said only you could cash it. Or else it had to be made out in my name."

She drew the corners of her mouth down and looked at the cigarette for a moment. Her hair was the color of a peeled almond, the sweep above her hairline a bulging sculpted ledge, like Lady Bird Johnson's. And then, with surprising sincerity, she said, "I'm very sorry. I'm sorry. You should have told me sooner. They don't know you. You should not have to wait for your money like that. I'll call them. Forgive me."

———

Alone in the house, I walked around, looking into the various rooms. I went into Feibleman's room to turn down his bed and lingered there, staring. His address book was open on the desk. Carol Burnett. Marlo Thomas. Warren Beatty. Why did this guy know these people? I had never heard of Feibleman. Hellman had told me several times that he was a writer, was in the middle of writing a novel. On his desk was a script for a show called *Madam A* that Hellman and he had written together, and in his typewriter was a page of his novel, a story about people in New Orleans. One character was named Breaux and another was named Moment and a third was named E.L. The names seemed odd to me.

Feibleman was quiet and spent a lot of time in his room typing. If I knocked on his door to tell him something, he came to the door in his underwear. He was pleasant and mild-mannered but a little nervous and seemed not to notice me much, which I was grateful for. I didn't want any undue attention now. Once in a while he asked me to get him a cup of tea or iron a shirt. He was always coming down to the kitchen to eat three plums or three peaches, then disappearing again. He ate very little during the day but a lot at night. He was always receiving packages from a place called the Sherry Institute. One overcast day he wore dark glasses all through lunch, like a guy in a spy story. I had heard him telling Hellman in the living room a few days before that Joe Alsop had called while she was out and had begun his conversation with Feibleman by saying, "Who is this?" which Feibleman thought was rude. Hellman had said, "Yes, Joe can be very rude." Alsop was coming to the house for a few days the next week, and Hellman warned Feibleman that he might or might not like him and that if Alsop got drunk in the evenings, Feibleman should just go to bed. "Joe is a fag," Hellman said. "There's no reason for my liking him except that he was very good during the McCarthy period." She said Alsop was naturally, not artistocratically, against McCarthy, that he and his wife didn't get along, that his wife was slim. "Everyone thinks she is very beautiful," Hellman said, "but I do not."

Alsop had been involved with the CIA and something else. He loved war, she said. He knew a lot about art, culture, and some other things. I tried to follow the conversation, but I couldn't understand why she invited him to her house if she thought he was a disagreeable pain.

I left Feibleman's room, wandered down the hall to her room, and checked to see if there was anything that needed straightening. The ashtray was clean, the bed was made, her clothes had been put away. Her wastebasket had two empty cigarette packs and a few manuscript pages in it. Rather than carry the whole thing downstairs and back up again, I plucked the trash out and left the basket there. On the way down the stairs I looked at the pages. She used nice paper, thick and waxy. In the stairway light I could see the watermark: Old Hampshire Bond 100% Cotton Fiber Extra No. 1 Grade. I liked the feel of it. The black felt-tip she had used to make notations and corrections had a purplish tint to its blackness. She had written at the top of one page: *Lillian Hellman, Notes to Follow "Scoundrel Time,"* as though it were a school essay. The text had been typed hastily and was pocked with misspellings, some of which I could see she had corrected the moment they happened by simply typing the right letter on top of the wrong one, giving the page a complicated Cyrillic look in places. There were five pages in all, comprising two versions of a beginning. I scanned it, feeling that I shouldn't, but my curiosity was too strong. I sat down on the bottom step and read. "I have now had over two years to think about 'Scoundrel Time' . . . But facts, it can certainly be answered, do not have to do with truth. I tried to tell the truth about myself, but I am not willing now or ever to say that I know such truth. But the charge that I 'misrepresented' myself is shallow, malicious and has never been more than an undocumented flat statement of dislike . . ."

She was defending herself, giving her opinions about intellectualism, the sixties, William Buckley, anti-Communists. It seemed people had accused her of dishonesty because, she said, they themselves had been dishonest. It intrigued me. There was always the possibility that people had lied to you. As far as I was concerned, despite all the books and plays and committees for public justice, she was no more honest than the rest of us. As I was heading for the trash cans to throw the papers away, I changed my mind, decided to keep them, went back to my room, and stashed them with my books. I didn't want to just toss them. Though I wasn't sure what it all meant, I knew the words were important. There was more than one version to the world. What people stood for wasn't necessarily who they were. What we saw wasn't necessarily what was real. For every view a person had there could be another view that disagreed, for every action there could be a motivation you didn't know about. I had believed that words in books offered the one true picture, but I could see now that there were other pictures.

Later, when they'd returned from the Styrons', Hellman and Nichols sat in the living room talking. I heard Hellman say, "I always wanted to write about Rose, but couldn't or didn't know how," and for a strange moment I thought she was talking about me.

Before he left for New York, Mike Nichols shook my hand, said goodbye, and handed me an envelope, one of Hellman's small envelopes the grayish green of a surgeon's scrubs with *Lillian Hellman, Vineyard Haven, Mass.* embossed on its back flap in handsome navy blue letters. He had dragged a line nicely through *Lillian Hellman* with one of Hellman's own black felt-tipped pens and scrawled *Nich-*

ols above it. On the front of the envelope he had written ROSEMARY *(Thanks)*. He had the gay and crookedly sprawling handwriting of a seven-year-old, which knocked my appreciation of him up a step into affection. His handwriting was nearly as bad as my own. When he had left the house, I carried the thin square into my bedroom and lifted the back flap: the shocking green of a bill was visible in the cleavage of the envelope. The sight of unexpected money always startled me. I sat on my bed and looked at it in a rush of wonder and satisfaction. In my fingers the bill seemed nearly alive with meaning, too precious to spend. Why had he given me this? Maybe because I had ironed a shirt for him. Or maybe he thought I was good at my job. Maybe he had actually liked me. To me it was an acknowledgment, an indication that I had succeeded in some small way. Nichols didn't owe me anything. It was my job to wait on him, that was why I was here, a fact that after all this time was finally sinking in. I wasn't a guest in this house. I turned the envelope over, read my name again, studied the short, tight parentheses like two monkey ears framing his sloping *Thanks*. The way he had edited the embossing on the back of the envelope delighted me. He had firmly crossed Hellman's name out. I could have spent an hour coveting this envelope, staring at Nichols's lettering, at Alexander Hamilton's far-seeing eyes and luxurious hair, feeling the starchy sturdiness of the bill, remembering Nichols's nose, but the faint sound of Hellman's voice calling to me from the top of the staircase snapped my head up and drew my eyes toward the door.

She was angry. Based on only one short croak, I could tell instantly now what her mood was. Dread made my body heavy. I put the envelope on my pillow and went quickly up the stairs. It was only ten o'clock. A whole day of climbing in the direction of her plaintive voice lay ahead of me like a rickety wooden ladder too narrow for my feet.

She was standing by her bed in the rectangle of muffled, pearly light that filtered through her long bathroom and through its door-way onto her bed. "Come in," she said in a voice so soft it made me light-headed with fear. I went in and stood just inside the door, a few feet from her.

She put a hand on the edge of her bed and lowered herself onto it with the precise movements of an unwell patient setting herself onto an examining table. "I'm going to sit down," she said when the act was completed. Bad moods seemed to lock her face into its true place, a default setting of displeasure. When she was angry, her face was menacing in its blankness, and her certitude caused her eyes to stare and the corners of her mouth to turn down. Her nose was like a great flesh-covered keel at the front of her head. My heart flopped helplessly, choking on fear.

"You left the bathmat in the bathroom doorway after you washed the floor this morning, Rosemary."

I was standing beside the bathroom doorway. I turned my head, expecting to see the mat slumped there, but she had returned it, saddlelike, to its place on the edge of the tub. I knew she was right. I had left the mat there and forgotten it.

"I tripped on it and hit my head on the door."

She wasn't yelling; she was speaking calmly, which was more terrifying. I knew this mistake was serious and that she had cause to fire me, if she wanted to. I had put her in danger. The fingers of my right hand found the fingers of my left. "I'm very sorry, Miss Hellman," I said. "I hope you're all right."

"I'm all right. But these things you forget could be extremely dangerous for me."

"I understand," I said.

She had been looking just to my right as she talked; my face was slightly in shadow, and the little veil of light that was here fell squarely on her glasses, certainly obscuring her vision. But now she looked hard at me, finding my eyes and staring into them, and gravely began to speak in that measured, announcing way. She said that I was obviously a very bright girl, that my memory was very good, but that I wasn't using it correctly. There were many things she had asked me to do, things that I had forgotten and should not have forgotten. Simple tasks. I should learn to write things down, she said. Make notes to myself. That way I wouldn't have to remember.

"Has anyone at school ever tried to help you with your memory and the way you use it?"

I crossed my arms. I had to think about what she had said, shuffling the words straight in my head. Nobody at school was thinking about my memory. More to the point, nobody at school had thought there was anything wrong with my memory. She was the first person who had ever said anything like this to me.

"Help my memory? No, Miss Hellman."

She placed her hands on her knees and leaned forward slightly, elbows jutting out in the posture of an exhausted coach. She stared at the floor. She seemed to be catching her breath, and when she spoke again, her tone had made a subtle crossover from anger to seeming concern. "Donna and I have discussed your work," she said in a kinder tone, "and we both agreed that we had to check the dinner table many nights to see that you'd done it right. I know that things like setting a table will be unimportant to you in your future; unconsciously you know that, too, and therefore you don't really care to remember it. But to do any job well, one must be interested and ready to remember what needs to go into that work."

She paused to dab at the corners of her mouth with the tip of one index finger, radiating a kind of parental sadness over my failures. The idea of Donna and Hellman dissecting my performance flooded my stomach with a tingling wash of anxiety—I was never more vulnerable than when I knew people were talking about me. "To me," she went on, raising a hand to her chest as if introducing herself for the first time, "all work is interesting. And doing it well is important. I am not criticizing you, Rosemary, only trying to enlighten you."

I said, "I see," like a zombie and blinked and uncrossed my arms. I was stunned by this speech. It was a mix of encouragement and criticism, self-interest and generosity, and a kind of baldly showy and impersonal authority that I instinctively mistrusted. Her words had sounded wise—*were* wise—and they seemed to hold the hope that I might absorb a similar wisdom. I was conscious that I was being taught, and I could see that she was playing the teacher and was pleased with the role.

"I believe that if people know their minds, how their minds work, they are ten years the wiser for it. You learn quickly, Rosemary. You're honest. And like all honest people you want to do your job well. But if you want to do your job well, you must take greater care in your tasks, in *everything* you do." She paused, touched her watchband, looked up at me. "Yes?"

She was waiting for a response, and though I hated the imperious Britishness of that *Yes?* I gave her what she wanted. I let my hands fall to my sides and looked into the corner of the room where the fireplace sat like a roaring giant's big black mouth and said, "Yes, Miss Hellman."

You learn quickly. You're smart. You're honest. Setting the table will be unimportant to you in your future. Her saying these astonishing things made me wary. They were the words I had hoped for all along, they described the person I had wanted to be, the person I wanted her to see me as, but they were backhanded and bittersweet, they were the pat on the head before the bridle was thrown on and the bit tucked into the mouth. I saw now that she wouldn't fire me, but I didn't know whether to trust her. What had made her say I was honest? How had I shown that? I didn't think I was so honest. And I hadn't been honest with her. I had never told her what I really thought. I never told anyone what I really thought. My entire life was a thing I didn't want people to know. My face was a camouflage of pleasantly arranged flesh, but just beyond my eyes, my thoughts teemed in contrast.

She raised a hand to show there was more. "When I taught at Harvard, the one student I was really attracted to was the one who knew how his mind worked. This is terribly important. I've learned that when one doesn't know how one's own mind works, one is just lying to oneself, not really looking. What you aren't interested in, be interested in in another way. Write it down."

She edged herself off the bed, feeling for the floor with her feet. "Think about this," she said, heading for her desk to begin her work.

"Yes, Miss Hellman," I said again and went out of the room.

Downstairs I stood at the ironing board and began mindlessly pressing clothes, while the pain and confusion did its ugly work of spreading to the farthest corners of my mind. Had Hellman seen through me? I was bewildered. I didn't know whether to trust her advice. I ironed a blouse of my own, the one I had bought at the thrift shop, smoothing its sleeves with the hot metal plate of the iron. The smoothing soothed my nerves. Was I lying to myself? That possibility frightened me. I wanted to know what the truth was, to be true myself. *Write things down,* she had said. She meant lists of things to do, like the lists she was always drawing up for me. I did write things down—I wrote in my journal, wrote letters and stories—but I never made lists.

The iron's steam floated up, collecting on my face, hot at first and then cool as perspiration. I tried to focus on those good things she had said about me: *smart, honest, future.* For all my unhappiness and disappointment I was fascinated that she had said these things, and even flattered: she had seen me. But what did she know about my future? What made her think my future wouldn't include setting tables? I was seventeen; there were a lot of years ahead. She had addressed me in a strange way, as though I were her student rather than her housemaid. She wouldn't have addressed Marta that way. There was a part of her, I thought, that needed to make these speeches and pronouncements, that needed to cast herself in the role of teacher. But a good teacher, I was certain, would include herself in the lesson, would allow that she could learn from it too, that she could be wrong. When I first went into my tenth-grade English class and saw Bob Edgar, our teacher, with his wry, fine-boned face and his horn-rimmed glasses, I knew the class would be interesting. I remembered him leaning over the *Norton Anthology* reading lines from "The Rape of the Lock," pausing to explain the words *cull* and *billet-doux,* smiling slyly, his slender fingers moving in a sifting motion over the pages as he read, "And decks the Goddess with the glitt'ring spoil," like a greasy-fingered burglar lewdly pillaging a jewel box. Once Pope's dense words, stacked up in forbidding columns on these tissue-thin pages, were filtered through the clarifying strainer of his reading, I could see that there was clever humor in them. I could see, because of the theatrical way Edgar read, that Alexander Pope appreciated the ridiculous, the foolish, the absurd, the mean aspects of life. He knew what an important joke it all was. Pope, like Henry James and all the other writers, was trying to figure out the point of the world. These sonnets and essays and poems were all about people, how interesting they were, how transparent and vulnerable and sad and brave. Edgar would write notes in a dry, slightly magisterial style, then photocopy and hand them out to the class, reminding us what our homework was and what quizzes and exams lurked around the corner of the next weekend. I remembered a line he had written toward the end of one of these notes: "You have an exam next Monday. If I were you, (which, I remind you, I

am not) I would read Pope's *An Essay on Man* and Shakespeare's
sonnets 29, 87, and 94." His immaterial and unteacherly aside, the
notion that we might mistake Bob Edgar for ourselves, had struck me
as funny and arch and odd. In addition to slipping us a valuable hint,
he was making fun of himself and us. I liked him for it and trusted
him. My mother was the same way, I knew. Her students liked her
because she entertained them, gave them the idea that they were all
in this together. She was persuasive and compelling, and whatever
subject she was talking about was like a train you wanted to hop
onto.

I finished the ironing, folded up the board, and went into my
room to lie on the bed for a minute. As soon as my head touched the
pillow, I felt a burst of electricity in my chest as I realized I had
forgotten to pick up the newspaper she asked me to get earlier. I
knew that when she finished working she would want to look at it. I
sprang up off the bed and ran up the outside stairs, hoping to God
she wouldn't see me as I slunk up the driveway. I ran all the way to
Cronig's on foot, too shaken and distracted to think of my bicycle. I
felt an awful sinking in my chest when I discovered that Cronig's was
out of the *New York Times,* as they usually were by that time of day. I
ran across the street to Leslie's drugstore, praying they'd have one.
They did, and in my excitement at the sight of it lying in its wire
rack, I picked it up and ran out without paying, sprinting back up
Main Street with all the speed I could muster. Sweat leaked into my
eyes and burned them. The ink from the paper rubbed off on my
hands and shirt, but I didn't care, as long as I could get back before
she noticed I was gone. I put the paper on the kitchen table and went
back to my room, exhausted and sick with confusion. I saw in the
mirror that my nose was smudged with ink. I didn't bother to wipe it
off. I lay down on my bed and put one arm over my eyes, and
suddenly in the blackness behind my lids I saw the road that wan-

dered through the Blue Hills near my mother's house, those crowded, unimpressive woods where the police were always searching for missing people among the ferns and muddy skunk cabbages and a woodchuck was always chewing on a pinecone by the side of the road.

Maybe Hellman was right about me. Maybe she should have fired me. She had hit her head on the bathroom door because I had forgotten the mat. I knew that was unforgivable, a bad mistake. What if she had fallen and been hurt? I knew how bad that could be. My mother fell all the time. When I was a young child, nothing snatched my breath away faster than the sound of her startled cry at the moment she realized she'd been sucked into the vortex of a fall, followed by the clattering of crutches and whatever local objects she took down with her. No matter where in the house she was, I knew what that tangle of noises meant, and I—and whoever else was there—went running toward her in terror of what we might find. This time would she be dead? I would run through the house with no recognition of the rooms I passed through, run so frantically fast that throw rugs skidded out from under my sneakers as I scrabbled around corners. I staggered into furniture and sometimes, in my panic, thundered to the floor myself. The sound of my mother's falling was always endless, and in the minutes that she lay on the floor, a cold gray feeling beset me, like a suffocating blanket of wet snow, that no one at all was in control of anything. Once she was back on her feet again, my mother's hands trembled perceptibly and her face was pale and her lips were dry with fright—my own hands, face, and lips responded in kind—and she glanced at the injured place on her arm or leg, already revealing signs of the livid bruise it would later blossom into. I was always overjoyed that my mother had come through the accident alive, and as she applied ice to her bruise I stared at her, wide-eyed and disproportionately light-hearted, thrilled that I too was still alive.

Hellman spent two days in Washington, where she made a speech at the celebration for Leonard Bernstein's sixtieth-birthday concert. I knew that the event would be televised, but I didn't bother to watch it. Instead I went to the movies by myself, saw *Heaven Can Wait* down at the Capawock Theatre, then came home and went to bed. The night before, she had called from Washington to speak to Feibleman, and I had had to tell her that he was out. She sounded sad. She sounded as if she was lying on her back with a cold. She spoke nicely to me, seemed happy that someone, anyone at all, had answered the phone. If she couldn't talk to Feibleman, there was always me.

The next day she returned in time for lunch. She looked tired. As she ate bacon and eggs and okra with Feibleman in the living room, she told him about the trip. It was awful, she said. *Rotten!* She told the story slowly and at length. When she got to Washington there was no car waiting for her at the airport and she bumped her head on something. When she got to her hotel she called Mr. Someone, who was one of Bernstein's secretaries, and Miss Nadia Somebody from the National Symphony Orchestra and yelled at them both and mocked Miss Nadia by imitating her foreign accent on the phone to her. And then she discovered that all of a sudden she couldn't see anything and called a doctor who said it could have been the bump on the head and told her to take two aspirins. And the next day went all wrong because the hairdresser was scheduled for five-thirty, which was too late, and because at six-fifteen Bernstein decided he wanted her to change the speech she had prepared. He didn't want her to talk about his wife for some reason. She said she was disgusted with the whole thing and thought Bernstein was grasping for popularity. She didn't change the speech and told Feibleman over and over how appreciative everyone but Bernstein was of her and how moving Bernstein's son had been when he came to her after the speech and cried and thanked her for thinking of his mother. A stage hand had treated her with great regard and said to the orchestra drummer, "Move out of her way! She is a famous lady!"

Early one morning at the beginning of September I sat in the kitchen, bored, with both elbows planted on the table, humming a tune, absently fitting the bowl of a teacup over one eye and looking out the window at the early morning light with the other, imagining what it would be like to have a black patch like Moshe Dayan. I thought about the fleet of beautiful hot-air balloons that had come flying so low over the roof of the house a few days before that their puffing jets of air sounded like a dinosaur's breath. As I was noting that with one eye covered with the teacup my humming seemed to sound fainter, Joe Alsop walked into the kitchen in his bedroom slippers and said, "Good morning, my dear! How *are* you!"

Embarrassed, I put down the teacup and quickly stood up to show him I was at his service. "Fine, thanks," I said.

Alsop rubbed his hands together, heartily preparing to take on the day. He had a cigarette holder clamped between his teeth and wore a purple robe with lilac piping. His slippers were dark leather. His hairless shins as he stood in the morning light gave off a high polish, and his heavy eyeglasses were two large tortoiseshell circles, round as coat buttons. He talked around the stem of his cigarette holder. "Perfect morning, wouldn't you agree, my dear?"

I agreed. Politely asked him what he'd like for breakfast.

He pursed his lips. "Something light, I believe." He smoothed the front of his dressing gown and looked with a searching curiosity about the kitchen, which, housing this dandy figure, seemed suddenly modest and dingy. "An egg, perhaps?" His eyes went from me to the stove to the window and back to me again. He seemed to be looking for something.

"Boiled?" I asked, hopefully. Boiled and scrambled were the only eggs I could do safely.

He frowned and breathed thoughtfully into his fingers, tapping his lips with a pale, well-manicured fingertip. I prayed he would say boiled. He smiled around the cigarette holder and said, "No, darling. I believe I shall have fried. A fried egg should do it." He looked around some more. "Splendid," he said, smiling at me. "Fried it is."

I wished he would leave the room so I could start the breakfast and make the mistakes I knew I was going to make coaxing a fried egg into existence. He made me very nervous. "If you'd like to go into the living room, I'd be happy to bring your breakfast in when it's ready," I said.

"Nonsense!" he cried. "I shall take my breakfast here"—he pointed at the bland kitchen table—"where I can enjoy your delightful company!" He sat and raised his chin, as if about to submit to the attentions of an expensive barber. His skin was pale and smooth and freshly shaved. He fascinated me. He looked pampered and preened over. I stared at the cigarette holder and the round glasses and thought to myself it could have been worse—he could have shown up with an ascot and a monocle. There was something soft about his inward-tilting lips. He had lost most of his hair, and his marmoreal pate shone in the light. What hair remained at the back of his head was tidily combed across his crown. His thumbnails were shiny and smooth as pennies flattened under the wheels of a train. I wanted him not to stay in here with me. I said, "But the newspaper is . . ."

With a theatrical flourish he cupped a hand behind the pink orchid of one ear, his head dipped attentively toward me, brows elevated, listening intently, as if for a distant trumpet call.

". . . in the living room, and you might like to read it."

"Oh, yes! I'll just pop in and fetch it." He jumped up, slippered out of the room, and came back in with the *Vineyard Gazette* creased and skewed under his arm. He sat down and rattled the paper. I struggled with the egg, frying it in butter. Though I knew I shouldn't let the yolk harden, I had no idea how to tell when it was properly done. I poked at it with a spatula. When I set the egg and some toast and coffee in front of him, he put down the newspaper, pinched the linen napkin between two fingers, shook it loose, and smoothed it across his lap in anticipation. "Lovely," he mumbled as I set the pitcher of cream in front of him. "Forgive me, my dear, your name again?"

I told him.

"Not in school?" he said.

The first week of September was coming to a close; I explained that I would be going to Ireland. In Ireland the school term didn't begin until October. He asked me what school.

"St. Paul's."

He chewed his egg and dabbed at his mouth and showed no sign of having heard me. Then, after a minute or so he lifted his coffee cup to his lips and said in thoughtful confirmation, "St. Paul's."

He talked loudly, as though I were deaf, and in return he appeared not to hear what I said. His accent was frightening in its majesty, impossibly aristocratic. He sounded like Thurston Howell III on *Gilligan's Island*. I wondered if he understood me; were my words too plain and small and simple for him, too primitive? When I opened my mouth to answer his questions I felt like an agitated ape clapping two coconuts together in frustration. This, clearly, was a person who knew a lot, had no doubts about what he knew. And yet he was humorous. He stirred sugar into his coffee with a fussy tapping of his spoon and held the handle of the cup delicately. He sipped and patted his mouth with the napkin. "Have you," he said, "by any chance had the good fortune to make the acquaintance of two lovely young women named Sarah Chubb and Corinne Zimmermann?"

I stared at him, stunned. Quinny Zimmermann and Sarah Chubb were friends of mine. "They're my friends," I said.

"I have the delightful distinction, the honor, of being their great-uncle."

It made sense. Quinny's middle name was Alsop.

"Their grandmother is my sister."

"I met her," I said.

"You met her." He poked at the egg with his fork.

"I had dinner with her once in New Hampshire."

"You had dinner with her once in New Hampshire." He straightened his glasses, then looked up at me as though what I had said was just dawning on him. "How lucky for my dear sister!"

His sister, Mrs. Chubb, was like him. They both had an angular briskness and surprising glasses. A mosquito landed on Alsop's forearm as he was eating his breakfast, and with a comical show of precision he pressed it smartly to death beneath the tip of his stiffened forefinger, as if pressing an elevator button. He had a slightly self-conscious brand of humor. He was formidable, but I liked him, and when he invited me to sit down with him, I did. He had been at the house for two days, and Hellman acted as though she liked him when he was in the room with her, but as soon as he was out of her sight she grumbled and sighed and complained about him. One day, when he turned to go out of the room, I saw her bare her teeth at his back and shake her jowls and hold her two fists in the air to vent her irritation. I could see how he might be a difficult guest, but he was nice to me. He asked me if I'd like some coffee, and when I said yes and moved to pour some, he said, "Let me." He was serving me. That was something new, and when Hellman came into the room I was laughing at some witty thing he had said, with the coffee cup raised to my lips and a piece of toast in my hand. I felt caught. Immediately I stood up. Alsop urged me to sit down, and Hellman said, "Yes, sit down. Drink your coffee."

What else could she say? I knew she was slightly intimidated by him, and I understood that that was precisely why she had invited him.

September crept along in a way it never had before in my life. This was the first September I hadn't been in school, and the freedom of that was both thrilling and frightening. The days grew cooler, and the falling temperature seemed to bring everything into greater focus, lending the days a clarity they didn't have at any other time of year. The ferry carried fewer people to the island and took more of them away. The streets cleared out, the traffic slowed to a trickle. Feibleman went back to LA toward the end of his third week. Vineyard Haven began to feel like a lonely ghost town. The evenings were shorter, the mornings a little less bright. In the afternoon as I walked to Cronig's to do the shopping, samaras coptered gently out of the trees over the roadway, and black and orange monarch butterflies began to appear in astonishing numbers over the wildflowers above the beach. In the mornings I had to pull on a sweater, and again in the evenings, but the ocean water was warmer than it had been all summer, and whenever I had a few free hours I went swimming off the jetty and lay in the sand and daydreamed about Ireland, suspended between this life and what seemed like my next life. With a start I would remember that between leaving the Vineyard and leaving for Ireland I would have little more than a week to spend at home with my mother. And then I would think of my mother, bringing her voice out of the rustling sea grass. It made me feel better to think of her. She was my best friend; more than that, I was certain that the best things about me had come from her. I admired her. I wanted to be like her. I wanted her to be happy. I knew she was alone, that the loss of my father had been difficult and frightening for her, and if what Sheila had said was true, it was worse. He was her husband, and then he was gone and she was forced to be both father and mother. When the voices in our house fought a little too harshly or a kick in the shin landed a bit too forcefully, angry footsteps would eventually pound down the front stairs and up the hallway, seeking asylum in my mother's face, and a bitter outburst of complaint would rain down on her from whoever had been wronged. My mother would put down what she was doing and turn in sympathy toward the face weeping in her doorway. She did what she had to. I knew that she tried not to drink, at least until evening, and she always got up in the morning and went to work, had gotten a second master's degree. Nobody in my family had been killed or arrested, nobody had died of neglect, we were far from starving, and with endless scholarship applications and reference books about the various schools and colleges, my mother made sure we got an education. I knew that she loved us. Even when things were difficult for her, she seemed to enjoy her life. Sometimes, when I asked her if she was afraid to die, she said, "They'll have to pull me off this earth kicking and screaming." I knew my mother would never give up, and there was safety in that.

Lying on the beach I remembered myself as a child, how anxiously I had waited for my mother to come home whenever she went out. At night, when everyone else had gone to bed, I would stand at the living room window in my nightgown, waiting, watching for her headlights to appear on our long driveway. I feared that if I went to sleep she wouldn't come back. One winter night I waited a long time. It had been snowing all evening and the snow was still falling. I was worried about the slippery roads. I fretted so much that finally I got dressed and put on my boots and walked down the driveway in the dark to wait for her. The world was utterly quiet, and the snow falling around my face in the darkness was like black ash coming out of the sky. I could feel it on my cheeks; cold flakes flew into my eyes. The snowy fields on either side of the driveway seemed to glow with light, and at the end of the road the street lights on Route 138 lit up the storm in swirling yellow patches. I stood halfway down the driveway, watching the occasional cars slide slowly past the end of it, praying that the next one would be my mother's. I counted to one hundred, convinced that by the time I was done she would arrive. When that didn't work I walked to the end of the road and back to the middle again, convinced that that would do the trick. Then I decided that her car would appear within the next ten cars. I sat on a tree stump and waited, the snow gathering on my thighs in long slender loaves. I prayed, promising God I would give him anything if he brought my mother home safely. I knocked snow from tree branches, walked to the end of the road again, and back to the middle again, and looked up at the sky for as long as I could without blinding myself with snow. Finally, when I saw her headlights turn in off the main street, I hid behind a yew tree. I didn't want her to know I had been waiting for her. I didn't want her to see me. I knew it would upset her if she knew I'd been worried, and I didn't want to upset her. I didn't want to add to my mother's burden. If my mother knew I was unhappy, she would be unhappy too.

On the beach I weighed sand in the palm of my hand. I knew my thinking had been childish and crazy and a little bit vain. To think that anyone could control the outcome of events, control another person's happiness or unhappiness. There was so little in life that you could control.

The second week in September the BBC came to interview Hellman. They arrived with cameras and cables and lights, a makeup man, a hairdresser, and three technicians. The commotion they caused put Hellman on edge. They rearranged her furniture and blinded her with tungsten lights. In the course of setting up their equipment they knocked over a lamp, scratched the wooden floor.

When Hellman discovered that one of the technical assistants had left the front door wide open, she berated the entire crew. One morning while they were shooting, the lights went out in Vineyard Haven, and when they had to stop and wait, Hellman grew even more impatient. I was glad they were here. They made my job easier for those few days, took her attention off me, and the crew was young and funny and joked with me in the kitchen. It was a relief to have the protection of their presence. Hellman wouldn't yell at me in front of them. While Peter Adam, the BBC guy, was interviewing Hellman in the living room I had to bring her coffee, glasses of milk and water, clean ashtrays, matches, the telephone. I stood in the hallway eavesdropping on the interview. The questions and cameras and bright lights made her nervous. I could hear it in her voice.

Hellman's mood had deteriorated to a new low. The complaints she leveled against me those last few weeks were endless, and the requests more insistent. After all these weeks of my working for her, she still couldn't get my schedule straight and was constantly asking me to work when I wasn't supposed to. Finally I gave up correcting her and just worked whenever she wanted me to. Once, during a terrible thunderstorm I sheltered my bicycle in the little cement hut that housed the outdoor shower, and the next day, when by accident Hellman discovered it there, I overheard her say to Hannah Weinstein, one of her guests, "Have you ever heard of anything like this?! What's wrong with putting it in her own room?!" Later she told me angrily never ever to put my bicycle there again. "People use that shower!" she snapped. Not a single person had used it all summer. Another time, when Feibleman was looking for some cherry tomatoes in the refrigerator, I heard Hellman tell him, "There aren't any. That pretty girl has eaten them all." The comment shocked me more than any other she had made about me. It was startling and strange. I hadn't eaten the tomatoes, and her saying *pretty* gave the sentence a sinister curve. *Pretty* wasn't a compliment coming from her.

At night I would pass the time in my room, reading or writing in my journal, or ride my bicycle downtown and eat an ice cream cone or call my mother on the pay phones by the ferry, then sit down on a greasy railroad tie at the edge of the beach and stare at the lights of the ferry, not wanting to go back to the house. One night I wrote in my journal:

> . . . *things around here have been horrid. Ms. H has all of a sudden got into a very bad humor with me and she is really picking on me and is very antagonistic and hostile. I don't think I've been too pleasant either, so. . . . I guess we just do not get along and who knows the reason why? She says I like to argue and win and I think the same of her, so where does that leave us? And if it is really so that I am arguing unnecessarily then it must be my reaction to her, because I never had this problem with anyone before. I think it really stems from a lack of communication due to the fact that her senses are not sharp and aware that's how the misunderstandings arise. She does things without knowing it or hears things wrong and when you try to explain she thinks you are arguing. I think now she is overly sensitive to me and overreacts when there is the slightest problem. Thank God it's only one more week. I wouldn't be able to last another day if it weren't. . . . This isn't as great as I thought it would be.*

I heard Hellman telling her friends on the telephone that she felt she was going through a depression. Everything she said now was a complaint about the people around her. And she seemed fearful. One night when she had no guests and just the two of us were in the house she asked me repeatedly if I was going out that night, as it was my night off. I told her several times that I was going out. And then I changed my mind. I was tired, and what I really wanted was to lie down and read. When I told Hellman I'd be staying in after all, an expression of relief flashed across her face, and then, just as quickly, as though she suddenly remembered who she was, the look was gone and she said briskly, "Well, if you're not going out, please turn off the outdoor lights now." She was glad not to be alone, I knew, even if it was only me keeping her company.

At the end of September, amid the turning trees and the brisk wind, I left the Vineyard. The day I packed my bag I felt for some reason that I should give Hellman a gift. I stopped what I was doing and rode my bike down to the Bowl and Board and bought the first thing that caught my eye—a painted serving plate in the shape of a fish. Hellman liked to fish, she liked to eat fish, she looked a little like a fish. The plate seemed appropriate and wasn't too expensive. In the kitchen the next day, as I was saying goodbye to her, I handed her the plate. She held it up to see it, pressing her glasses to her face with one hand and tilting the plate toward the window light. "It's a . . . a fish," she said, "how clever," and she smiled at the plate and then at me and told me how thoughtful it was of me to make the effort. Her appreciation of the gift seemed sincere, but I didn't know why I had felt compelled to buy her anything, and now that it was done I was embarrassed. To her it must have seemed a cheap little piece of clutter. Though I didn't like her and had felt humiliated by her, I had had an urge to do something for her. I had a suspicion that some of the sourness between us was my fault, that I had given up trying to make things better, given up trying to do a good job.

Ten minutes later, as I was heading out the door, she came down from upstairs and stopped me and presented me with a bottle of perfume in a box. I knew it was a bottle someone had given her a month or so before, because I had seen it on her bureau. When she handed it to me and thanked me for all the help I had given her, I wondered if she felt sorry for me too. She shook my hand and wished me a good trip, a good year in Ireland, and said, "Next summer, well, perhaps . . ." and raised her hands in a way that suggested it was all up in the air what would happen next summer. I didn't want to come back next summer and wondered if she knew that by now, and I didn't think she wanted me back either. I said, "Next summer," smiling and nodding in blind agreement. And then we said goodbye, and she turned back through the kitchen doorway.

I put my bag on my bicycle and wheeled it slowly down to the ferry. I had felt bumbling as I said goodbye to Hellman. I was glad to be leaving her, but I wasn't happy. When I thought of how I had looked forward to this job, the unrestrained fantasies I had created around it, my cheeks reddened in shame.

As the ferry dragged away from the Vineyard Haven dock, I stood on the deck and watched a cormorant standing on a mooring ball with his wings held up to dry. It made me sad to look at him. He was ugly. He looked like a baby learning to walk. Like a witch drying her cape. I was one of a lifetime of young women who had come to help keep Lillian Hellman's house in order, and I wasn't even very good at the job. As a domestic I had been an outstanding dud. I didn't care. I knew I wasn't a dud in plenty of other ways.

I could see Hellman's house as the ferry passed around the tip of the jetty, the little white box tucked above the sand. I felt I was seeing it from a great distance. A lone gull with opaque yellow eyes hovered low in the air above me, waiting for me to toss him a crumb. I had nothing to throw him, and I went inside to sit down. The ferry was not crowded; I had plenty of seats to choose from. I sat near the back and stared out the window. The island looked very low and flat, but it was pretty dressed in its fall colors. Whitecaps broke in the sound, leaving veiny webs of lather behind. I put my head against the window, feeling the vibration of the huge engines below. I could feel my body relaxing with the relief of going home, could almost feel how the lock on the front door gave so easily when you turned the key. I knew that when I went into the house that night my mother would be sitting on her bed with her legs stretched out, reading, and when she saw me she would smile and toss down her book with theatrical haste and lower her eyeglasses and lift her arms to welcome me and say, "You made it, Rose!" And I would sit down on the bed with her, where I felt safe, and tell her everything.

ACKNOWLEDGMENTS

I am indebted to Estela Abosch and Pat Towers for their kindness and support, and to Betsy Lerner, whose friendship and editorial gifts have been invaluable to me.

ABOUT THE AUTHOR

Rosemary Mahoney is the author of *The Early Arrival of Dreams* and *Whoredom in Kimmage,* a National Book Critics' Circle finalist in 1993. She won the Charles E. Horman Prize for Fiction Writing as an undergraduate at Harvard and is also the recipient of a Whiting Writer's Award. She lives in New York City.